METROPOLITAN HOME

# RENOVATION STYLE

**Books by**
*Metropolitan Home*

*Renovation Style*
*The New American Cuisine*
*The Apartment Book*

METROPOLITAN HOME
# RENOVATION STYLE

Written by Joanna L. Krotz

Villard Books   New York   1991

All rights reserved under International
and Pan-American Copyright Conventions.
Published in the United States by Villard
Books, a division of Random House, Inc.,
New York, and simultaneously in Canada
by Random House of Canada Limited,
Toronto. Originally published in hardcover
by Villard Books, a division of
Random House, Inc., in 1986.

Library of Congress Cataloging in
Publication Data
Krotz, Joanna L.
    Metropolitan home renovation style.
    1. Dwellings—Remodeling.
    2. Interior decoration.
I. Metropolitan home.   II. Title.
TH4816.K76 1986   643'.7   86-40108
ISBN: 0-394-54941-4
ISBN: 0-394-75819-6 pbk.

All the photographs in this book were
previously published in *Metropolitan Home*.

Manufactured in the United States of
America
9  8  7  6  5  4  3

# ACKNOWLEDGMENTS

The inspiration for this book comes from a community of professionals. For years, the staff of *Metropolitan Home* magazine has been thinking hard and imaginatively about what it takes to make a home—starting from the premise of a feeling rather than a place. Home is hardly a photograph stuffed with drop-dead chic. No. It's where you kick off your shoes, snuggle in, and feel contented. So before any house or loft or apartment is published in the magazine, we ask ourselves the tough questions. Does it look good? Sure, it's stylish. But can someone really live here? Does the design solve problems? Does it have ideas readers can adopt? Those are the kind of real homes pictured in *Metropolitan Home*.

And since we begin with the philosophy that it's the individual home-owner who turns a house into a home, the magazine has a particular affinity for renovation. In the past half-dozen years, every fall we've published a special renovation report —"Elegant Renovation"—with the work of the most innovative readers and designers and architects across the country. And in issue after issue, we explore the creative possibilities of the resurrected home, devoting pages and pictures, ideas and intelligence, to our belief that renovation is the contemporary route to getting personal style into a house.

*Metropolitan Home*'s enthusiastic endorsement of renovation is seasoned by experience. More than half the editors on the magazine have themselves been through the messy and scary process of tearing down the walls, pulling up the floors, shutting their eyes tight against the destruction in order to better see the finished plan. As editors, we are therefore also our readers. We know the uncertainties that go into hiring designers and contractors. And no matter how expert we are, no matter how many times we've advised friends, we never forget that when it's your own kitchen, choosing the appliances, the countertop, and the color and pattern of tile to live with for the next ten years is bound to cause anxiety. High anxiety.

*Renovation Style*, then, is the direct result of the magazine's collective wisdom. And if this book motivates readers to look at houses with new and wide-open eyes, it is due, first, to the guiding vision of *Metropolitan Home*'s Editor-in-Chief, Dorothy Ka-

lins. Successful projects, renovation and otherwise, start with grit and end up with glamour. No one knows this better than Dorothy, who has a remarkable talent for taking a dream and turning it into reality.

The editors who produce the photographs in the magazine, and sometimes the room designs too, created the backbone of this book—and its visual glory. Thanks to Carol Helms and Donna Warner, Ben Lloyd and Steven Wagner, the romance of renovation glows through the plaster dust. I'm especially indebted to Donna, whose in-depth knowledge was so crucial for the Source Book chapter.

Next, there are the editors who tell the stories behind the pictures. Skillfully and stylishly, writers Michael Walker and the late and dearly missed Don Vining put real life into the photographs, giving readers the facts, figures, and fantasy that are the foundation of every home.

All the pictures and words in the world don't yet make a magazine. Someone has to put the two together —to make sense of it—and that's what Art Director Michael Jensen and Design Director Don Morris do. *Renovation Style* also pays homage to the influence of Art Director Emeritus Bob Furstenau. Then there are the people who actually make the magazine: Executive Editor Marcia Andrews, Barbara Graustark, Charla Lawhon, Pam Hanks Kenyon, Dayna Dove, David Staskowski, Richard Ferretti, Cathleen Munisteri, Mary Beth Jordan, Donna Sapolin, Larry Peterson, Newell Turner, Diane Benson, Marna Ford, Celesta Peterson. Thanks are particularly due Pam, the computer whiz, who went eyeball-to-eyeball with the electronic age and made the machines blink.

Thanks, too, to crack City Editors: Nancy Adams, Chicago; Linda Humphrey, Seattle; Diane Dorrans Saeks, San Francisco; Rochelle Reed and Barbara Thornburg, Los Angeles; Bonnie Warren, New Orleans; and Patricia D. Rogers, Washington, D.C.

As part of Meredith Corporation, *Metropolitan Home* is fortunate in having enlightened business and corporate management. Steve Burzon, publisher, exudes energy and ideas, and convinced us just how elegant renovation can be. As publishing director, Burt Boersma has been a helpful guide. Thanks as always and especially to Jim Autry, poet and president (of magazines), for his

unfailing support. Thanks, too, for the sage advice of Jack Rehm, executive vice president, and to Meredith's president Bob Burnett for keeping the fire burning bright.

The book came out of the pages and philosophy of *Metropolitan Home*, but special expertise was needed to produce it. Paul Hardy designed *Renovation Style* from first page to last. He made editorial sense out of an avalanche of material. Paul's imaginative perfection and dedication to quality is evident on every page. We couldn't have done without him or the help of his assistants Miles Abernethy and Margery Greenspan. Thanks also to Mary Knowles for her floorplans.

The Source Book chapter was researched and written by Michael Walsh, writer extraordinaire, who, along with Donna Warner, plotted every inch of its progress. A mini-book in itself, the Source Book was wrestled into grace and order by Michael's judicious skill.

Always on call, Mike McClintock is the reassuring Voice of Experience. Conversant with muntins and medallions, brick and brackets—everything, in fact, that the up-to-date renovator needs to know—Mike's help has been invaluable.

At Villard, our editor, Diane Reverand, has made us feel special, smart, and accomplished as only a consummate editor can. Thanks to her insight and vision, *Renovation Style* is a definitive book, a real, substantive guide—with no gaps and no missing pages. We're grateful also to Villard's editorial director, Marc Jaffe, who had the great good sense to get excited by our project and then the even better sense to let us do the job the way we knew best. The hard work of Patricia Barlow, Linda Rosenberg, and Anet Sirna-Bruder has resulted in a book we're all proud to hold. Thanks to Dan Surdell for his magnificent color work at Orent Graphic Arts. And, of course, this book wouldn't exist at all without the efforts of literary agent Bob Cornfield, who put us all together.

Last, though hardly least, there's my huge debt and gratitude to First Reader and Ace Problem Solver Wayne E. Kuhn, who, alone, knows its full measure.

*Joanna L. Krotz*
*Spring 1986*

# CONTENTS

**ACKNOWLEDGMENTS**     **vii**

**INTRODUCTION**     **xi**

**BIG HOUSE DREAMS**     **2**
The Once and Future House • From a
Porch to a Postmodern Parlor • Preserva-
tion Hall • The New Family Home • The
New Glamour of Comfort • The Enlightened
Tudor • New Wing for an Old Farmhouse

**RENOVATING THE RANCH:
TRACT HOUSING AND THE
SPLIT-LEVEL**     **32**
The Suburban Loft • The Magazine Make-
over • Customizing the Colonial • Re-
inventing the Split-Level • A '60s House
Lightens Up • Raising the Roof on a Ranch

**THE SMALL CITY HOUSE**     **60**
Tradition with a New, Fresh Air • The
House That Roared • The Urbane Renewal
• Brave New Bungalow • Adding on the Ritz •
The Outdoor Room • Building on the Skyline

**THE LOFT MOVEMENT**     **89**
The Revisionist Loft • New View on Los
Angeles • The Movable Design • The
Salon Loft • Living on Top of the World •
The Neo-Classic Loft • Saladino on Lofts

**THE CONVERTIBLE HOME:
CHURCHES, CARRIAGE HOUSES,
AND ADAPTIVE RE-USE**     **116**
Home in a Village Church • The Design
Factory • Living in a Landmark • The Gas
Station, Revisited • Converting a Carriage
House • A Bowling Alley Moves into the
Fast Lane

**THE URBAN PLANNER:
LIVING IN A HIGH-RISE**     **138**
The Streamlined Condo • The Engineered
Apartment • The News in Detail • Private
Penthouse • The New Classics

**THE GREAT VICTORIANS:
TOWN HOUSES, BROWNSTONES,
AND PAINTED LADIES**     **160**
The Light-Filled Gingerbread • State-of-
the-Art Town House • Perfect Retrofit •
The Victorian Impulse • Town House with
a Secret • The Possible Dream House •
The Greenhouse Effect • The Urban Villa
• A Labor of Love

## CHARM AND HOW TO GET IT: COTTAGES AND BUNGALOWS

**203**

The Romantic Cottage • Instant Heritage for a New House • The City-Slick Barn • Shaker Chic • The Appeal of Handcrafting • The Sunshine State

## THE THINKING COOK'S KITCHEN

**235**

Installing the Kitchen Sync • An Old-Time Kitchen That Cooks • A Contemporary Way with Wood • The Chef's Special • Building on Your Dream • The New Power Look • A Kitchen to Live In • Limited Addition • The Module Plan • The Euro-style Kitchen • Building into the Backyard • Opening Up the Galley • Pink and Black Is Coming Back • The Warmth of Wood • The Surprise of Concrete • The Neo-Fifties Kitchen • The Semi-Professional Kitchen

## THE PERSONAL SPA: BATHS AND DRESSING ROOMS

**278**

The Masterful Bath • The Wet Room • The New Retreat • A Japanese Bathhouse • Bath, with a City View • Bath, with a Canyon View • The Glamour Bath • The French Line • The Bedside Spa • A Solution in Bold Strokes • A Solution in Old-Fashioned Fantasy • Roses and the Retro Look • California, Country Style • Japan, Contemporary Style

## THE RENOVATOR'S SOURCE BOOK

**303**

Appliances • Cabinets • Columns • Countertops • Doors • Faucets • Fireplaces and Mantels • Flooring • Glass Block • Greenhouses and Atriums • Hardware • Heating and Cooling • Lighting • Moldings • New Materials • Paint and Wallpaper • Roofing and Siding • Sinks • Skylights • Stairs • Storage • Tile • Tubs and Toilets • Windows

## INSTANT ACCESS: A PRACTICAL GUIDE TO RENOVATION EXPERTS

**335**

How to Hire an Architect, Interior Designer, or Contractor • How to Finance Your Renovation • Directory of Architects, Interior Designers, and Contractors • Directory of Wholesalers, Manufacturers, and Retailers

## INDEX

**355**

## PHOTOGRAPHY CREDITS

**359**

# INTRODUCTION

The starting place, of course, is the dream. The ideal place. A home that has your personal taste, feel, and style written all over it. A place to come home to. You open the door and—immediately—the mood says welcome. Relax. You belong here.

That's the goal of this book. It's dedicated to the principle that dream houses can come true. And we mean individual dreams, those you have when you look around at the too-familiar walls of your unsatisfying rooms and fantasize about change: the Victorian bedroom you always wanted, with wainscoting, a window seat snuggled into a bay window, a canopied bed, and the lure of history; the semiprofessional kitchen, with a restaurant stove, mosaic tile floor, marble counters, and Eurostyle flair; the living room that positively yearns for friends, with inviting French doors, lush parquet floors, a plump, overstuffed sofa, and a sleek stack of electronic wizardry built into the wall. It's all within your grasp. You can perform the magic and leave your mark on any space, even the most ordinary. It's possible. This book proves it.

With land and new construction costs soaring, and with space at a premium everywhere you look, especially in the major cities, the dream house has more and more often become a superimposed one—a new vision, your vision, proudly growing out of an existing structure.

And that's renovation.

It's been a while in coming, this burgeoning interest in converting lofts and brownstones, ranch and carriage houses, condos and factories into places we can call home. The early days of the movement, in the 1950s and 1960s, were awash in exposed brick walls, cheaply paneled basements, tacky "additions" hardly worthy of the name. Preservationists railed against the loss of landmarks, but bulldozers blazed down Main Street (and Broadway) nonetheless. The idea was progress; make way for the new. And renovation, then, meant only making do.

How times have changed. America is no longer so infatuated with everything brand-new and shiny, clean-edged and modern. We've become enlightened about our architectural legacy. We care, now, about roots and giving the past its due. But there's more to the change than that. Self-interest has contributed the strongest motivation of all. The economics of owning a house have changed drastically since the postwar boom times.

You've heard it countless times before: in 30 or so years' time, the percentage of income Americans spend on shelter has jumped from 25 percent to 40 percent. More money, as you well know, is buying a lot less house. The number of people in each household is shrinking, from 3.14 in 1970 to 2.71 in 1984. Two-income families may account for greater income today, but every dollar is needed for rising costs. And then, many more people are living alone, nearly 20 million at last 1984 Census Bureau count, out of the 85.4 million households in the country.

What does all this mean? The obvious lesson is that it takes a lot more money and work to fuel the American dream house than ever before. More dollars, certainly. More years to attain it, probably. More juggling of priorities and schedules. Compromises. Trade-offs.

The moral of those statistics, however, is more uplifting. Despite the cost and strain, America refuses to quit dreaming. A recent poll conducted by CBS and *The New York Times* concluded that 76 percent of the public believes that those who never own a house are "missing out on an important part of the American dream." A *Metropolitan Home* magazine survey a year or so ago revealed that most of our readers would rather renovate an existing place than purchase a new house, by a 65 percent to 35 percent majority. That's not just wishful thinking, either. The dollars going into home improvement all over the country are rising dramatically—from $49.3 billion in 1983 to $64 billion in 1984 to a record $76 billion in 1985.

Nowadays it makes more sense to put money into the place you own than it does to purchase a ready-made, brand-new house. Ever since the inflationary years, roughly 1979 to 1982, you can no longer count on making a killing when you sell your home. That's the real change in the country's housing economics. Buying an older house "with potential" for less money and literally making it your own—renovating it with your personal stamp— now offers a better investment and more livability than most new houses that money would buy.

Partly from economic necessity then, partly from a new-found yearning to see a bit of history in our homes, and definitely the stuff of dreams, renovation has taken on a new glamour. Romance, even. It's the search for new canvases that draws us, the urge to carve new living spaces from old. For what is more breath-catchingly exciting than the misty-eyed promise of rooms that just might be?

The singular impulse of *Metropolitan Home,* the magazine, is that renovation is now the most heady, satisfying, and, usually, cost-effective way to get the home you want the way you want it. It's the impulse that influences page after page of this book. Here are concrete ideas and design strategies about changing and using space. You may see an idea for a window in a Victorian house that would be perfect for your ranch house. Clever solutions for storage or floor treatments, for wall color and room dividers, for kitchens or baths can all move easily from one kind of structure to another. Very few of these ideas are limited to the architecture of the houses. Whether the project takes 20 minutes or 20 months, the house town, brownstone, or suburban, this book serves as an intelligent planning guide to all the details of undertaking a renovation, including how to estimate a budget, the conflict of dollars versus design (or, how perfect does everything have to be?), which improvements help resale value, a source book chock full of products and options, and how to deal with the team of experts—the architects, designers, contractors—you'll need. Because, along with the glamour, renovation has undergone yet another transformation.

Today, we're far more likely to pick up a telephone than a hammer to begin the work. So we've included supportive and sage suggestions throughout about how to manage the project, how to work with the people you hire, how to let them be the experts when it's a waste of time for you to worry. We offer advice about the ongoing psychodrama —how that home team becomes, for a few weeks or too many months, the most important people in your life. We explain all you need to know to get the job done.

Ah, yes. Getting the job done. "The worst part of the renovation," says architect Patrick Pinnell in Washington, D.C., "is like participating in a gang rape of your house." The living-through-it process brings home the brutal fact that, like any romance worth the name, renovation includes its share of heartache. Subcontractors will decamp. Patient instructions will become scrambled. And the golden rule of any house project will hold sway: everything takes twice as long and costs twice as much as you expected.

Not for one minute does this book underplay the pain of the process versus the glory of the results. While most of the pages you'll see are saturated with glorious "after" photographs designed to inspire you, inform you, and perhaps cajole you to pull down a wall, enlarge a bath, make your kitchen more workable, or even to buy a place with, um—potential—we would be unbalanced and unfair if we did not say, loud and clear, in renovation, getting there is not half the fun. Whoever said the dream was going to be easy?

And yet. Ahhhh. The rewards. The shivers of delight. The downright pride. Just remember this about any present and future renovations. As you begin to lose all creature comforts, to be deprived of the basic sweetnesses of American life, like home-cooked meals, hot baths, clean clothing, money in the bank, and peace of mind, take it from friends who know: it will all be worth it someday. And *Renovation Style* will be there to help.

METROPOLITAN HOME

# RENOVATION STYLE

# BIG HOUSE DREAMS

Ah, the grand old glories. The houses that cry out, "Save me." There's a new tradition stirring in those musty rooms and marbled halls, a spirit that respects history but stops far short of the museum. The past has never looked this good before.

Using imaginative hindsight, architect Robert A. M. Stern has given new character to this classic 1893 Shingle Style country house (*above: a rear view*). The parade of French doors at either end is new, as is the trellised loggia *(opposite)* that reconnects the house to the garden.

"The new American dream house," says architect Robert A. M. Stern, "is the old American dream house with better plumbing." And that comment explains much of the current interest in revitalizing those rambling, century-old Tudor houses, or four-square Colonials whose rooms know no bounds. They offer architectural quirkiness and the confirmation of time. They have thick real plaster, not dry-wall. Stately clapboard siding and inlaid parquet floors. They have deep porches, window seats, bays, and even turrets. Just looking at one conjures a feeling of heritage and hearth.

The venerable giants are clearly family homes—the places to move in the dogs and the cats, the kids and the caboodle, the endless things that clutter up a house and make it familiar. And these grand old houses will embrace everything you own and throw in a big backyard too. Here's the chance to found a manor, to embark on a committed love affair with a house that will give roots to the next generation.

In contemplating the revival of a sprawling old house, accentuate the strong points—ample light and generous space—but resolutely stare down its potential for baronial heavy-handedness. A refreshing, helpful impulse is now emerging in the rehabilitation of older houses, one we call "the New Traditional." More than a style, the New Traditional is an attitude that puts its feet up, living with the past, not in it. Just because the house is large and old doesn't mean you must obey all the historical imperatives and install period-perfect rooms. The New Traditional look is a sensitive marriage of precedent and panache, of historical and contemporary.

We're not suggesting any disregard of old-house glory. Many large-scale sirens have seen some "modernizing" already—and these intermediate renovations may be costly to undo. In the 1950s and 1960s, additions were frequently tacked on willy-nilly while vintage trim, molding and porch railings were often covered up or simply stripped. "Bastardizing old houses makes no sense," says New York interior designer Mario Buatta, who has an abiding love for old English country homes. "Do the whole thing right, or don't do it at all."

Sometimes easier said than done. The historic details you do want restored can be cranky and temperamental to replace. Old veneer floors, for instance, are difficult to match, since aged wood doesn't look at all like new wood. Few materials, in fact, are exactly the same size, shape, or color they were a generation or so ago. Fortunately, because Big House Dreams like yours are more common, acceptable reproductions of woodwork and hardware, moldings and medallions now abound.

So as you envision your Dream rising out of the loose and rusty flashing on the house's roof (which, by the way, might indicate water damage inside), think hard about the challenges. Remember the cost of upkeep—heating, for example. Big houses generate big bills. In the end, you'll have a special house that's worthy of all the work.

**ON THE ROLE OF THE ARCHITECT:** "When you design a house, you have to tailor it to the owner, but not to his psyche. Because then, you're not doing your best job for the client. I like people to spend as much money as they can on a house. I love to see them spend money on the very finest craftsmanship, the most beautiful moldings I can devise. Most people live in a house about ten years, and nobody wants to buy somebody else's psyche down the road. Don't build a house around it. I don't want that kind of ego trip for them or for me."

If this 1890s Shingle Style house looks just as it should, that's because architect Robert A. M. Stern's sensitive restoration developed the personality it was meant to have all along. "Basically," he says, "the American house hasn't really changed that much in look and character. The house has always been a shrine to the family. And in a way it's becoming even more important. It's a solid edifice, a thing that people still gravitate to."

Inside, the house proves his point. Stern put into the interior all the emotional elements a country house should contain, whether they were there at the start or not. This house is more comfortable today than it has ever been.

At the rear, old walls were removed to turn two small rooms into a large, easy-going living room; stripped and refinished floors and the light woods of the furnishings also update the house. The combination of a flat-weave rug and the flowered-print fabric is an altogether modern notion.

New French doors allow the enlarged living room to open into the garden. The small panes filter the strong light as well as fragment and frame the garden view. Paradoxically, the doors promise both safe enclosure and tantalizing access.

Simple columns, painted glossy white, replace the old walls in the new living room (note the one just to the right of the straight-back side chair). The house's handsome proportions and glittering windows (like the leaded fanlight in the stairwell, *previous page*) mask an essentially cottage interior. Evoking English country homes, old roses and lilacs bloom on the sofas and chairs, but the mood is definitely contemporary.

**GRACE UNDER PRESSURE:** Architect Stern took one column and multiplied it into a loggia along the rear of the house. Open to the sky, the frame will eventually be filled in with wisteria blooms.

**"I** think the International Style architects swallowed a bitter pill with the historic preservation movement," says Robert A. M. Stern. "Because what the public was saying to the architect was, 'We'd rather save any old building than have one of yours.' It was a clear mandate."

The cabinets, while new, are charmingly dated with glass doors and the blue-painted interiors of a bygone era. The tile, readily available, was designed in a country mood—but the diamond punctuation is techy black, not calico blue.

Although we think of the country house as an open one, it often harbored a warren of little rooms, as this one did. To open it up, at the opposite end from the living room, a new dining area/sunroom and kitchen replaced the outdated "service" area. Former servants' quarters, laundry, pantry, small kitchen, and back hallway went the way of the servants—out. Instead, this divided space has been converted into the two large rooms one imagines at the heart of any country house.

The new sunroom is the old kitchen space freed from confining walls with side-by-side French doors, a theme of the house. It seems strange that such an essential room was omitted from the original. Characteristic of the Shingle Style house, the new ceiling is built of tongue-in-groove slats. And, characteristic of Stern, the old-fashioned details are added by using new-fashioned design savvy.

Separating the sunroom from the kitchen is a freestanding divider that holds the refrigerator on the kitchen side and the counter-level fireplace on the other. Aside from the warm glow of an eye-level hearth, the fireplace has swing-out grills for over-the-coals cooking.

Though the kitchen has the usual up-to-the-minute appointments, many details recall the house's history. Wide decorative moldings lend a sense of age to the new counters, as does the antique hanging lamp. A big black restaurant stove stands in for the old hearth.

**VOICE OF EXPERIENCE:** In addition to providing a continuous summer breeze even when the air is still, ceiling fans also help stretch heating dollars by returning the warm air that rises back to the floor level. In a large space, a fan with a reversing switch can send warm air down in winter or up in summer, drawing cool evening air through first-floor windows.

# FROM A PORCH TO A POSTMODERN PARLOR

THE PRICE: Architect Stephen Knutson estimates that this 642-square-foot addition, finished in 1982, would cost about $75,000 done today. Construction for the renovation took four months.

The addition (9 feet by 20 feet on the rear; 33 feet by 14 feet on the side) wraps around this 80-year-old house and then opens the new room to a backyard deck.

It's an old trick. Slap some walls around a recessed back porch and you've got yourself an extra room. This L-shaped addition to a 1900s Carpenter Gothic cottage in Evanston, Illinois, brings in the eaves with such success and daring that the old trick has turned over. "This isn't just another room with pine furniture and oak floors," says interior designer Larry Boeder, who collaborated with architect Stephen Knutson on the new design. "This is a room without sharp corners, where everything—architecture and furniture—is arched and shaped. And the feeling of a porch, an elegant indoor porch, is still there."

The peaks and pitch of the addition were designed to mimic the original architecture, making it hard to see any division between new and old structures. Twin gables, one in the back and one on the side, contain large, Palladian half-moon windows that add a neo-classical yet still contemporary feeling. The high windows allow a view to the outdoors from inside the main part of the house. And the open-to-the-rafters design allows the windows to fill the room with light. Only the arched windows were custom built. All other windows and doors are ready-made choices. Finding existing sizes—before the design plan is completed, of course—can be a significant cost-saver.

The former exterior wall of the house was left intact but drywalled and painted to match the interior of the addition. Thoughtfully, the openings of the original kitchen windows (one on the far right) were retained, to keep the kitchen sunny and to overlook the new room.

Function, not mere decorative whimsy, dictated the details in the new room. "It wasn't, gee whiz, where can we get a column in this scheme," says Knutson. "One of those columns encases a steel post that holds up a steel beam that holds up the second-story overhang."

Everything works to promote the idea of an indoor porch: the overhang was constructed from a remnant of the original stoop. The added neoclassical cornices and columns call to mind old-fashioned verandas.

VOICE OF EXPERIENCE: There are three ways to acquire intricate, large-scale moldings like the ones here: find a house where they're part of the original architecture and start the laborious process of refinishing; buy simulations and reproductions "cast" in plastic that are widely available and surprisingly non-plastic-looking once in place and painted; or combine different shapes and sizes of smaller stock moldings, straight from the lumberyard, and build them up on the wall.

# PRESERVATION HALL

**TRICKS OF HISTORICAL DETAIL:** The original pine subfloor in the hallway was made to look like American walnut flooring of the period with a couple of easy devices. Walnut stain did one trick.

Before the sanding and stain, a less obvious idea was fake "pegging." Floors used to be laid by pounding wooden pegs into precut small holes to connect the subfloor and the finish

floor. Then, after sanding, the pegs became flush with the floor, making round, end-grain details underfoot. Here, in imitation, wooden pegs were pounded into the pine for the same effect.

The porches were torn off in the 1920s. The third-floor ballroom and its mansard roof burned in a fire in the 1950s. The sloping front yard, with a circular drive for carriages, was sold off to land developers in the 1970s. That's the way great houses die—bit by bit—until someone comes along to turn the tide.

This Chicago mansion is a grander, more formal Victorian than the familiar oak and gingerbread houses. In carefully restoring it and making the most

of its former glories, the new owners still faced the same problems and suffered the same anxieties that any meddler—and keeper—of the past would feel.

The overall design decision was to combine careful innovation with the period details. That way, the house's historical integrity is given its obvious due, but not to the detriment of present-day comfort. Imagine the hall on the right with dark woodwork, big-patterned wallpaper, and green wall-to-wall carpeting. Too moody, for sure, though that solution would make it restoration-perfect.

Instead, the interior was lightened up. The mahogany-grained doors and frames, their finish too far gone to save, were glossed in pale yellow paint like the walls. Luckily, the good pine subfloor had always been covered, and after removing the wrecked top layer, the owners found the unfinished pine. Smooth sanding and a dark walnut stain make it more than presentable. Meticulously restored, the walnut balustrade is original to the house—and a grand bow to the Victorian period.

Although this house will never again look as it did when owner Captain Rumsey, then 77, posed on horseback in front of his Italianate mansion, The Evergreens, on July 4, 1913, the pride of the owners remains undiminished.

The current owners installed a fountain (left), just outside the front door, perhaps as symbolic replacement for the long-lost porch (above).

**VOICE OF EXPERIENCE:** Looking for a particular paint color? First, take the paint chip out of the store, which probably has fluorescent lighting. Tape it to the wall at home and live with it a few days to see how you like it. Second, don't judge color from a wet sample. Many colors have a much different tone when dry. Finally, more and more paint stores now use a color-matching computer. It scans any paint sample and reproduces the shade accurately. One friend brought in her son's prized sneaker and got a match to paint his room.

At first glance, the living room below has the look of times past, though it's thoroughly modern. If the house isn't to feel like a museum, the owners' style should come through. Given the restorers' choice of carpet, all else has grown pale. New wing chairs and a good-as-old reproduction Regency chair (on the right) feel at home with English antiques. The draperies, hemmed with cord, are tied back from behind to frame the tall windows.

However updated, the living room falls into easy conversation with the more formal dining room. In a room like this, with lots of hard surfaces—high ceilings, plaster walls, bare floors, even unique parquetry—the walls need some sort of soundproofing. A simple solution for the inevitable echoes was to cover the walls with the moiré-patterned, cotton-acetate fabric stretched over quarter-inch foam. The walls now look rich, but sound acoustically soft.

Two different sets of Victorian "Chippendale" chairs, a dozen in all, ring a late-nineteenth-century table. It's a grand and less costly way to fill the room than a matched set of twelve—easier to find as well.

Personal style takes this Victorian living room from the past to present perfect. The atmosphere and furnishings seem to be period, but they're not. All the individual choices add up to a modern, welcoming room.

**VOICE OF EXPERIENCE:** A heat gun—an intensified version of a portable hair dryer—is a good alternative to caustic chemical paint removers. It's faster, easier to control, and less dangerous. Like the chemicals, the heat gun will clear away layers of paint from baseboard moldings, carved mantels, and even from marble and metal ceiling tile.

**W**hen original moldings, doors, balusters, and the like are gone from a house, fine reproductions can fill the gap. Look for design, workmanship, and materials that re-create the vintage details. Period furnishings can also add the amenities missing from an old house.

Delight, to paraphrase Mies van der Rohe, is in the details. And this house is blessed with many—some of them restored by dint of much effort, some found by accident, and some provided by the furnishings:

Refinishing a balustrade and newel post is always a labor of love. The one above *(top row, left)* is made of turned black walnut. It was taken apart, removed from the house, and sent out to be dipped and stripped of its

cracked varnish. The only finish now is wax.

Although this particular swagged drape window treatment of festoon and side jabots *(top row, middle)* is more eighteenth century than the nineteenth-century house, the heavy curtains suit a lushly decorated bedroom. The draperies and cornice are velvet, and the "sheers" are lace.

As for the hardware, the owners were about to replace all the black metal doorknobs they found throughout the house, but the project proved too expensive. Instead, they began polishing. The knobs *(top row, right)* and escutcheons turned out to be nickel silver.

The newly installed white Cararra marble mantel in the living room *(bottom row, left)* recalls the Italianate roots of the house's original architecture. During renovation, the tile fireplace surround was discovered under layers of black paint.

The exterior shot of the bay *(bottom row, middle)* reveals rounded window tops and decorative brackets at the roof. The design devices come from Renaissance models, while the bay window, like the mantel, speaks in the vernacular of the classic Italianate style.

On the inside of the bay window *(bottom row, right)* balloon shades have replaced heavy, fringed "Victorian" draperies. Once let down, they look like shirred curtains. When raised, their soft folds are an informal touch in the more formal setting of the second parlor.

**Occasionally, simple decoration can take over for renovation. Here, the only redeeming feature of the bath was the solid porcelain tub. Exposed pipes, however functional, were an eyesore. A floor-to-ceiling veil of shirred cotton muslin hides the problem. The result is a lot better—and cheaper—than a new wall in such a confined space.**

# THE NEW FAMILY HOME

**VOICE OF EXPERIENCE:** Sunspaces are probably the most popular bump-out additions: roomy, light, energy-efficient. While custom sunrooms are expensive because of spe-cial-order glass sizes, and the labor required to insure long-lasting, waterproof installation, an array of pre-fabricated kits now offer lower-priced alternatives. Most can be ordered in modules of varying widths, heights, and glass patterns, all fitting into the same framing and waterproofing system. The choice is now so extensive that a prefab can be almost like a custom version.

Sometimes big houses are made, not born. With the considerable help of a canny architect, this unassuming 1920s building, "little more than a dark cabin, really," dared to think big.

"At first I was a little taken aback at such a major job of remodeling," says Bay Area architect Elida Schujman, who turned the Marin County two-bedroom house into a four-bedroom, two-bath manor. "The house had a good location, but it was close to the road, and the first floor, in front, was up to the property line. One of my prime concerns was to ensure privacy and still have the amount of light and windows that the owners wanted."

Her solution was to build both up and out, following the slope of the back hill, to create a loft-bedroom mezzanine in the front and a skylit, two-story living area at the back *(below)*. In all, the roof was raised five feet to make a brand-new upper story, a ten-foot-wide skylight and multipaned glass wall was added, and the downstairs bedroom walls, in the back, were moved out four feet to allow for better light. The house went from 1,413 square feet to 2,500. Two of the bedrooms are downstairs and two are on the mezzanine. "The effect," says Schujman, "is an indoor garden. There's plenty of cross ventilation, and there's natural light all day even though there are lots of trees around the house."

Wisely, the owners moved out during this renovation, which took about eight months, although six months had gone into the planning stage by then. "Costs are a little higher in California than other parts of the country," notes Schujman. Today, you'd need to bank on "at least $100 per square foot for any renovation here and $120-a-square-foot for highly detailed work. This house cost a little under $200,000 to complete."

At the back of the house, a custom-built greenhouse extension and an angled skylight allow glamorous dining under a 17-foot-high canopy.

Pulling furniture away from the walls and arranging it on the diagonal reclaims the middle of the room. Here, the angled fireplace calls the shots and the Eileen Gray rug does the organizing. The fireplace was already in the house, but it was replaced. The stones—which the owners picked up from a nearby riverbed—were added during the renovation.

**WORKING SCULPTURE:** Furniture can stand alone as form if you pare away the end tables and lamps. Here, fat upholstered wing chairs and the camelback sofa look so good because of the air around them. Tailored, solid-color, men's suiting fabric helps show off the fine shapes.

Whether they replace walls, as here, or sliding glass doors, French doors will open a room to the outside and provide architectural detail without the dizzying feeling of a sheet of glass.

I n the last two decades, the biggest revolution in the home has happened in the kitchen. Since the whole family now cooks and entertains here, this room has moved from backstage to center stage. What goes into the kitchen is now just as important as what goes into the living room —and just as many people are likely to see it.

This new kitchen was installed by using the space of a side patio on the 1920s house. The original kitchen had been in the back, where the dining area is now (previous page). The owners, accomplished and frequent cooks, asked for and got a real working space that also looks good.

The custom-made cabinets are patterned on Shaker lines and are nicely updated with enamel pulls. The glass doors provide a feeling of the pantry —and are also convenient. There's a great deal of economical storage here. Note, especially, the upper level of cabinets that reach to the ceiling.

**The view from the front of the revamped house (left), and the bedroom within (above): The old roofline has been transformed into decorative molding and a charming window was installed in the new wall.**

Small tiles make the floor, and then climb the wall in a larger scale, creating the bold checkerboard. Above the tile, the walls are painted in a semi-gloss enamel white.

An impressive restaurant stove and a built-in refrigerator/freezer with stainless steel doors does the rest of the work.

**The overscaled custom range hood here, seven feet long, works as a design element—to focus and punctuate the white space. But it's also a powerful exhaust system for cooking odors. Open-plan kitchens make effective ventilation increasingly important.**

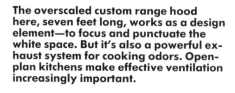

**ON COUNTERS:** The wood counter below (on the right) was made from a plywood base and covered with an oak veneer—flooring material. A veneered edge wraps around to cover the plywood on the side. It looks great, but it's not very durable, especially so near the sink. It's vulnerable to rot.

**ON VENTING HOODS:** "A commercial hood and a custom-built one will both cost about $2,000," says architect Schujman. "So, if you need a large hood, you might as well have one made." People get a little overanxious about hoods. While a good idea, they're not crucial and depend more on the chef.

# THE NEW GLAMOUR OF COMFORT

**T**his was a totally nondescript house," says designer Ann Dupuy, who completed the renovation along with a team of her designer partner, Ann Holden, and contractor Michael Carbine. "We added everything—it's all new inside."

Built in 1910 in one of New Orleans's now older residential neighborhoods, the wood-frame house was designed as a duplex. It had two two-story units, side by side, that were rental town houses. Little by little, the current owners began taking over more and more space in the 3,500-square-foot house; now they occupy just about all of it.

"I was inspired by a recent trip to Mexico," says Dupuy. "I was struck by the houses of an architect named Marco Aldoco, who's done a good deal of work around Cancún. He uses a lot of columns and soft colors, and his rooms are all open to the sea. I wanted to get that look in this house." The result is a traditional style, but done with a sumptuous ease. Lacking any stiff formality, this is now a house where you want to live.

**In this 30-foot-by-25-foot family room, adjacent to the dining and kitchen areas, New Orleans designers Dupuy and Holden installed French doors, bold aqua cove molding and columns, creamy linen draperies, all-new recessed lighting, and the forties flavor of rattan chairs.**

"We began with the idea of flagstone floors in this room," says designer Dupuy, "to get a feeling of the outdoors." The two-toned flagstone floor also has a contrasting border.

**THE PRICE:** "It took about eight months to complete this renovation," says designer Ann Dupuy, "over the winter of 1984–85." The cost was about $75,000.

**THE COLOR AQUA:** Surprisingly, a jolt of bold color often works very well in small spaces, although, as in this kitchen, it needs to be used with judicious care. Perhaps even more surprisingly, the new palette of strong colors is neutral enough to blend with a broad range of furnishing styles and periods. Who would have thought aqua could look so traditional.

**High windows in the kitchen *(above)* bring in natural light while still leaving space for storage. The theatrical island *(above and below)* has a flagstone top that echoes the floor and a plaster surface painted in the aqua theme.**

"**M**ost of what this house needed," says Ann Dupuy, "was to be opened up and to gain some character. We took out four of the downstairs walls to get more space and light and to connect the two apartments. There was a lean-to attached to the back of the house, no more than a shack, really. And we used that as a basis for the dining/kitchen areas and the big lounging room, where the family really lives.

At the back, we raised the ceiling from eight to sixteen feet, and then we installed decorative columns and moldings and the stone floor. What the house really needed was a strong dose of some architectural character."

The dining area *(opposite),* off the kitchen, has the same open-air access to the backyard as the large family room. New French doors and the background floor create the outdoor atmosphere that the designers and the owners wanted.

In the new kitchen, 25 feet by 10 feet, Egyptian-inspired columns frame the wide-mouthed opening to create a sense of entrance and provide a novel divider without closing in the space. The columns afford the kitchen equal status with the adjoining family room *(previous page, left).* Creamy painted wood cabinets and walls offset the stainless steel double sink and the center-stage working island.

All three areas—kitchen, dining, and second living room—are unified by the flagstone floor and the bold aqua color. The spacious suite has an element of fantasy, a whisper of thirties nightclubs, but it's all amply suited to present-day comfort.

# THE ENLIGHTENED TUDOR

Before the great Crash, before the big bite of the income tax, in that glittering decade called the twenties, those who aspired to live in style aspired to Tudor. A Tudor house said East Coast establishment, English ancestry, and dressing for dinner. With its haughty façade of Flemish brickwork and massive oak doors set in stone, the Tudor home was everyman's suburban American castle.

Twenties Tudor houses still abound. Indeed, the style is being built today, though usually on a smaller scale. The old ones are baronial, large, and dark, characterized inside by low, timbered ceilings, dark paneling, varnished stucco walls, dark wood floors, and carved stone fireplaces. Nowadays the large interior spaces seem burdened by the very details that once made them so appealing.

The design challenge of a Tudor home is to retain the character without the uncomfortable heaviness of the style. For contemporary tastes, this means letting light into the deep recesses.

In this suburban house just outside Pittsburgh, Pennsylvania, the owners found a delightfully startling solution

for both the Tudor's woes of low ceilings and dark interiors. They removed the low, first-floor ceiling, leaving the stairway and what is now a back-of-the-house balcony for upstairs bedrooms. The terrific results look much like the two-story space we often see in renovated city town houses. A quarry tile flooor emphasizes the house's new, lighter mood.

Then, with a witty wink and a nod to the past, the owners left the fireplace and baseboard of the old second-floor bedroom in place as a reminder of what the house had been. An up-to-date hanging lamp makes long use of the new height, and since the original details were usually painted gray, the light gray here is an in-house code for antiquity.

Unafraid to trifle with convention, the owners here had the daring idea of tiling the ceiling with small, glossy white squares, which look particularly crisp against the dark wood window trim and railing. The once gloomy stairwell is now opened up to reflected light from the ceiling. Two modern hanging lamps and a wall cutout illuminate the area even further.

# NEW WING FOR AN OLD FARMHOUSE

Also accomplished by Wagner and Emmerling, the hallway's plywood floor was first painted a creamy background color. Light gray paint was then speckled on by hand, using a natural sponge. Afterward, the cattle brand pattern and border was sketched in charcoal, then painted with a darker gray. Finally, another, even darker gray was sponged on overall for an addi-

Founded on an intensely personal vision, this stylish renovation of an 1881 farmhouse in Portland, Oregon, is a testimonial to the clear-thinking owners. Tiger and Geraldine Warren had the brave idea of adding an ultracontemporary wing to the venerable house. In collaboration with architect David Jenkins, they came up with this very modern addition and passageway *(above)* that still echoes the peaked, saltbox lines of the original. The Warrens then installed their very tasty interiors without falling prey to the dictates of farmhouse-rustic. The solutions are both structural and decorative, rounded out with rich artistic details and unusual finishes.

Besides the ever-present desire for more space, the Warrens also wanted a wall-to-wall window on the new wing to capture a sweeping view of downtown Portland, which includes the controversial Portlandia building designed by architect Michael Graves. Rather than use their own carpenters, the Warrens figured out an ingenious, and inexpensive, solution: they hired a firm that makes storefronts. The glass and metal grid took three days to install and cost far less than a custom-made window wall.

Both inside and out, the new hallway *(above and opposite)* joins the old and new sections of the house, and features a new front entrance. Recessed lighting—with some fixtures more hidden than others to spotlight artwork—provides a welcome. Pacific Northwest Indian masks, contrasting tones of wood, and a uniquely reclaimed sofa set the tone of the New West style that's a lovely surprise behind the rustic door.

The creamy, glazed walls lend a special warmth. Completed by paint decoration specialists Ron Wagner and Philip Emmerling, the glazed color comes from mixing colored oil paints into a transparent varnish, called a glaze coat. Here, orange, yellow, and off-white glaze were dabbed on with a brush and then blended over the wall with a natural sponge.

A curved door, salvaged from a downtown Portland hotel, has new brass hardware and just the right new/old mood for the entrance.

tional speckled effect. All the paint was enamel and the cost was only $6 per square foot.

**VOICE OF EXPERIENCE:** If renovation plans include a soaring space with a peaked roof, you'll need to leave some exposed horizontal beams, called collar ties, even if it means blocking part of a glass wall. They're needed to tie the house together. In any building with a peaked roof, rafters tend to push out on the walls. For structural safety and to minimize surface maintenance, such as fixing cracked wallboard seams, leave at least every other collar tie in place when removing a ceiling to make a vaulted room.

**ON FABULOUS FAKES:**
Two marbleizing techniques color the floor below. The green borders were achieved by blotting the wet top-coat, revealing the dry, rubbed colors underneath. Two shades of mustard paint, swirled in a film of turpentine, create the yellow areas. The marbleized look comes from applying kerosene to the still-wet floor, which retards the drying process. Then the color is sponged on so that the undercoat and the new color bleeds into a soft, marblelike finish. Polyurethane protects the finish overall.

**"W**e often wondered if we were doing the right thing, but we stuck to our vision," says Geraldine Warren, owner of this farmhouse renovation in Portland. "It was, for example, a leap in style from a wood mantel to faux marble floors—but we took it."

A great deal of the drama inside this updated farmhouse comes from the owners' deliberate avoidance of rustic gestures and from a canny way with color and finish. Architectural detail on the baseboards and molding is picked out in a glossy, outlining white paint. In the library *(opposite)*, the wooden mantel was stripped and then left alone—austere and yet inviting. Terra-cotta tile in front of the fireplace and the glory of those original wooden doors warms the spare space.

The decorative choices evidence the owners' anti-traditionalist style. A leather Chesterfield sofa and the leather armchairs recall the rough comfort of the Western frontier, but the confident green brings us back to the present. Oriental drawings of horses echo English hunting prints.

In the dining room *(above)*, a similar hand is at work. Color and shape are carefully mixed. The room is softened by balloon shades at the original windows, wooden doors, and curving, neo-classic furnishings.

But it's the marbleized floor, providing a very bold and intriguing background, that really makes both the library and the dining room. The green and yellow faux marble is totally unexpected in an 1881 farmhouse.

**Seen close up, the terra-cotta tile and faux marble finish show how closely the floor color mirrors the room's furnishings.**

# RENOVATING THE RANCH
## TRACT HOUSING AND THE SPLIT-LEVEL

Renovation's urban lessons are on the move. The innovative solutions we loved in brownstone and loft space are now coming home to the suburban tract. As you see, Ozzie and Harriet don't live here anymore. With some 40 million houses built since 1946 in close-in, desirable suburbs, the country's most plentiful and most boring housing stock is ripe for renewal.

"It was a catalog of the period's worst architectural features," says architect Daniel Solomon, who masterminded the soaring transformation *(right)* of this mild-mannered fifties artifact *(above)*. But the fault was less in the house—the shell remains intact—and more with the old floor plan. Who said double-height town-house space should or could exist only in century-old buildings?

I t should come as no surprise—yet somehow it does—that the new frontiers for renovation in this country are no longer the buildings of old, but some 40 million new houses built since 1946. Call them ranch, split-level, Cape Cod, or Dutch Colonial, they're a housing resource so obvious we've all but ignored it. Why? Too many of us left the suburbs seeking freer lives, newer values, and wider open spaces, if mostly in the mind. Turn 180 degrees and a decade or two. The need for space is mostly in the living room. And what better canvas than the straight plasterboard walls and pine floors of a Suburban Ranch?

Those houses were built for eager young postwar couples setting up an idealized life to fit the old American Dream—their very own house, brand-new, with three bedrooms, minimum: a master; one each for the requisite kids-to-come; and a guest room aka "the den." Then there was the Nuclear Family room and a mandatory dining room. Used rarely because of the eat-in kitchen, it became show-off space, little more than a still life of table and chairs. And even if all that chopping up and labeling of rooms resulted in cramped, ungainly little spaces, there was, for sure, a room for every function.

Now look at values today. The American family is no longer a man, wife, and two kids. Any and all permutations of that mix make a family these days. And so, too, with the spaces we live in. Any place is dining room enough as long as it has a table. Space is still important, but the functional imperative is gone, along with the notion of solitary woman-in-the-kitchen. Just as roles have blended and blurred in the last decade, so has our need for the rigidly defined little rooms of the 1940s and 1950s.

Having found this freedom in our heads, it is inevitable that the Suburban Ranch, seen with new eyes, loses its bourgeois implications. What's left is affordable, solid living space—a new canvas for us to work our enlightened magic on.

And that's just what's happening across the country as once urban pioneers rethink the suburbs: knocking down walls and raising ceilings, adding frankly pleasurable amenities, building out into banal backyards with glorious kitchens, sybaritic baths, courtyards, and pools. We're blowing away fifties constraints to apply sophisticated architectural thinking. Renovation style, once rooted in the cities, is coming out to play in the suburbs.

# THE SUBURBAN LOFT

Whatever emotion you felt upon entering a classic, fifties ranch house, you never had to catch your breath. Fifties houses weren't designed to dazzle. But current-day ideas can create that dazzle.

Here, it's hard to imagine that this loftlike space, located in a Bay Area suburb, was once an all-too-typical Cold War survivor—"The very essence of banality," judges architect Daniel Solomon, who engineered the cost-conscious renovation. The exterior of the house didn't change at all *(page 32)*. Instead, Solomon reorganized a floor plan that had shoehorned too many rooms into limited space.

The airy colonnade below was achieved by gutting the kitchen, living room, and dining area and replacing the walls with supporting column-and-truss dividers. A new, higher, barrel-vault ceiling lets the columns and arches support the roof and play off the exterior's plain Jane shape.

The original, misplaced kitchen robbed the living room of precious space. Now it resides in its own "house" at the rear of the room, with an interior window to provide light and to overlook the living area.

**The old entry opened into a gloomy, windowless hall. Now a tiled floor and panoramic sight lines create a graceful transition from the front door to the stair-stepped dais.**

# THE MAGAZINE MAKEOVER

**A granite exterior dated the house (*above:* the before state) as much as did the shrubs and planters. We substituted a coat of stucco, painted lavender and yellow, bigger windows, paving tile, and simpler plantings in stucco-clad, concrete blocks *(right).***

I n 1982 or so, *Metropolitan Home* first began touting the potential of ranch houses. Interest rates, you'll remember, were sky-high. Mortgage and home improvement money was tight and expensive. The better shape the original house was in, the more likely you were to find the financing to customize it. Houses with pedigrees cost a packet and then took another small fortune to update. Air and light had entered the movement, so that renovation was no longer the sole concern of rigid preservationists. At the same time, paying for the privilege of living well in cities across the U.S. was on an upward spiral. Older suburbs, just outside the city, began to look a lot more glamorous.

Indeed, a host of interlocking points suddenly opened our eyes to the lowly tract home. As we scouted for homes to publish, we saw amazing proof of how a ranch could be transformed. Avant-garde owners from Connecticut to California showed us examples of redone ranches with the paint still wet. And they overwhelmed and excited us. We were taken then, just as we are today, with how a bold, new home can be carved out of an ordinary house without much travail

or cost. So, as a magazine, we decided to back our editorial policy with cold cash. We decided to tackle one ourselves.

We found this 1952 house, a gabled version of the familiar flatroof, in Houston, Texas, suffering from all the problems of the genre: featureless rooms, not enough light, and a lazy floor plan that squandered space. We purchased it and proceeded like anyone else. We interviewed and hired local architect Val Glitsch and contractors Bill Martin and Burke Windham to perform the work. We renovated this ranch in 1984.

**Return of the front porch: a deeper threshold and a solitary column heighten the importance of the front door after the changes.**

canvas. Which means whatever style you fancy, and however much you have in your budget, your renovation dollars will go further.

"A lot of people don't see the potential in these ranch houses," says Houston architect Val Glitsch. "They are not destined to remain ugly."

**A**rchitect Val Glitsch removed two walls, added skylights, columns, fresh color, and a new hallway. "When we first started," she recalls, "a neighbor said, 'Well, you sure are wrecking a perfectly good house.' His attitude has changed remarkably since then."

**THE ALL-OVER FLOOR:** For unity and a contemporary mood, ceramic paving tiles cover a concrete floor in all the heavy-traffic areas—the same tile as on the front walk.

**VOICE OF EXPERIENCE:** For the best sculptural effect from staggered wall surfaces, specify a three-coat taping job. Too many contractors get by with a heavy first coat of joint compound and one finish coat after sanding. To do it right, the first coat embeds and covers the tape, filling up the recess where drywall panels meet. After sanding, the second coat feathers out the joint. After another light sanding, the third coat makes the seams smooth and flush with the wall. A final light sanding completes the job.

The old entrance *(above)* was typical: no light, no feeling of openness, and lacking any sense of drama or discovery that opening a front door should bring.

The temptation with a ranch house is to leave well enough alone. That was precisely our reaction when we first laid eyes on this one. Everything worked—in fact, was in very good condition—and, well, it wasn't that bad. But look at it this way: a ranch will cost less (sometimes a lot less) than a place with more personality, detailing, and architectural interest. So the money saved can be put to work making it into the home you really want.

Most of the ranch's charm comes from its low and lean silhouette, so we did not alter the exterior significantly. Instead, the bulk of our money went toward rearranging the inside. As soon as you step through the new French front door of the revitalized house, a flood of light greets you. Larger windows on the side wings and the addition of skylights bring in daylight. A flowing floor plan disperses the extra light and provides views across the house. Usually, doorways in a ranch are staggered, the better to fit in all the chopped-up rooms. Moving and enlarging the openings changes the sight lines. Immediately you've added a vista, and a new sense of how the house works.

A dramatic floor plan inspires bold furnishings and color. A sassy red leather armchair and black-striped curtains play off the salmon, blue, and terra-cotta. Two types of tile, quarry and ceramic, give the new fireplace the look of a classic facade. And the angled arrangement of the armchair and plump chaise makes the most of a long, narrow space.

Looking from the living room into the old, dark hallway *(right)* shows how a new, grand entrance *(below)* can restyle the house.

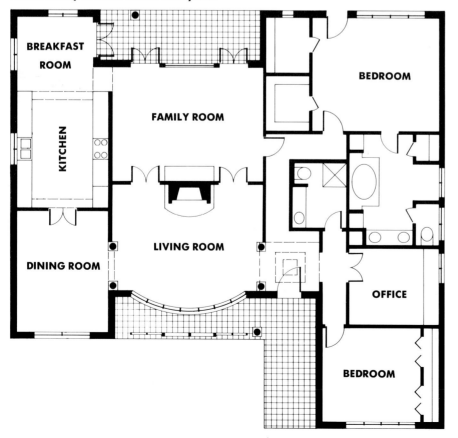

Once cut off from the rest of the house, this den *(above)* was transformed into a practical family room with better light and French door connections to the living room *(right)*.

With older-house renovations, the objective is at least partly restoration. But ranch houses have little historic architecture to preserve. What they do have are rooms out of touch with the way people live today. There was nothing inherently wrong with this dark-paneled den *(left)*, it just didn't work hard enough. And it ignored the adjacent backyard. We wanted to put that prime location to better use.

What we did was remove the dark wood paneling and the T-square parquetry. We took out the functional—but boring—sliding glass doors. In place of all that, we installed tile floors, here and throughout the house. We added more storage and the charm of French doors. Then, for more sun and light, we put a skylight in the roof. The result is twice the entertainment space and a room you want to be in, day and night.

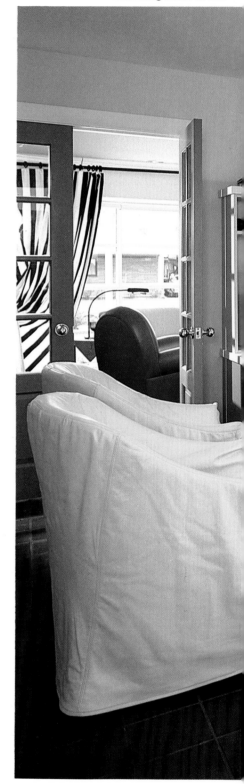

The new floor plan shows how the spacious 2,400 square feet have been put to use: dining, living, and entrance areas are now lined up through larger, open doorways. The kitchen and dining rooms were also opened up and joined. A new family room is off the backyard.

**BREAKFAST ROOM**

**KITCHEN**

**FAMILY ROOM**

**BEDROOM**

**LIVING ROOM**

**DINING ROOM**

**OFFICE**

**BEDROOM**

ack for large com-
uter cables, the rule
seems to be custom-
uilt housing. The
solution below is a
canny one, readily
available. Originally
seen in restaurant
kitchens but now
found in retail stores,
a rolling wire shelving
unit keeps the VCR, TV,
compact disc player,
turntable, speakers,
and assorted power
units comfortably
ensconced—with nary
a snarl of wire or cord.

In the revived family room, amenities
and Eurostyle furnishings have been
added to update the room and make it
work as the informal living center:
entertainment area, audio/visual room,
second living room. The casual center-
piece is a glove-soft, fabriclike leather
sofa that has lost all straitlaced inhibi-
tions. Two armchairs, draped in canvas,
complement the leather. The generous
coffee table provides a touch of luxe.
And the black Aalto chair across the
way recalls the house's fifties roots. The
old fifties corner counter—the wet bar—
always had a tiny sink that no one ever
used much—except during the odd
party. This new bar area offers storage
that's custom-built, with salmon-colored
laminated cabinets and drawers below.
Above, a painted glass-door kitchen
cabinet puts glasses and bottles right at
hand. In between, a laminated white
counter serves out the drinks.

Fifties aficionados may wince at giving up the original pine cabinets and classic chrome wall oven in the former kitchen *(right)*, but the new kitchen *(above)* now works much harder for its supper. The inefficient cabinets were removed to make way for a larger entrance to the dining room. For better flow and work space, we also discarded the right-angled divider.

**C**o-contractor Bill Martin says to "be sure to work your plan hard before you get into construction. Decide schedules at the front end. And before tearing down a single wall, ask yourself: 'Am I over-renovating the house? How will this change enhance resale value?' "

The kitchen should be high on the list of any renovation plans. That room, and the bathroom too, are tied most directly to a home's resale value—and, of course, to its livability. Although we spread our money throughout the house as evenly as possible, we gave our baths and kitchen a higher priority when apportioning funds.

In the kitchen, we wanted more storage and more space to work. Custom-made laminate-clad plywood cabinets in up-to-date colors provide more storage but actually take up less room than the originals *(below, left)*. That permitted space for today's wider range of appliances, including the stacking microwave and oven on the wall. It also expanded the counter space. A new double sink replaced the old, single variety.

Yet this lighthearted and hyperfunctional new kitchen is still in touch with its mid-century roots. The chairs around the oak table (which works for eating or preparing food) are by fifties master designer Arne Jacobsen.

A view of the former dining room, looking toward the living room *(above)*, reveals how the original floor plan meandered. Note the staggered doorways and how the new ones have changed *(below)*.

With dash and daring, the new dining room *(right)* now opens directly onto the kitchen and combines wide-ranging elements: a traditional mahogany china cabinet behind Joe D'Urso's marble-topped sleek table; a kimono stand (left side of room) contrasts with the post-modern palette and columns; and chintz-draped formal dining chairs are supplemented by the Richard Meier black side chairs in the back.

# CUSTOMIZING THE COLONIAL

Built in the mid-1960s, the front of this bland, "builder's Cape Cod" in Connecticut was enlivened with an evocative white latticework frame fence "to unify the front elevation and to lend foreground," says the architect.

THE PRICE: "We completed this house in two phases," says Floyd, "but the actual work took about a year, with three or four months of planning. Today, it would cost about $150,000 to renovate, including the kitchen and the front walkway."

"I had just returned from a trip to the Loire Valley in France when I started to work on this house," says Connecticut architect Chad Floyd, "and the strange coincidence was that the owners had just traveled there too. The design here emerged from our joint interest in the Loire châteaux—the grand scale, the huge fireplaces, everything. We wanted this little house to live big, to remind us of a château."

"It's on a fabulous site," Floyd goes on, "overlooking a harbor, but it was a nothing house—grim, dark, terribly proportioned rooms with low ceilings, a long, narrow living room. The idea was to open it up, to make something special out of the 2,800 square feet."

Besides righting a scarcely believable indifference to the backyard view, Floyd sliced through the center of the house, dividing the inside with a floor-to-roof "great hall" that explodes with light and space. What came out were the front door (to make a more sensible entryway), a stairway up to the left upstairs hall *(below)*, and a narrow guest bedroom.

Three new skylights now emphasize the wash of sunlight. All the major rooms have been turned to open into the center gallery. "I changed a lot of the doors," says Floyd, "because I like French doors. They're not buttoned up. I like doors to take up space, just as a person does, to make the gesture of entrance and exit."

"It all looks lush and superscaled from the first floor," Floyd concludes. "It's one of my favorite houses. I thought slicing through the house and blowing everything up was an elegant, inexpensive way to transform very ordinary space."

Throughout the house, architect Floyd installed supersize, half-round moldings with a five-inch radius, made from eight-inch-by-eight-inch sheets, turned on a lathe by the contractor. The outsize moldings change the room proportions, making everything seem much bigger.

**ON COLOR:** The palest pastels, soft washes of paint color, can often change the lighting in a room. Here, researcher Brenda Huffman spent months plotting the subtle colors in this vertical slice of sunlit space *(below)*. She finally chose two— a light blue-green for the chimney mass and stairwell and a pale ochre for the surrounding walls. The result is a slight shift in perspective, a gradual and soft toning as the light changes. The different colors also define the central hall, setting it off as an object in space.

# RE-INVENTING THE SPLIT-LEVEL

Before the changes: views of the house from the front *(opposite, right)* and the back *(far right)* show that the familiar suburban silhouette wasn't altered. New windows, however, and the verve of exterior decoration give this standard suburban a completely updated face.

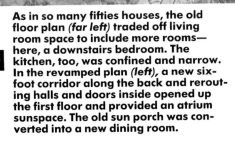

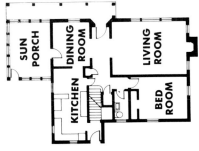

As in so many fifties houses, the old floor plan *(far left)* traded off living room space to include more rooms—here, a downstairs bedroom. The kitchen, too, was confined and narrow. In the revamped plan *(left)*, a new six-foot corridor along the back and rerouting halls and doors inside opened up the first floor and provided an atrium sunspace. The old sun porch was converted into a new dining room.

In this postwar split-level in Des Moines, Iowa, a minimum of add-on construction made an ample house a whole lot bigger. And a whole lot smarter, both inside and out. The unused backyard was put to front-stage use with a multi-level terrace that blends into the new alley-wide addition *(above)*. Both the addition and the terrace shift the emphasis of the house from the front to the back. A decidedly unsuburban color palette, as well as the exterior grid motifs, serve as a postmodern welcome mat. "I showed the owners a lot of pencil sketches," says architect Cal Lewis, "and they saw similar uses of color on other projects I did, but they took a lot on faith."

Don't forget. It's not how much space you have that counts; it's the way you treat it that makes the home. In this case, a six-foot-wide extension across the back redefined the house. Says Des Moines architect Cal Lewis, "The owner wanted a feeling of volume and openness in a typical split-level with eight-foot-nine-inch ceilings. And the real heart of our solution was planning. The owner had a lot to do with it. We originally came up with a plan that reorganized the upstairs and opened up the rooms, but it didn't include the galleria, and because the owner knew what he wanted—that feeling of volume—we could go much farther. Planning was the key. The rest was details, by comparison."

The only major new construction in the house, the back extension grew out of an existing lean-to. "We took off the lean-to," explains Lewis, "and reused the foundation, extending it along the back of the house. We then added new walls on top." The resulting galleria changes the feeling of the house altogether. A balcony on the second floor (*opposite*) connects the new space to the old.

Other changes are more than cosmetic—enlarged room openings, new windows, the eye-catching charm of postmodern detail, glass blocks for interior light and interest, skylights for the same reason—but the ingenious six new feet is what makes the house breathe freely in the present.

**A bump-out bay was the solution to cramped space in the kitchen. The new bay separates the eating area from the spacious cooking galley (below). Note the two kinds of windows. And note, too, the playful, open shelving that echoes the exterior's gridwork.**

"The new galleria," says architect Cal Lewis, "is ninety percent of the effectiveness of the renovated house. It solved both the emotional and functional problems of the space." It also added private living space and a sense of place to the often overlooked back of the house.

**THE PRICE:** New construction began on this split-level in the late fall, stopped for winter, and was completed by spring. The cost today, says architect Lewis, would run about $140,000.

**ON THE RISING BOTTOM LINE:** "After you get the price from the contractor," says Lewis, "invariably, upscaling will occur. I always tell clients to expect at least a ten percent increase. I know that as the client gets into the project, as he learns more, he'll decide spending that extra ten percent will be the best value." And if it's only ten percent, the client's lucky.

Adding dramatic space needn't bring down the house. In the living room *(opposite and right, top),* a standard, builder-issue picture window was replaced by a large, graceful bay window, but the bay was inexpensively rigged to fit into the existing opening. Subtle color changes on moldings and walls throughout the first floor help smooth the transition from room to room. The view from the center hall, just inside the front door *(opposite),* benefits from enlarged, arched openings that are associated with gracious, older homes and never found in ranch houses. The hall itself once took a meandering course to the rear of the house, but it now runs unimpeded from the front door through the kitchen and on to the back terrace. Most of the major first-floor rooms were reorganized to open onto the hallway. On the hall and kitchen floors, unglazed, terra-cotta Italian tile, with a lighter-colored border, adds warmth and also extends the improved vista.

The new dining room *(right, below)* still carries the peaked roof of its sun porch origins. "Oftentimes," says architect Lewis, "you get more interesting solutions in a renovation because the original house imparts restrictions and you can't afford to be dictatorial or rigid." The mix of colors here, both on the walls and in the furnishings, shows the careful balance of cheek and charm displayed throughout the house.

# A '60S HOUSE LIGHTENS UP

**ON THE BENEFITS OF EXCAVATION:** In the living room *(below)*, owner Beug exposed the galvanized flue during the construction phase and liked it so much, he left it that way. Be careful not to overreact while everything's in chaos, when all you want is to cover the mess, quick, with drywall. One techy, silver flue—or its equivalent—can do wonders in a neat, white room. The trick is to remember that, inevitably, the room *will* be neat and white again.

F ilm producer John Beug is accustomed to managing projects with a myriad of details. Which may be what prompted him to act as his own contractor in the reconstruction of this straight-lined tract, built in the early 1960s by a student of International Style architect Richard Neutra. "We skinned the interior and exterior walls," explains Beug, "replaced glass, added a new roof, an office, a greenhouse, and two decks. But these changes were subtle. I didn't want to alter the house's character." Sounds like a snap, but the actual process went a great deal more slowly.

When Beug first laid eyes on the house in 1976, he was sure all the windows had been tinted with beige glass. That turned out to be a nine-year accumulation of nicotine left by the previous tenant. He also found rugs ruined by dogs, rain-rotted window frames, and a leaky roof. But Beug liked the house's plain, modern lines. And he especially liked the location—high in the Hollywood Hills. After a cursory clean-up, Beug lived in the house for three years, "to get a sense of the space."

He then worked with local architect Peter de Bretteville, who is noted for an innovative way with heavy metal houses that still live light. Together, the pair shaped the renovation battle plan.

**Located in Los Angeles' coveted Hollywood Hills, this modest, plainly modern house went from bunker *(top)* to breezy with the addition of two decks, one in the back *(above)* and a larger one in front *(opposite, top).***

As a contractor, Beug supervised every detail of the two-and-half-year remodeling. The entrance to the house was rebuilt, becoming lighter and more inviting with the addition of glass doors and a skylight. The prob-lem of how best to use the hillside site's almost full acre was solved by extending the house with two decks— a small one near the first-floor office in the back and a larger one with a hot tub at the entry.

Now, having gone through it, Beug says: "I spent nine months out of the house entirely, and you could say I lived in squalor for the rest of the time. I really didn't mind, though. I liked the process of living and working in construction. My friends, of course, thought I was crazy."

Crazy like a fox. Beug paid $60,000 for the house in 1976 and spent $110,000 to $120,000 on renovating it (which, he says, is double the original estimate). The result is a house with flow-through light and space that blends easily into the neighborhood. And that Hollywood Hills neighbor-hood, don't forget, has more than its share of multi-million-dollar, movie-star homes.

The new front deck creates a double-take welcome: sunlit, wire-glass doors and a skylight on the deck lead to the original, Mission-style front door *(below)*. A change in the flooring, from cedar planking to terra-cotta tile, emphasizes the transition from the outdoors.

# RAISING THE ROOF ON A RANCH

VOICE OF EXPERIENCE: Conventional roof framing uses rafters every 16 inches. The spaces between rafters, called bays, are filled with insulation before wallboard is applied. One interesting alternative is using larger timbers (3½ inches wide instead of 1½ inches) that are four feet apart, as used in this house. The heavy rafters are spanned by 2-inch-by-6-inch plank-ing, then covered with rigid insulating board before finish roofing is applied. Inside, the rafters and planking can be stained, painted, or protected with a clear sealer.

I f ever you doubted either the amazing state of the Los Angeles real estate market or the resale power of renovation, this is the story that will change your mind. Designer Barbara Barry and kitchen design specialist Margy Newman work as a team for home interiors, but they began branching out. They formed a partnership—Nouvelle Maison—to purchase houses, renovate them, then resell the houses for a profit. "We like renovation," says Barry, "and this way we get to complete the whole package. We have the luxury of a cohesive design and we become our own clients. We never need to worry about pleasing the clients.

Impressed by the "good bones" of this 1952 ranch in Santa Monica, Barry and Newman decided to purchase it. "Ranch houses have their own integrity," says Barry. Because of the prime, near-the-beach location, the cost for the 2,500-square-foot house was $375,000. Renovation lasted for about five months, which is a rather fast turnaround. It helped, of course, that there was no major electrical or plumbing work—which is a prime advantage of renovating the modern ranch house. "We put in about $150,000," says Barry, "maybe a little more. And we sold the house for $615,000"—unfurnished.

Within those five months, the designers accomplished a thoroughgoing airing of the ranch and its unacceptable layout. They added a wing at the back for an up-to-date master bedroom/

An enlightened entryway was added during the renovation *(top)*, with new French windows flanking the front door. The window in the garage is original. In the back *(bottom)*, the new redwood deck off the bedroom suite is in perfect harmony with the original deck that leads to the kitchen.

bath suite, with access to a redwood deck. They took off the old flat roof and replaced it with a peaked one that raised the ceiling height from 8 feet to 14 feet. New light and space came from bigger and more windows. "Adding windows makes an ordinary house light, bright, and pretty terrific," says Barry. The designers also opened up the ranch's boxy, small rooms, designing a new entryway in the process. Their careful weaving of old and new transforms the house without rending the fifties fabric.

The living room *(opposite)* was once three small rooms, which says a great deal about the shortcomings of ranch design. But straightening out the crooked floor plan was only half the task. "It had weird green walls and dark wood floors," says Barry. After scraping off the accumulation of avocado wallpaper, the designers took on the floors. The dark hardwood was bleached and then lightly rubbed with white paint to let the grain show through. "The palest banana-yellow paint simply changed the whole mood," says Barry. And new, fixed windows, installed just below the raised roof line and shaped to fit in the peak, bathe the room with light.

In the new wing, at the back of the house, the master bedroom suite opens onto a redwood deck. Both the deck and the wing follow the lines of the original house.

**W**e try to look for simple solutions," says designer Barbara Barry. "We don't want to get too tricky, which can be a problem at resale. Always match the windows and match what went before. Don't try to change everything. Open it up, clean it up, and leave it alone."

**DESIGN SAVVY:** Appliance manufacturers are finally catching on to consumer demands for design that works in tight spaces. The refrigerator here has the motor on top, instead of in the back, which makes for a more efficient use of the small space. This narrow kitchen works as well as a big one.

The half wall in the kitchen/ dining room, seen on the working side *(left)*, offers a hard-working lineup that's compact without being cramped. A new window alongside the counter and a new, divided door flood the room with light.

As so often happens in ranch design, a cramped and dark kitchen was moved to the back of the house to glean more space and breathe light into the room. Here, kitchen designer Margy Newman used the former den for the dining area and converted a back porch for the kitchen's working galley. That still left the room open to the original redwood deck.

A half wall of cabinets, dishwasher, and sink was installed in the room to make a design-efficient kitchen work area. The top of the half wall is also a serving and preparation counter. And the island also works as a divider, separating the cooking from the dining space.

In setting up the budget for the kitchen renovation, designers Barry and Newman used the major dollars for big-ticket items and made clever design choices to save money on the rest. The 30-inch-wide single sink, for example, is the cheapest available, but expensive ceramic tile surrounds it. Each of the porcelain cabinet pulls cost a mere $1.50, but the cabinets themselves are solidly crafted of pine.

Open pine shelving and ceiling molding, to match the cabinets, keeps all the California sunshine warm and mellow, while the white paint on the window and door trim provides a subtle contrast with the creamy wall color.

# THE SMALL CITY HOUSE

The problem? Finding an affordable home. The smartest solution: one of those undiscovered houses that exist, faded and neglected, in cities across the country. What you need is vision. Take that unprepossessing house in a nondescript neighborhood and reshape the interior. It's a lot of house for the money.

Typical of the housing built in New Orleans in the 1890s, this shotgun house in the Garden District has tiny front gates *(opposite)* and a mere 1,200 square feet of lined-up rooms—which gave rise to the name: you could sight a gun right through the house. Moving the entrance (up the new stairs, *above*) deftly sidesteps the inconvenient floor plan.

**S**ome friends of ours, diehard renters for years, recently went house-hunting and knew just what they wanted: "Two or three bedrooms, a fireplace, a big backyard, lots of light, high ceilings, a big *front* yard, a nice quiet neighborhood, some sort of clean-lined architecture, and, of course, a $100,000 price tag, tops, at around ten percent fixed." The punchline is that our friends didn't want to move from Venice, California, where real estate runs, roughly, $100 per square inch. "To her credit," says this now-enlightened dreamer, food and wine critic Colman Andrews, "the realtor at least waited until we were out of her office before dissolving into helpless laughter."

But finding an affordable first house these days is no joke. This chapter answers that dilemma. The Small City House. They're called by quaint names: bungalows, cottages, little bricks, shotguns, two-story, wood frames. Places like Atlanta, Des Moines, Tulsa, New Orleans, Minneapolis, and, yes, Santa Monica and Venice, California, grew up around modest older homes and then all but forgot them in the boomtime of high-rise and hustle. Mostly built in the 1920s and 1930s, though some date from the turn of the century or even the 1940s, the small city house might once have been a barber shop or a seed store; it might have been, in 1923 or so, the proud, new castle of some up-and-coming merchant. The histories vary, but the bargain doesn't.

Once renovated, the results are obvious, but these houses don't stand out much at first. You'll need a shrewd, assessing eye to measure the potential. They demand imagination. That makes them affordable.

The beauty is you can literally devise your own interior design, reshaping stingy cubbyholes and doorways into more inviting archways and open-plan rooms. You'll need to rethink the traffic flow, removing walls and doors for better, more contemporary use of space, and, quite possibly, you'll want to install more generous windows and rooftop skylights to pull in light. A frequent trick in these small homes is to redirect the focus of the house—from the front to the back (the fancy front parlor has moved to the relaxing back deck). Just exposing ceiling joists might yield quite a few extra feet overhead, and, often as not, the attic space can be called on to give the living room a new horizon. The best thing about these old houses is that they'll take an enormous amount of modification without so much as a peep of protest. As for our friends—well, a modern ending. They found their dream: a leaky stucco cottage. "It was too small, the windows didn't quite fit their frames, the garden looked like something out of *Apocalypse Now,* our alley was a veritable gallery of graffiti—but other than that it was perfect. We could even afford it." And, after moving in, they knew just what to do. "We called a contractor."

# TRADITION WITH A NEW, FRESH AIR

Railed on three sides, the old front porch of the shotgun house now looks inward through the new French doors. Skylights at both ends boost the natural light that reaches into the shaded rooms. Glossy gray deck paint foreshadows the gray interior.

**ANTIQUES IN A MINIMAL MODE:** Traditional furniture here is used as if it were contemporary. Connections of period, style, and color are replaced by the gray envelope of the house and by the anchor of white sofas and striped chairs. There are five lamps (all different), seven assorted tables, and seven chairs—a variety that keeps the room from looking self-consciously designed. Yet everything's accomplished with a light, spare hand. Despite the richness of the furnishings, this room clearly has a modern sensibility.

Down South at least, a shotgun house is, by definition, not worth bothering about. Certainly not worth renovating. It was cheap worker-housing built during the 1890s on minimum size lots— 1,200 square feet of living space. But to New Orleans contractor Michael Carbine this little house was just right —for one. Its two front rooms, thrown together with an open side porch, yielded one grand room, 19 feet by 32 feet. Carbine raised the low, 8-foot ceiling into a Bermuda tray ceiling (it's still flat at the top, but the sides slope). He then sealed up the central front door, turned the two small windows on either side into floor-to-ceiling French windows, and added the octagon-shaped window at the roof peak as a light scoop.

Finally, he moved the front entrance to the right side of the house, which turned the original front porch into an open-air extension of the living room. The outcome is spacious, loftlike living in a place you'd least expect it.

These highly colored and patterned Louis XVI chairs, covered in a faded crimson tapestry, provide a good lesson in using virtuoso pieces. Without the competition of richly textured rugs, draperies, or wallpaper, the effect is startling. Designers Ann Holden and Ann Dupuy cleverly let these chairs be the loudest voice in the room.

VOICE OF EXPERIENCE: Painting wood floors permits the use of bold colors not available in wood stains. But paint under foot traffic generally requires more frequent maintenance than paint on interior or exterior walls. Wood floors colored with a penetrating stain, and then sealed with two or three coats of hard, clear polyurethane, will look better longer.

# THE HOUSE THAT ROARED

**THE PRICE:** Architect Robert H. Taylor was given the problem of opening up this house on a very small budget. His ingenious, quick-fix solutions came to a total of $50,000 in 1983.

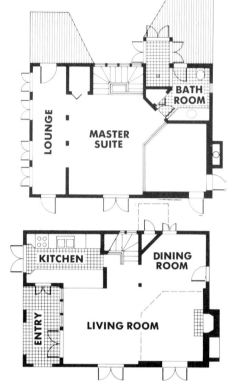

This little house in Los Angeles had big problems and nothing much going for it but the Spanish tile trim and a good location. There were far too many tiny rooms and no light at all. Clever tricks with inner space and a new, low-profile, peaked roof line solved the tight squeeze. Piercing the new roof and old side walls with glass allowed daylight into the once dark downstairs. The major breech in the old house's shell is the floor-to-roof window that was installed in the wall of the new stairwell. Now, both floors are illuminated by its long reach.

To open up the house even more, half the second floor was removed, which created a mezzanine suite of bedroom, bath, and deck. Entered through an angled corner wall of the bedroom, across a bridge *(below)*, the bathroom opens in turn onto the new,

private, second-story deck that supports a windowed, open shower room.

On the first floor, most of the interior walls were taken out to make way for a living room finally worthy of the name. And removing half of the upstairs level provided two-story height for part of the first floor. Two skylights directly overhead transform the new tall space into a light well. Where the ceiling wasn't removed outright, a precious ten extra inches was added to the seven-foot-six-inch ceilings by exposing the second-floor joists. The first floor now breathes with revitalized life.

Such rearrangements, of course, demand careful compensation. Increased pressure on the exterior wall from the heavier, unsupported

One wide-open living room took over a warren of first-floor rooms, including the old stairwell but excluding the kitchen. A two-story light well, bedroom balcony, glass curtain walls, and a couple of skylights did the rest.

roof is countered by crossed tie rods that work as decoration but are mostly functional. On the mezzanine, above the joists, sheets of heavy plywood replaced narrow oak planking to make a more rigid, structural floor. The "bridge" to the bath is also built up to accommodate plumbing pipes and the heavier beams now required to replace the missing floor and support walls, both above and below.

In all, the little house grew up quite handsomely.

The key to the second-floor mezzanine *(left)* is the pyramidal roof. Kept low to be invisible from the street, the new roof preserves both the house's facade and the Spanish flavor of the tile-topped parapets *(opposite)*.

# THE URBANE RENEWAL

**ON RESTORING WOOD:** Liberating old wood from old finishes isn't always worth the effort. In this case, though, it was clearly the right approach. Ebony stain and glossy urethane revived the sanded-down pine floors. Three coats of beeswax was enough on the cypress window frames.

A 64-foot-long, 6½-foot-wide central hall *(left)* was wasted as a mere corridor to connect the four downstairs rooms. By broadening and raising the hall's four doors to archway dimensions, the former tunnel turns into an interior courtyard with cinematic vistas.

A well-honed plan and crafty changes in this turn-of-the-century New Orleans city house emphasize how little renovation is really needed to go a very long way, thus saving the money and major construction for a gleaming kitchen/deck addition. And yet, in both the old and the new space, architect Ronald Katz's design sparkles with pizzazz.

Just widening the passages between rooms—nothing so major as yanking out walls—produces spaces that offer long-distance views in every direction. Originally two-foot-by-seven-foot openings, the doorways were enlarged to five-foot-by-nine-foot portals. The new woodwork on the archway matches the color and cut of the original cypress on the living room's window frames—what you can't restore, you can reproduce.

Once the new/old woodwork and the generous doorways were in place, little in the house was tampered with beyond the addition of contemporary finishes, colors, and materials. But these make all the difference. First it was necessary to get down to basics by peeling away generations of flocked wallpaper. Then the walls were painted slate gray to pull the room into the here-and-now without inducing shock to the historic roots. A plump rolled-arm sofa and chaise evoke an earlier period, but their cleaner lines and sophisticated color live for today.

**SOME FURNITURE IS AN ISLAND:** Because the spaces in this house flow gently into one another, the centered furniture groupings amount to islands in the stream—clustered together with space all around. It's a neat technique that enhances the visual impact of both the furniture and the vintage architecture.

**THE WALLPAPER STRIP:** Forget steaming it off. Today, wallpaper stores stock solutions that dissolve old paste. Directions may say to apply with a sponge, but a spray bottle is easier, faster, and almost drip-free. You'll still have to coax the old paper with some sort of wide blade. And patience. Afterward, patch, prime, and paint.

**VOICE OF EXPERIENCE:** When removing partition walls or widening existing openings exposes unfinished subflooring patches must be made using new boards. Since this raw wood will absorb stain and surface coatings much more readily than the surrounding area, the new boards must be primed with a thin coat of stain to match the adjacent, old boards. Then, when the entire floor is refinished, the patched areas won't be noticeable.

**In striking juxtaposition to the cozy gray dining room, the white kitchen rises pristine and palatial beside it—a new addition to the old house. Yet there's no sense of stepping out of the nineteenth century and into the present.**

Some architectural details simply outlive their usefulness and can be removed without jeopardizing either historic or visual integrity. In the dining room *(opposite)*, as throughout the house, the ankle-high baseboard that abruptly separated floor from wall was replaced by more contemporary quarter-round molding. That lengthened the walls (like turning down the cuffs on a pair of pants) and turned them into uninterrupted solid surfaces—a much more graceful look. It also eliminated the monumental task of refinishing the baseboard to match the rest of the woodwork.

Decoration is characteristically light in the dining room—and characteristically old/new. This is the only room with a bay—the wall opposite the doorway curves outward—thus lending space beyond the center for three sculptural *Yucca rostrata*. The dining table is custom made of blue pearl granite and set on a black, lacquered base, chosen to extend the presence and material of the fireplace.

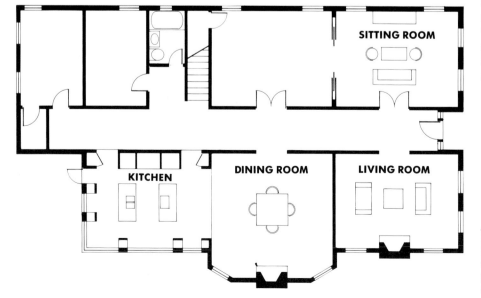

**The concept of the double parlor—two big rooms (15 feet by 20 feet) connected by pocket doors—was fairly standard in Victorian homes. Here, the front-parlor idea of big rooms connected by big doors has spread throughout the house.**

Planning a renovation turns into a series of tough questions. What do you remove and what do you restore? Which gets torn down and which retained? This vintage city house answers with a successful recipe for combining century-old architecture with today's sensibility.

Seen close up, the custom details are as handsome as they are hardworking. *Top, right:* Architect Katz had the floor tiles made to order and designed the pattern. Squares in the border and hexagons in the center are worked in a classical Greek key motif to set a Mediterranean mood. *Top, left:* As in the entire renovation, the dining table and setting is a mix of grand and plain styles. A basic black-and-white theme is enriched by the red mats, the granite table, and the fanciful wine glasses. *Above:* Made of half-inch birch plywood and painted white, the lightweight storage unit allows an open display of kitchenware that simply tames clutter.

I f redesigning is an exercise in innovation, with limits and challenges set by the existing house, then adding a room becomes creative architecture. And this kitchen, quite dazzling and quite contemporary, is creative indeed. Yet the addition lives harmoniously with the period architecture of the original building.

Actually a foot shorter than the height of the house's main rooms—13 feet, floor to ceiling—the kitchen's soaring columns, windows, and center skylight give the illusion of much greater space. It's as exciting at night as during the day, since the garden and pool at the back are lit to connect the outdoors with the inside.

If it looks like a stage waiting for actors, that's the idea. Obviously this is a household where cooking and entertaining are one and the same.

The kitchen is, however, thoroughly practical. The double-island work spaces play off each other, sink in one, cooktop in the other. Down-draft venting in the cooktop island eliminates the need for an overhead hood, while the ceiling fan helps out too—which means there's not a bad seat in the house.

The structural columns work double time as both open and shut storage pantries. And the stage metaphor is furthered by the 15-watt, bare showcase bulbs that surround the skylight like dressing-room-mirror lights. The lights can be dimmed for dramatic effects.

The glory of the kitchen, though, setting off everything else, is the new tile floor. Hand-set in grout, piece by mosaic piece, it defines the area of culinary performances. It looks like just the kind of floor that might have been installed when the house was built—yet it is somehow far more stylish. The neatly built custom shelving, placed between the ovens and the refrigerator, punctuates the kitchen wall with a sharp geometric design, like a Mondrian painting—perfectly in keeping with the tiled floor.

Ingeniously, the roof of the kitchen addition becomes a deck just outside the master bedroom. Overlooking the backyard garden, it's a perfect after-dinner setting.

**THE RIGHT CHOICE:** Although the first impluse is to purchase all major appliances in the same color—and that's usually a good notion for the large blocks of space appliances take up in a kitchen—here a double-doored white refrigerator/freezer contrasts with a black stack of microwave and conventional ovens. And it looks appropriate. The recessed black adds drama toward the window, and the white blends into the storage unit without disrupting the flow. Colors need not always match.

# BRAVE NEW BUNGALOW

**Built in the mid-1920s in Venice, California, this two-story bungalow with clapboard siding had been divided into two rental units, upstairs and down, before the new owner renovated it.**

The owner here is something of an architectural aficionado," says Los Angeles architect Frederick Fisher, who designed this witty transformation in Venice, California. "He gave me general parameters for the major changes, but when it came to the finishes, the owner got very involved. He likes bright colors and textures, and he was always pushing me to do more and fancier and riskier finishes. He was great to work with."

Indeed, within a modest budget, Fisher accomplished quite a bit of fancy work. "This was a duplex, with a complete living unit on each floor," he says, "so first we got rid of the redundant rooms—the kitchen and laundry area upstairs, for example. We eliminated the extra street entrance and broke through the vestibule walls. Then we reorganized the space, since we were converting the house for one person. Downstairs, we took out several small rooms in favor of a more open, one-room plan.

"My philosophy," continues Fisher, "is to take advantage of light once you get it into the house. I think it should be milked for all it's worth." In addition to several windows and smaller skylights, Fisher installed a central, peaked skylight. He prefers the peaked shape because it "follows the roof line of the house, and it also allows you to retain the rafters. That makes structural changes simpler and less expensive, and the peak also lets the light bounce off the sides of the skylight, filtering it. That way, the sunlight doesn't make huge blocks on the floor, but hits the rafters, which means the light comes in patterned. I think it's prettier and more natural."

**The living room floor was stained white *(opposite)* to create a "natural, brighter look," says architect Fred Fisher, and to make a neutral background for the showy furnishings and the showpiece fireplace mantel *(left)*. Made of Brazilian blue granite—"absolutely the most rare, exotic, and expensive granite there is," says Fisher—and *rose Aurora* pink Italian marble, the mantel covers a quite ordinary, prefab fireplace.**

**THE PRICE:** Completed in 1985, this Venice, California, bungalow cost about $50,000 to renovate, says architect Fred Fisher, including the new asphalt shingles for the roof and a new fence around the house.

**ON ZOLATONE AND PLEXTONE:** Developed for industrial use in the 1950s, Zolatone is a multicolored, lacquered paint made up of blobs of color—chemicals—that won't mix. When the paint's sprayed on a surface, the colors remain distinct, imitating Formica or granite. It's extremely strong and will resist chipping and also hide any flaws. Since interior designers have begun using Zolatone in the last few years, a consumer version has emerged, called Plextone, which produces similar results. Plextone is available at paint stores across the country.

Throughout the house, architect Fisher has artfully played with stone textures and materials to make the crisp design softer. Mostly, in the past, expensive marble and quarried materials were used only in grand and rich spaces—hotels, lobbies, cathedrals, and the like. But increasingly used in the home with restraint and in small portions, as here, the cost becomes manageable and the strong shapes and rich colors have a powerful impact.

Granite is the stone that gets Fisher's full treatment—from genuine to faux. A slab of the real thing makes the dining tabletop *(opposite)*, which casually sits atop a run-of-the-mill restaurant pedestal. The look of granite is repeated on a stepladder that leads to a guest-room loft. The same faux granite finish appears on the kitchen cabinets *(below, right)*. Both were produced by a currently fashionable paint called Zolatone. It's a flecked spray-paint that creates a look Fisher describes as "shelf-paper granite."

"It was too expensive to replace all the kitchen cabinets," says Fisher. "The Zolatone finish hid the imperfections yet added warmth just as wood or marble would have." All the appliances were good enough to leave in place, and, adds Fisher, "we figured the original gray ceramic tile was neutral, so we left it alone." But it's the new, speckly vinyl floor that really sets off this kitchen. "It's an old pattern dating from the thirties," says Fisher, "but it's still being made," and against the Zolatone, the vinyl looks very new wave.

**"We brought along four colors of the vinyl tile as samples," says Fisher, "so the owner could choose two for the pattern. He decided to try all four—and when we started laying it down, we didn't even know we'd end up with that basket-weave pattern."**

**In the kitchen *(right)*, architect Fisher's fondness for bringing in lots of California sunlight is evidenced by the new French door, generous number of windows, and, overhead, a small skylight that boosts light directly into the center of the room.**

# ADDING ON THE RITZ

**THE PRICE:** With close to 1,300 square feet on the main living level—194 feet wide and 66 feet long—this renovation took five months of planning and seven more for new construction. The cost was about $80 a square foot, including a revamped, small kitchen.

A tall, arched French door in the living room is flanked by two sets of regular French doors, making a wide-open wall to the backyard an inviting possibility.

**A**ny city house is bound to tell tales about the former owners. This plain Jane building in Washington, D.C., began as a turn-of-the-century corner store, with a windowed bay at the front to display goods, the asset of 12-foot ceilings, and the storekeeper's second-story flat. Then, for years, it saw service as a laundromat. By the time architects Michael Holt and Robert Lewis were called in by new owners, the building had already undergone a residential renovation—five years before. "In theory," says Holt, "it was a pretty good design. The downstairs had been turned into one large space and the kitchen floated, but it was a paint and patch job, without any quality in the materials or craftsmanship."

Those earlier modifications meant the little store was already a livable house, making it harder for the owners to decide how much more to do. "As the clients became more involved," Holt explains, "the project changed scope. Through the course of the design's history, we increased the budget four times over."

After months of planning, Holt and Lewis gutted the small structure, taking out ceilings and floors, raising the living room and entryway floor about 15 inches to pull it off the street. The existing systems for heating and air conditioning remained, but the architects radically changed the ductwork. "We didn't pay as much for equipment as for all the rerouting," says Holt. They also removed the clunky, old staircase to the shopkeeper's quarters and installed a new, curving one to garner more space downstairs. Since the side walls are the bearing walls, the Palladian design was possible at the end of the living room, where glass and airy French doors replaced the rear wall.

Finally, Holt and Lewis installed the exciting trim and details that made for a high-impact transformation. "The clients were a little uncertain about how the columns and arches were going to look—they couldn't visualize it," Holt recalls now. "We provided drawings, but no models. In the end, they were willing to take the chance, and we're all pleased."

The architects' freshly minted classical spirit works its way down the hall and frames the curved-out dining area *(opposite).* Made of birch veneer plywood boxes dressed with poplar trim and painted white, the columns are classic Doric sliced into cross section, which lightens their look and turns them into something refreshingly new. "We even had two extra columns for the dining room that we didn't end up using," says Holt, "because they blocked the side windows when you looked down the vista." More than gratuitous decorations, the columns and arches act as airy dividers, so spaces flow into one another but the living and dining rooms are still defined.

Look to the original architecture for ideas on restyling exteriors. Architects Holt and Lewis drew on the shape of the second-floor windows for the new, arched doorway into the backyard *(above* and *below, left).* In front, the old square bay, originally a store's display case, was left untouched *(below, right).*

**ON REAL-LIFE RENO-VATION:** Every project will demand some compromise between the perfection of design and the limit of dollars. Be prepared. In this case, it was the flooring. The yellow pine floors were sanded, lightly rubbed with charcoal-colored stain—a neat trick for instant aging—then sealed with a urethane finish. They look great, yes. But "they're too soft," says architect Holt, "and really should have been replaced. As the design changed, the money for the project grew and grew. So we made the decision not to change the floors. I think, in retrospect, the clients are sorry they didn't."

# THE OUTDOOR ROOM

This sweeping pano-
rama of indoor/out-
door room in Venice,
California, right off the
beach, was accom-
plished without exten-
sive remodeling. A
cost-conscious plan
and an inventive use

of space removed only one view-blocking support. Doubling as a landscape designer, architect Steven David Ehrlich pruned the lot's luxuriant shrubbery, substituting bold stucco walls that march down the property lines to the beach. There, an 8-foot-by-12-foot sliding wood door offers privacy from a "very public" stretch of sand. Besides shielding the owners from close neighbors on either side, the new walls create a ceilingless room. And as you move from inside to out, walls and ceilings gradually disappear.

You don't get unusual problems in small houses. As always, the owners wanted more space. As often, the budget was tight. What you do get are imaginative solutions.

Reviving this ordinary stucco bungalow, built in the 1960s, was the result of judicious editing by architect Ehrlich, not a massive overhaul. Exploiting an indoor/outdoor theme ignored in the home's original design, Ehrlich joined the pool deck and the house by extending the interior's Mexican tile floor into the transitional open room and by then adding a step-down that doubles as seating. The only element he removed was a column in the middle of the rear wall that supported the second-floor balcony. That single column had managed to break up the ocean view quite efficiently. A stucco-sheathed horizontal beam, slung beneath the ceiling, replaced the support without obstructing the vista.

Additions were kept to a minimum as well, which means the money saved on construction went a long way toward refining the basic outlines of the house. Cement tile on the deck

Upstairs, the master bedroom opens onto the balcony's proprietary view. The French doors, refreshed with white paint, are original. Steel cable on the railing is new. The other rooms on the top floor include another bedroom, two baths, and a study.

was added in a crosshatched pattern to break up the boxy lines. Stucco walls went up along the property lines to add intimacy and the feel of a Mediterranean courtyard.

The architect was equally restrained —and deft—on the upper level. An exposed wood balcony roof was covered with stucco, both to lighten it and to make it more organically part of the structure. And the railing's superfluous vertical supports were banished in favor of metal nautical cable, stretched horizontally.

Quite simply, and with a few gestures, the backyard became a courtyard and the ordinary bungalow was transformed into a little villa.

The downstairs rooms of the 2,000-square-foot home flow together, pulling one visually toward the outdoor room deck, and pool.

A good coat of indigo blue paint on the pool shell, seen on the borders, makes the water take on the mood of the Côte d'Azur.

**R**eworked from a jumble of California beachside clichés, this lyrical Mediterranean scene is architect Steven David Ehrlich's response to a formidable challenge: turn the prosaic bungalow and lot into as provocative a setting as the oceanfront location.

# BUILDING ON THE SKYLINE

Jane Siris and Peter Coombs, husband and wife architects who built this house for themselves, wanted a suburban space without the commute, the city amenities without apartment living, and a place where their children wouldn't feel cramped. They got all that and more. Their fairy-tale co-op in the clouds is a whole new house constructed on top of a New York City building.

A studio penthouse, little more than a tin shed, was the beginning. It had water, sewage, electricity, and heat—the essential services that made the project possible. Bringing up new lines from below would have been so disruptive that the co-op's board might well have vetoed the plan. Along with the $38,000 penthouse came a toehold on the roof, wiring, plumbing, and a freight elevator to the thirteenth floor. For another $10,000, they bought 400 square feet of rooftop for expansion.

To construct the steel framework for the new three-story house, materials were brought up piecemeal on the elevator. The Tinkertoy I-beams alone (the longest was 28 feet) took a week to move and many had to be cut to fit into the elevator. A full-blown steelyard was set up on the north terrace to reweld the spans before assembly. After that, actual construction of the frame took another week. A boom crane, rented for one day, might have been cheaper transport from street to rooftop.

Two pieces of the new frame were already in place. The architects tied one wall of the house to the water tower, incorporating two of its steel supports into the west side of the house. Two new columns (one in the living room) support the east side. These four uprights make the new foundation. Including interior and exterior railings, the subcontract for the steel alone cost $30,000.

Privy to sweeping cityscapes and breathtaking sunsets, this small three-story house set atop a New York City apartment building pioneers a startling frontier of urban renovation: rooftop real estate. It's a unique solution to getting a dream off the ground.

Four tons of steel girders, a daring plan, and downright determination created this stucco penthouse with panoramic views of the Hudson River and midtown Manhattan.

**THE PRICE:** For $150 a square foot, this family got a roof over their heads and a roof under their feet—with three bedrooms in between.

**VOICE OF EXPERIENCE:** Built-in adjustable blinds are a worthwhile extra for skylights to protect against brilliant sunshine. In high-ceilinged rooms where heat builds up, an operator skylight offers cross ventilation. Opening the skylight will create a natural air flow, allowing the warmest air to escape.

**LESSONS OF THE NEW FRONTIER:** The first step to high-rise suburbia is to hire an architect and do a feasibility study. That includes an engineer's report and preliminary drawings, required in the planning. The architect must also investigate zoning laws, which regulate mass and setback. Then comes a lawyer to negotiate with the landlord or co-op/condo committee. Finally, you're ready for a contractor and the business of building.

Careful and clever design makes the small rooms live bigger. Everything that can be built in is, like the dining banquette *(left)*. Everything that can be stored is put away to cut down on visual clutter. Where privacy doesn't matter, interior walls were omitted to create the illusion of greater space. Beyond the dining area wall is the children's "backyard," an enclosed deck. The adult or "evening" deck *(top)* is laid over the building's old roof on a plywood subfloor, shimmed for proper water runoff. Paving tiles set in mastic make the final weatherproof surface.

The new living room *(above)* sinks below the roof line and is the original tin-shed penthouse. Low steps now lead directly to the terrace and set up the level for built-in seating and the raised fireplace hearth. Lightweight armchairs keep the small room open.

# THE LOFT MOVEMENT

To walk into a loft is to covet one. The space is bold and breathtaking. The possibilities are high and wide. Your floor plan and furnishings, your imagination and desires, are limited only by your bank account.

In a turn-of-the-century New York warehouse *(above)*, a new, simple skylight brings in the sun, so the original factory window *(opposite)* can hold onto its charm. New drywall, painted white and clean, hides the old ductwork.

No question about it. Living in a loft has mystique. An aura. Whether you buy raw space, carve your initials in it, and travel a bit to find groceries, or whether you pay the price for a finished loft in an area already sporting a Benetton and a chocolate chip cookie shop, you'll no doubt be living smack in the heart of town. Restaurants are close by and so's the office. If space is the ultimate luxury in the city—lofts deliver lots.

Best of all, you basically get a canvas. An appealing, wide-open invitation to install exactly the kind of home you have always envisioned. Tin ceilings don't come with the place? You can add them. Fancy a few Palladian columns? Speak to the designer. It can all be done (with the proper respect for budget, of course). Lofts used to be just shelter, bare brick-walled hangars for the proverbial starving sculptors. Nowadays, the postmodern influence has brought us back to human scale, and the bare, empty flaunting of space that used to be loft design is disappearing in favor of walls and modules, clever dividers, and little interior houses. We now want doors that close and rooms of our own. The second and third generation of owners are moving into sleek and satisfying homes.

Understandably, then, the cost of buying a loft is on the rise. In New York's trendy Soho neighborhood, where the rage began in the mid-1970's and has not yet abated, lofts are turning over at the rate of $350,000 a clip for an average 1,500 to 2,000 square feet. Los Angeles or Boston or Minneapolis or Chicago lofts don't match that dizzying height, but prices are climbing everywhere.

Since lofts mostly occur in buildings about a hundred years old (younger than that as you move from east to west), you get good, solid construction to build in the privacy a loft needs. Age does, however, have some disadvantages. "The trouble with any loft," says Alan Buchsbaum, a New York architect who's become expert in loft conversions, "is that there is no such thing as a single major expense. There are many in several major categories."

Everything might need work: installing or relocating kitchen and bath could require moving the plumbing stacks—that's expensive; electrical capability might be enormous because of previous industrial needs (200 amps, 3 phase, for example) or it might be too weak to run so much as a hair dryer—that means money. Possibly there's handsome wide-plank flooring underneath the rust-stained linoleum, or, just as likely, you'll find concrete floors. The dollar vs. design question then becomes new flooring (pricey) or wall-to-wall carpeting (less pricey).

There is a way to cut through the uncertainty: hire a structural engineer to inspect any loft you're strongly considering. A professional inspection will make sure you get the mystique, not the mistake.

# THE REVISIONIST LOFT

Adding a central kitchen, mezzanine, and stairway to a long, narrow factory space in New York—just under 1,500 square feet—turns an empty tunnel into home. Living/dining and cooking areas are on the upper level. The lower one has an open suite of bedroom, bath, and luxurious whirlpool.

**THE PRICE:** Completed in 1980, this loft would run about $125 per square foot today. "The most important budget consideration for installing utilities in a loft," says architect Buchsbaum, "is locating the plumbing risers and stacks. That's where the real money goes."

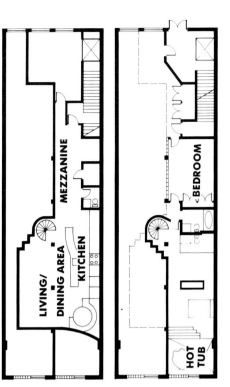

s original as the idea was to turn old factories into homes in the 1970s, it took a surprisingly long time for design to catch up with the notion. Raw space became its own design motif. A passive, "less-is-better" solution ruled for years. Not so any longer. Here, the old clichés of sanded floor, white walls, and exposed brick are gloriously ignored by New York architect Alan Buchsbaum.

In this dark 70-foot-by-20-foot corridor, which has windows only at one end, the severe limitation provoked an inward design focus—an imaginative implosion. Tall 16-foot ceilings in an 1865 building were the first inspiration for Buchsbaum. He split the space horizontally, constructing an upstairs mezzanine that includes a kitchen near the entrance and, beyond, the living and dining areas. A few feet of room-divider walls were built just inside the front door, giving the necessary feeling of an entrance. The dividers tame all that wild space into the human scale of a hallway. They also make the living area more intimate. Sometimes, as here, when you draw attention to a liability—the corridor shape—it turns out to be a design solution. Retaining the original tin ceiling, which was stripped and repainted, heightens the mood of adventure.

In a key departure from white-box loft design, color is used generously here in witty ways. Pastel hues on the large background areas—semigloss latex paint on the walls and glazed ceramic tile on the floor—allow the furnishings to supply intensity. They stand out like sculpture.

**"D**ividing tactics are critical when you're designing a loft's open space," says architect Alan Buchsbaum. "Try to keep one very generous, public space—the ideal is a balance between livability and architecture."

The loft's flavor is stirred by an unexpected blend of textures: rough wood beams and welded steel pipe railing; crisp ceramic tile and a loosely draped hand-painted slipcover; Oriental rug and clean-painted metal. The furnishings, chosen with a highly personalized style, highlight the English wicker chairs, circa 1920. All the attention to tiny detail reinforces an atmosphere of relaxed elegance.

As owners of all kinds of living spaces are currently busy pulling down the walls between the kitchen and the rest of the house, the loft kitchen makes them envious. It's an open-ended option. Here, the kitchen is carefully located in the center of the mezzanine level, planned as the exciting focal point for the entire loft. A very practical, real cooking kitchen, the open setting and the mix of old-time and up-to-the-minute industrial wares and materials turns food chores into pure theater. One is reminded of a good restaurant kitchen.

The long island, laminated on the sides and top, takes a sharp turn to form a low-rise divider for the kitchen

and dining areas. No walls come between guest and host, but the eye is comforted—the "rooms" are defined. Broken only by a pale gray double sink, the countertop works overtime—for preparing or serving food and as a second eating area.

Useful objects are displayed for their own sake, handsome, honest, and close at hand. A big black commercial stove rules the stage, so that other appliances and the work counters fall into easy, supporting roles. Shapely industrial lamps add drama as well as focused, working light, and platoons of shiny, intriguing tools, pots, and wire storage racks banish all thought of hanging cabinets.

**IT'S OKAY TO SHOW OFF THE WORKS:** That terrific cast-iron sculpture with the brass fittings under the window, the one that creates such a neat, low line to finish off the tall, narrow space, is, of course, the loft's new heating unit. What makes it look so special is that the clean, straight-edged box that usually houses a radiator has been discarded, so the works inside are exposed.

**It's the planning that ensures you a room you can live in:** keeping the downstairs bedroom open lets in the daylight and avoids a feeling of confinement from the new, low ceiling. But the stairway sets off the room from the whirlpool, just on the other side, making it cozier. Notice that the second step to the bath platform spreads out and smoothly turns into a generous bedside table.

Seen as a whole, the two levels create a private club mood. Remember the pool view, even while dining. Soft-colored ceramic tile on the floor is pretty and practical in the kitchen and bath, but a nice surprise in the sleeping and sitting areas. The all-over tile gives the loft the sense of unity it needs given the wide variety of materials. It's a good idea—tile is a willing companion to most materials. And just as the bath step widens into a table, the dividing wall grows up to become the back of the dining banquette.

Double-height windows at the back provide the only natural light for both the mezzanine and lower levels—and were a prime motivation for keeping the two areas open. The windows have another trick going for them—clearly, they aren't the same. Glass block, a favored solution for lighting spaces that still need privacy, holds its own to the right, while a more traditional, double-hung window, on the left, was fitted with opaque glass and then etched with acid. The juxtaposition makes all the difference between the ordinary and the extraordinary.

Like the wall paint and the striped floor tile, the blue tile border that circles the apartment is a subtle use of varied background color.

Looking like a vintage fixture against the clean tile, it's a good punctuation point for a lesson learned from tech: everything doesn't have to be kept under wraps, hidden away, smoothed out. The iron pipes of the radiator have their own functional beauty.

**VOICE OF EXPERIENCE:** Along with the several concerns of adding an oversize soaking tub or whirlpool bath (getting it into the building, for example), remember the engineering one. Floor joists wil need beefing up to support the spa plus people plus the weight of all that water. A 20-inch-deep spa tub may easily hold 250 to 300 gallons of water, weighing about 2,000 pounds.

# NEW VIEW ON LOS ANGELES

VOICE OF EXPERIENCE: When adding new windows to older buildings, compare the thickness of the frame to the wall. It may not have the depth to match a thick plastered wall built with two-by-fours that actually measure two inches by four inches. New units may require extra pieces of trim, called jamb extensions.

This is recycling at its most witty. April Sheldon and Rocco Cappeto applied a giant dose of imagination and just $6,000 to the "piles of concrete rubble and twisted reinforcing bars" of this bunker of a former brewery. And that was enough to turn it into a fashionable home.

Although the large, inviting doorway may look like the result of renovation, it was the brewery's original loading dock, cleverly left alone. (The garage-like door can easily be rolled down.) Instead, a concrete slab was removed from the east wall to make the new, multipaned window. The upper part is stationary while the lower windows slide open toward the center. With one stroke, the factory walls stopped looking like a factory, yet the new window doesn't jar. Since all the other windows are above eye level when seated, the new one provided a much-needed view.

Rather than carting away the concrete slab carved out for the window, the young couple put it to work. Two sections were cut to make the table base —a hefty, grainy contrast for the delicate glass. And the glass top was etched by an artist neighbor in a pattern Sheldon designed.

"I found these fifties-era dining chairs on Santa Monica Boulevard," said artist Sheldon. "I enameled them pink and replaced five layers of vinyl with a fabric that I hand-painted."

"Through an eighteen-foot-by-eighteen-foot roll-up door, we get the fine Los Angeles weather and a great view of the downtown skyline."

# THE MOVABLE DESIGN

**VOICE OF EXPERIENCE:** Sandblasting is a time-saving if costly alternative to laborious hand-scraping and wire-brushing to restore both wood beams and old brick. But a draw-back may appear once the job is done: on brick, particularly old brick, the force of the blasting (a pressurized stream of fine sand) may pit and scar the surface; on wood, the blast effect can exca-vate little rivulets in the grain. Both materials may emerge dramatically altered.

"I don't so much work out of my house," says Chicago interior designer Richar about this grand space, "as live in my office." Quite consciously, this rented loft was left raw and techy, to showcase the sensual mix of furniture and art. "Black is dramatic and elegant," says Richar. "And that elegance balances the roughness— the sandblasted beams and brick, the exposed ducts and sprinkler pipes."

We may all have seen glowing wood floors and brick walls a time or two in lofts, but the innovation here is using them as a background for expensive, designer furniture and a very personal art collection. All familiarity vanishes as your eyes move from fussy gilt carving to the engineered lighting, from the Italian Bugatti chairs, circa 1900, with hand-painted vellum backs, to the slick laminated storage unit. The heart of this conference/living room is a cluster of three black leather love seats and a ribbed, wool rug. Toward the back, gilded console tables provide a surprising double take against plain white walls and the Italian desk and work light.

The effort here went mostly into the furnishings and lighting, while the loft itself was minimally changed to set off the furniture and to function as work/ living space. The low-voltage track lighting, for instance, has an expensive extra complement of fixtures so that each piece of furniture, all the artwork, even each accessory is spot-lighted by a beam from above. Whenever Richar acquires a new piece, another light fixture is added. The result? Drama, especially at night. The 2,300-square-foot rectangular box was divided only by a couple of inexpensive drywall partitions; one behind the desk, to provide more office space, and the other, on the left, to form the semi-private bedroom.

"I want to send the message that I'm comfortable with decoration, but I don't use it in traditional ways," says the designer, who lives and works in this Chicago loft.

**MATCHING FURNITURE HAS A NEW SET OF RULES:** A Eurostyle mix of furnishings and colors, more than any structural changes, makes this loft uniquely personal. A case in point: a gilded reproduction Louis XV chair sits in perfect harmony with a lacquered, new wave table.

# THE SALON LOFT

ON BIEDERMEIER: Europe's last neoclassic gasp, Biedermeier was the final ripple of the dominant French Directoire and Empire styles in the mid-nineteenth century. It was made for the middle masses, not the upper classes—the first furniture specifically produced for the homes of the upwardly mobile, not for palaces. Because of the light-colored woods, smaller size, and spare

A rehabbed warehouse near the waterfront, Seattle's Merrill Place houses lofts, stores, a theater, and a restaurant.

An elegant bridge between the Old World and the New, this loft is located in Seattle's resoundingly modern Merrill Place, a resurrected warehouse that's now a mixed-use building. Designer Terry Hunziker has transformed the rough-hewn, 1,200-square-foot, high-ceilinged space into a warm, finely finished home by some artful tricks with canvas and by a spare use of early-nineteenth-century European antiques set against a very contemporary room.

The key to this theatrical yet inexpensive design is the use of freestanding stretched-canvas panels that become new, lightweight walls and dividers, bringing the large space down to human scale. The building renovation revealed the pattern of old bricks on the walls, but they're nicely subdued by the gray-beige color of the canvas. Designer Hunziker painted the canvas panels with a hand-held sprayer, applying more color at the bottom and less at the top to lighten the look. The panels are held away from the walls by epoxied dowel rods. Half-round moldings soften the edges of the frames. All of the heavy wooden beams overhead have been sandblasted to make them appear rougher, more textured.

Acting as both backdrop and artwork, the canvas panels graphically silhouette the champagne-colored fruitwoods of the Swedish Biedermeier and Russian Empire chairs. The furniture's strong lines and eccentric shapes stand as sculpture all by themselves. Techy hanging lights bathe the wood in a warm glow.

Everything here points to the signature style of the American Northwest: the muted "oyster light" palette, the up-front presence of natural materials, and the Oriental accessories. Northwest design mixes cultures and periods with ease, but owes particular allegiance to Japan. In this loft, Hunziker blended that style with the drama of neoclassic European furniture.

A two-faced fireplace divides the living and dining areas. Giant pieces of black pottery, above the woodpile, help the division and echo the ebony details of the Biedermeier chairs. Hand-stenciled calfskin covers the seats.

decoration, Bieder-
meier antiques are
often chosen by
designers today to
invoke the grand
European tradition.
The style sits in perfect
harmony with the most
up-to-date furnishings

and is even comfort-
able with the rough
beams in this loft.

# LIVING ON TOP OF THE WORLD

The inside story here is the novel idea of lowering and raising floor levels so that the big-as-a-barn space is divided horizontally instead of with eye-stopping, vertical walls. A custom-built sofa *(right)* helps with the low-rise divider—making the living room area more intimate.

You don't make friends by complaining about too much space, but it does present a delicious dilemma: how do you keep all that openness without feeling as if you're living in a hangar? This New York rooftop loft offers a solution. Install multi-level, open rooms and an outdoor deck.

Cedar planking, unsealed so the wood grays naturally, makes the deck, as does the panoramic sweep of the Hudson River. That trendy-colored aqua border on the brick parapet is copper roof flashing, weathered by the years—the luck of the original 1908 rooftop.

f each detail in this loft looks effortless, it's because its English owner-architect, Angus Bruce, spent three years lavishing attention on every one. Renovation here was a cost-conscious labor of love, completed in stages. All the curving, sculptural shapes take time, care, and thoughtful planning. You need to do a lot of painstaking work—and you need to be patient—to achieve these built-in platforms and arches. The process may be studied, but the results look easy as a breeze.

"We had the initial idea of forms that would break up the main space," says Bruce. "Then we decided to raise the rooms so you could see the wonderful windows and the even more wonderful view from anywhere. After that, we used only materials that would keep the room bright and open. Of course, eighteen-foot ceilings helped make it possible, but when we walked in, we found an existing dropped ceiling that was four feet lower than the actual one. We removed that."

The success of this renovation rests on many more levels than just space arrangement. Sight lines are channeled up and down, yet traffic flows easily around and about the platforms. Although this former industrial space is hugely scaled, very few brushstrokes are used to warm up a cool white canvas. The trick that works is to make them big and bold. Arched openings, laminated curves, the maple on the floor and oak on the trim, the judicious Japanese screens all quickly take the edges off the boxy architecture.

Spare furnishings leave breathing and entertaining room—and let the glorious view command. Choice details, such as the 1850s French Country clock *(page 104)*, make a personal statement. In all, the loft is vivid proof that a wide-open plan can still be intimate.

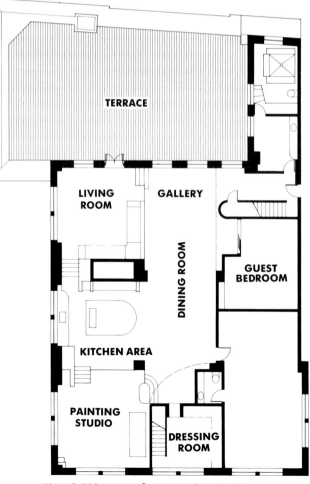

How 3,500 square feet turns into 4,500: a raised living room was built across from the mezzanine studio, steps up from the kitchen. A balcony bedroom overlooks it all.

At this end of the main-floor dining area, the loft's three levels mesh like a highway interchange. Through the arched doorway, veneered oak stairs lead up to the bedroom.

Throughout the loft, living space focuses on the terrace. An updated version of the Adirondack chair and a light dhurrie rug maintain the outdoor mood.

Custom-designed details enrich a spare setting: architect Bruce's stereo console is made from plastic laminate molded into deco's streamlined curves.

An inspired solution in this space, Japanese shoji screens soften the square lines and keep the walls from becoming bulkheads. One is arched and hung above the front door.

**THE PRICE:** Obviously the owner-architect had the skill and the time to do much of the work himself here, but he estimates that the loft would cost about $100 to $120 per square foot if it were done today for a client —or $350,000 to $400,000 for the entire job.

Wherever possible, architect Bruce has thrown a curve into the boxy lines. "My style works," he says, "because it's relatively simple and yet I pay a great deal of attention to detail."

Centrally located on the main floor, the kitchen was set between the two higher levels. Here, the studio is to the left and the living room off to the right, while the view looks down from the balcony bedroom. "Primarily, the kitchen was designed as a center-piece," explains Bruce. "We wanted to use it for entertaining—so everything was installed to work off the kitchen and we put the dining table quite nearby." It's a few feet away from the rounded edge of the island *(right)*.

Since the advantage (and liability, too) of a loft is that most of the fixtures are added, the owners were able to custom tailor the room to their own needs. The counters and work spaces are overscaled to the proportions of the large room and to accommodate the tall occupants. There's nothing sacred about counter heights. Bruce designed and constructed the cabinets himself. On the sturdy, cottagelike hutch, he added a butcher-block counter and, on top, opaque glass sliding doors.

Sunlight from the generous windows pours in across the stainless steel double sink and a butcher-block counter, but there's still a narrow window ledge for plants and herbs. Natural light is supplemented by an overhead lamp *(below)* and by a soft tech table lamp for the dining area on the island. The island itself echoes the overall theme of curves, becoming cousin to the rounded stairs of the mezzanine, the sweep of the balcony, and the laminated stereo unit.

Designed by the owner, the laminate-covered island harbors two butcher-block counters, an inset stovetop, warming oven, and a trash container. The rounded front is reserved for informal dining and for serving. Above the sink, the light/art hanging is an Italian lamp swathed in white linen. The beech pegs act as counterweights, allowing for adjustable heights. Though the lamp is no longer being manufactured, one could readily apply that trick to any hanging factory lamp.

**"T**he problem with a loft," says architect Angus Bruce, "is how to build in storage without breaking up the space too much. Besides dividing the loft, the varying room levels also create 'attic spaces.' Beneath the platforms, there are shelves and pull-out drawers."

Further evidence of the architect's love and care for detail is the grooved archway *(inset)*. Sliding doors, from left and right, join in the middle to close off the opening.

In the bedroom, a smoothly curving balcony, not four walls, gently hems in the room. When the four-foot dropped ceiling was removed, structural metal pipes were revealed under the real ceiling. The architect smoothed over the pipes with plaster to form the wavy ceiling, which subtly changes all the right angles.

A built-in bookcase offers storage and also punctuates what might otherwise have been an overwhelming white expanse.

# THE NEO-CLASSIC LOFT

**VOICE OF EXPERIENCE:** Boxing in exposed pipes and wires, a perennial story in how-to magazines, can sometimes create more of an obstruction and distraction than the materials it covers. Painting radiators, steam pipes, and sprinklers to match the background is less expensive, faster, and often works better.

In Manhattan, loft conversions have just about peaked, with purchase prices running at least $175 per square foot, sometimes more when the location is very prime. In Chicago, Philadelphia, and Los Angeles, however, loft conversions are on the rise and it's still possible to pick up a bargain.

**W**e can think of compelling reasons why you wouldn't, necessarily, want to build everything into a loft. You've just moved from cramped rooms, and the idea of breaking up that fabulous sweep of space is anathema. Maybe you don't plan to stay long, and the sizable expense of custom building rooms and walls won't pay off. Possibly, you just like it big and wide open.

This loft, then, is an extremely stylish response to that need. No new walls, and yet not a compromise in sight. Nothing about it screams "loft"—meaning you don't have to look over your shoulder all the time because your footsteps are echoing in a lonely hangar.

If you've decided against installing a conventional room or two, lofts demand bold strokes and furniture to do the organizing of absent walls. But the point to remember is that raw industrial space doesn't always require new, techy design. This drawing room setting could easily sit in a vintage Georgetown row house. Don't let the structure dictate your taste.

The hardest-working element here is the floor, a sparkling tuxedo of a choice, classic yet quirky. The main checkerboard consists of 12-inch black and white tile. But it's the 8-inch tile of the border's diagonal pattern that makes all the difference. As you see, it's not an all-over frame. It starts, stops, changes its mind. Two black-tiled rows, on the right, neighbor a diagonal white/black line. Toward the back, the black tile drops to one corridor. Alongside the dining table, it alternates again. The flooring, confidently spurning a rug, demands your attention and then rewards a second look. So the box is broken up, the work of the missing architectural elements and interior walls is done.

Other, very simple solutions satisfy the same need. An inexpensive device, the high molding stands in for the familiar eight-foot ceiling, bringing the actual one down to human scale. Painted glossy black and nailed on, it's just three-inch round, straight from the lumberyard. That and the rich creamy paint remind us of traditional rooms and very quickly set a mood.

Like the tiled floor, the neo-classic furniture is carefully chosen to hold interest; each creates a shape that catches the eye and complements the whole. And, last, the color scheme pulls the room together: the crisp black and white backdrop is broken by large-scale jolts of warm wood and the hot turquoise of the coffee table and the screen. Note, too, that the art-furniture screen can be moved anywhere to lend an instant sense of room.

**YOU CAN IMPORT ARCHITECTURAL INTEREST:** Neo-classical shapes dominate the room and stand in for missing custom-built details. The instant architecture: columns and pedestal bases, whether standing alone or, as here, using a plant as a capital; rough-textured urns; Sheraton, Hepplewhite, and Duncan Phyfe reproduction pieces; the Parthenon's pediment shape atop the bookcases; the gilded dolphin arms on the love seat.

# SALADINO ON LOFTS

"**W**hat I do is appropriate," says designer John Saladino, perhaps the most deft practitioner of the art of infusing the past into present-day rooms. "I like to juxtapose Asian materials, natural materials, classical materials, material from a nontechnological civilization, and very slick, highly technological things. I like to put very beautiful, articulated Italian lighting fixtures in with scratch-coat plaster. But the point isn't preference; it's range."

It was because of that very philosophy —the range—that *Metropolitan Home* invited the designer to create a loft stage set, a design he loved that others would see as inspiration. The result *(right),* constructed in the magazine's studio, is what Saladino calls "a loft/fantasy office."

And the lessons are worthy of the creator. "First, I looked at the potential of the existing conditions, and the strong points were the column and the ceiling height. I decided to feature the column." But it was disguised by white paint—masquerading as something else. It was stripped and left alone, with tiny bits of the white paint still evident. "The walls of European cities," explains Saladino, "trace eons of civilization—Roman, medieval, nineteenth century—and we race over there to see it. As you peel back the layers of the past, traces of other homes will show. If you're remodeling, let time show."

Next, "I wanted something to do with a garden, a powerful evocation of space," Saladino goes on. And the lattice, composed of quarter-inch-by-one-inch stock molding, has the feeling of a "trellis, a garden environment. I think the reason we see so much latticework today comes from our revived interest in pattern."

Last, "exposed and natural surfaces are beautiful," says Saladino, "and also cut down the budget." So the sugar pine joists were left "unmasked for honesty." And the plywood platform was left unfinished.

ON CEILINGS: "They're the forgotten landscapes of the twentieth century. Ceilings are simply anonymous surfaces that we punch holes in to install systems. Think of a Robert Adam ceiling, and what we've come down to now. How about wood ceilings, floating ceilings, revolving ceilings—or illusionistic ones—just drawing a perfect circle in white high-gloss paint over a dark matte finish will make a poor-man's dome."

ON ROUGH SURFACES: "We built the divider with wire mesh over wall studs, then covered it with scratch-coat plaster, the unbleached plaster that's conventionally used as an undercoat."

**ON FLOORS:** "Floors are a wonderful way to put color into a room—especially if a wood floor has been rubbed or pickled with paint."

**VOICE OF EXPERIENCE:** Rough surfaces on concrete or brick, particularly old brick stripped of its plaster veneer, can shed fine dust and powder unless sealed. A range of products— from many coats of paste wax to a single, thinned coat of shellac —can solidify the surface and give it a bit of a gloss. The most neutral sealer you can use is clear liquid silicon, which will darken masonry a shade or two but it will leave natural color gradations intact.

**ON LIGHTING:** "I always say there should be three kinds of lighting: ambiant light, which generally illumines the shelf; art light that throws patterns all over the ceiling, like light underneath plants; and tool light, to read by or even like the light for treads on a stair. The effect is like three-dimensional chess. Some light should be pervasive and some should be specific."

# THE CONVERTIBLE HOME
## CHURCHES, CARRIAGE HOUSES, AND ADAPTIVE RE-USE

Who would have imagined a 1900s storefront in Washington, D. C., or a 1920s gas station in Illinois would be the latest link in the chain reaction of urban renaissance? All kinds of older commercial buildings are fast becoming unique city homes.

This storybook New England church was originally built in 1862, then grew with the community. In 1900 the belfry was added, as was the front extension. In 1924 the gabled vestibule was attached. And the new owner, an interior designer, turned it into a one-of-a-kind home by adding the arched leaded window *(opposite)* that now lights up a dining room.

ver walk into an old small-town bank, say 1930s vintage, and stop in your tracks, struck by the gracious details? Marble floors, probably. Ornate cornices, likely. Proud and historic chandeliers? A grand, serious entrance? If you've had these thoughts in a bank or a church or even an ex–bowling alley, you're halfway to a new idea of home.

And if renovation, by definition, means imprinting your personality on a space you'll end up calling home, then recycling an older commercial building—or adaptive re-use—is surely the definitive form of the art. Each and every place will be special, unique, custom tailored.

In Seattle, an architect makes his home in a nineteenth-century carriage house. In Denver, a young attorney now lives in a turn-of-the-century schoolhouse that his grandfather once attended. In Connecticut, a young couple carved out a vacation home from a century-old barn. And in western Minnesota, a fallow ten-story grain elevator has been converted into 1,000- to 1,700-square-foot condos going for not much under $200,000 each. Hotels, hospitals, cotton mills, court-houses, printing plants, grammar schools, parking garages, laundro-mats, piano factories—you name it; they're being snapped up and turned into one-of-a-kind homes.

Why? Because any commercial or public building will offer the romance of living with history, plus a lot more. "The intrinsic building materials become obvious," says Michael Buckley, president of Hal-cyon Ltd., a Hartford, Connecticut, consulting firm that specializes in helping developers all over the country to convert old buildings to new uses. "You can actually *see* stone, brick, wood, and architecture that were, until recently, being designed out or disguised." You get, in other words, home with a whole lot of character.

In old buildings that were never used as houses, unforeseen prob-lems always crop up. The structure only reveals itself as you tear away at the innards, which makes estimating a realistic budget very difficult. If the building was used for industry, for example, be careful about toxic materials—lead paint, among other now forbidden sub-stances, was frequently used in the past. If you are dealing with a church or a barn, remember that conversion is a lot like building a whole new house inside a venerable structure. Bringing utilities into places where none existed can be tough on your budget and your patience. You'll need to check on local water supply, whether you can hook into sewer lines, if the electricity is up to code. Old lead pipes will need replacing, and, finally, you need to make sure that the cost in insulating and heating an expansive space isn't prohibitive.

An older building will demand a great deal of early attention. But look at it this way—character breeds character.

"I had been looking for a second home for about two and half years," says David Eugene Bell, the designer who bought this Litchfield County, Connecticut, church in 1978 as a weekend house and who now lives and works in it full-time. "I wanted a place where I could showcase my imagination. I like unusual spaces. As soon as I saw this church, I thought it had great possibilities.

"Actually," he says, "the church was in good shape when I bought it. It wasn't a wreck. An antiques dealer had been living here, sort of part-time, and he put in new plumbing. But the electricity was terrible, much too weak. I had to add all new wiring and move a great many outlets. I think it's important to get an electrician who knows what he's doing. And you should always get several estimates.

"The other problem with the church was that it was, of course, right in the middle of town. So I added a deck in the back, which overlooks a river. And that's better than a backyard. It gives me complete privacy on my three quarters of an acre."

Bell mostly left well enough alone inside the Colonial Revival church, which has seen a few later changes. Except for the blazing addition of a fireplace and oak mantel on the long wall, the solutions were decorative rather than architectural. Cleverly, Bell used stock molding and standard pieces from the lumberyard to form the imposing broken pediment over the dining room entrance (page 117). He also installed the Palladian, arched window (pages 116 and 117). Original details like the wainscoting and window molding were highlighted with battleship gray paint, as was the new molding. Picked up that way, with the simple addition of darker color, the details work like a picket fence to set comforting limits on the grand scale.

"People always ask me, 'What does it feel like to live in a church?' " says Bell, laughing. "And I have to say it has good vibrations. There was a lot of love here."

# THE DESIGN FACTORY

**THE PRICE:** Acting as both architects and contractors, the partners saved 15 percent on construction. Completed a few years ago, the conversion cost under $150,000 a unit. If done today, with the same communal arrangement, the units would cost a bit over $200,000 each.

**Just on the edge of a posh Chicago neighborhood, the unassuming brick facade of a 1920s former shoe factory hides eight unique town-house units, each with its own entrance.**

In this tale of risk-taking and unusual professional cooperation, ten Chicagoans—seven of them architects—lifted a page from the urban developer's handbook and then rewrote the rules. They banded together to purchase and revamp a shabby old factory at the border of the city's lush Lincoln Park area. After an on-paper division of the property into eight tidy condo spaces, the alliance agreed on an exterior mode and then went their separate ways to ensure the realization of the original aim. And the goal was achieved: uncommonly individualized interiors for city dwellers looking for special space.

Two of the shareholders, architects George Pappageorge and David Haymes, fashioned a razzle-dazzle habitat from their vertical slice of the building *(opposite)* that won them an award for distinguished architecture. Besides the independent entrances, each of the three-story town houses has a roof deck and a custom-designed, completely unique interior.

**KITCHEN**

**DINING AREA**

**LIVING AREA**

**BEDROOM**

**BEDROOM**

**Looking down from the top of the town house *(opposite),* the view shows off the architectural elements built into the space to give it distinction and strength. Four-decker contemporary railings echo the shape of the columns, and offer contrast, too, in material and weight. Inset in the wooden stair landing, a quartet of glass blocks allows some light into the bathroom below. The stair enclosure zigzags alongside the steps and, in the same spirit as the flooring strips, makes all the angles feel orderly.**

VOICE OF EXPERIENCE: Yes, a skylight opens up a dark room, increases the sense of space, provides solar energy benefits, and more. But it is also a hole in the roof. Many develop small leaks even after competent installation. For the best wear, look for these features: copper flashing; double-glazing or provision for an interior storm panel to save winter heat; a built-in blind to control solar gain in the summer; and instead of air conditioning, an operator skylight complete with screen that can be cranked open to ventilate hothead cathedral ceilings and stairwells.

With the lure of a loft and the sensibility of a town house, this three-level, 2,100-square-foot space capitalizes on a central light shaft from the new skylight. A paddle fan, straight out of a 1900s workroom *(inset, opposite),* glides above the soaring, Y-shaped staircase. The vertical plaster slab gives the very opened-up space the feeling of stability it needs.

Necessity inspired invention, and the upside-down cutout required for the blades' motion also prompted the playful face in the stairwell, "We try to make a lot of fun with a low budget," says Pappageorge. The eye-, nose-, and mouthlike openings also allow light from above to spread throughout every layer of the interior.

However pristine it looks, the punched-out wall is painted in an evocative, chalky lilac.

On the first, living room level, a curved central partition, the bottom core of the light well, begins as a wraparound for a first-floor powder room and then climbs to define second- and third-floor spaces. Stepped, gray, laminated shelving deftly turns into the skeletal staircase that funnels natural light into the virtually windowless first floor. Another curl of a wall descends from on high, then bumps into a bare-beamed ceiling, unmasked, along with the wood floors, to recall the building's heritage. The trim dining corridor links the living area and the ribbon of a kitchen. Stretched across the back wall, the galley kitchen is behind a large cabinet with wheels, which houses (and moves) the refrigerator.

A look across the stairwell from one bedroom to another *(right)* reveals the openwork of the steps and how the stairway divides into two. Four ingenious doors of frosted glass swivel to close as effectively as vertical louvers.

# LIVING IN A LANDMARK

Located in the small town of Kirkland, outside Seattle, Washington, this restored building is now listed in the National Register of Historic Places.

THE PRICE: The owners both live and work in this historic building, with about a third, or 3,300 square feet, given over to residential use. The renovation cost "in excess of one million dollars for

the whole building," with approximately half of that spent on the living areas. It took a full year to complete.

**A VISIONARY REHAB:** The inspiring point about this renovation is that the owners had nerve and confidence enough to design the home they wanted inside. It's clearly contemporary and yet everything works within the landmark façade. Interior shutters replace draperies to complement the commercial face, since the owners' business offices are on the first level.

**VOICE OF EXPERIENCE:** Landmarks and buildings in historic areas may qualify for low-cost loans and tax credits. Find out through local building department or preservation groups. Also inquire about restrictions. Façade regulations may control window size, type of siding, even the color of exterior paint.

On a dark, rainy night in March 1982, a hopeful couple first set eyes on this 1891 former bank. It had fallen on hard times, including a mid-1940s "remodeling" into a dozen small apartments. "We were totally naïve," says the now proud owner.

"Demolition alone took four months. We took out the existing apartments, false ceilings, mezzanine floors, borderline electrical wiring and plumbing, all interior walls, floors, roof, broken and dry-rotted windows. New construction included three new staircases, a two-person elevator, two skylights, new floors, exact replicas of the original windows, all the modern mechanical equipment. And, finally, we had it painted, sparingly, within the limits of the vast natural brick wall spaces."

The big kitchen uses the entire area of one of those "remodeled" apartments, but it still cooks small. Within four steps of the maple-topped range island are the sink, dishwasher, and refrigerator. Nine feet of country table and eight primitive chairs balance the slick laminated surfaces. The giant hood keeps odors out and adds work light.

# THE GAS STATION, REVISITED

A lone red gas pump, moved from its original position, reminds the owners that their home has gone the distance. Exterior lighting is appropriately techy.

**"W**e had trouble convincing the banks this could be a luxurious home, but we never doubted it," say Jim Carlock and Bob Graziano of their high-octane rehab. A former Texaco station built in the 1920s and now in an outlying Chicago neighborhood, this conversion gives new meaning to the renovator's need for vision.

For the exterior, the owners added sliding glass doors to domesticate the gas station's bays, but the facade is still dressed in its original white porcelain. Where gas pumps once stood, green grass and a birch tree now grow. The new, triangular deck adds a bit of width and a sense of entrance to the low, narrow building.

Inside, the owners opted for a loft strategy without really changing the interior space except for the addition of kitchen and bath amenities.

Viewed from the back *(inset),* the small gas station looks more like its former self. In some neighborhoods, it's street-smart not to advertise renovation.

THE DISCREET CHARM OF ADAPTIVE RE-USE: Converting a commercial building is bound to produce special problems that simply don't occur in more conventional structures. In the case of this former Texaco station, says owner Jim Carlock, "It cost us $3,000 just to fill in the 50,000-gallon gas tank buried out front."

The design solution inside the gas station was to treat the space as one rangy room. New walls were kept to a minimum, both for space and for financial reasons, and the rooms were defined by new levels, as in the elevated kitchen *(left).* A unified white and black color scheme keeps the room airy and open, while the black techy lamps add drama.

# CONVERTING A CARRIAGE HOUSE

VOICE OF EXPERIENCE: Walls can be removed to make larger spaces as long as the structural loads carried by the wall are supported. Here, headers (the horizontal beams between the posts) collect the loads and transfer them to the columns. But think twice before removing walls holding wiring and plumbing. Rerouting those lines (for example, a drainpipe from an upstairs bath) will be more work than removing the wall itself.

A nineteenth-century carriage house, before *(above, left)* and after *(above, right):* The original arched transoms of the doors cost $500 per set to renovate, but the money was well spent. While the exterior remains unchanged, walls were added to seal up the doors.

Until the renovation, what this carriage house had going for it was its own inherent charm and a verdant setting in a great Seattle neighborhood. Not bad. But it also had an awkward, dark, stingy, and very gloomy interior.

This was clearly a time when moving the furniture would not solve the problems. The walls and the ceiling had to be moved instead.

And that's just what architect George Suyama did, in a glorious rebirth that bestowed everything you crave from a renovation: space, light, and detail—plus, of course, the inherent charm. He raised the roof several feet and then flattened it to rescale the atticlike second floor, which, reversing the convention, became the main living level. The interior was treated to a general and extensive gutting, with most of the walls removed or replaced by load-bearing columns. Light now pours into the house from a generously proportioned skylight over a two-story center well. The overhead natural light lends new life and focus to the whole structure. Today, it's a delicious surprise to find that sweep of light and architectural distinction residing in a small carriage house.

ADDING EMOTIONAL DETAIL: Bold wood trim and columns (only some in a supporting role), seductive fanlight windows, and streamlined steel railings add up to architectural drama—and also the feeling of home.

The raised fixed-pane skylight roof and the lunette window *(right)* are the prime ingredients of this radical and stylish renovation.

**A**n advocate of design that fits the existing neighborhood, Seattle architect George Suyama still wanted to open up this dark carriage house. His idea? "An envelope pierced by a corridor of light." The solution? He left the exterior unchanged and installed a massive skylight.

The classic renovation problem of needing load-bearing walls to support floors and roof was solved here by structural columns of steel sheathed in graceful wood at the corners of the central light well. They replace the wall supports that once divided this second floor into small rooms. The columns also do the work of first-floor walls, which were removed in the general gut. You can now walk unimpeded all the way around the light well in the lofty living quarters, while natural light streams down to the lower level of central hall, kitchen, and bedrooms.

**A new, gracious ceiling height for dining, and, indeed, for the entire front of the house, was found by raising the roof. You can see the old roof line in the corner behind the column (above and right).**

**THE NEW WINDOW TRICK:** Extraordinary windows are the cost-conscious renovator's first choice for high-impact detail. Shapes like the half moon *(below)* are the key.

The rolled steel railings are delicate counterpoint to a wooden column *(below)*. The freestanding staircase floats to the upper level *(left)*.

# A BOWLING ALLEY MOVES INTO THE FAST LANE

From the street, the little brick building in Chicago looks just as it did when built as a bowling alley in 1906. Behind the weathered door and the white, plexiglass windows, however, are two outdoor rooms and a new home.

"When I found the building, it was just a long, narrow city lot with a roof on it," says Chicago architect Martin Sexton. Now his home is a surprise package of introspective renovation—a bold-stroke solution.

Hemmed in on all sides, the turn-of-the-century building was about 125 feet long by 25 feet wide. Its anonymous façade nudges the sidewalk in front, while the back wall abuts an alley. The side walls stand shoulder to shoulder with the neighboring buildings on either side. There wasn't any room here to move out. Within the limited space, Sexton's innovative ideas used the space in a novel way.

"I relied on architecture by controlled demolition," says Sexton. He left all the exterior walls intact, but then shortened the house by 10 feet in the front and 10 feet in the back by removing the roof and floor. So the building is now about 105 feet long,

but the outside walls are left standing where they were built. That created two light-filled patios at either end of the house. Now Sexton has both a front and a back yard—both set within the walls. To enclose the house where he had left openings, Sexton installed floor-to-ceiling glass doors at both sides, which opens the living area to the light and to the yards.

Inside the now smaller house, the original maple bowling lanes were filled in and carpeted. There's a galley kitchen on one side with a narrow studio room running along the opposite wall. In between are two baths, a closet/laundry room, one bedroom, and the living/dining room.

Inside, architect Sexton replaced the old walls on either side with sliding glass doors for access to the courtyards *(above)*. Landscaped and decked, the rear yard also has a garden.

After stepping just inside the front door, you're in the privacy of a courtyard, facing a freestanding concrete wall that's about four feet wide *(left)*. An L-shaped wooden bridge spans the graveled courtyard and a reflecting pool, then takes a right turn to the front door of the house proper.

# THE URBAN PLANNER
## LIVING IN A HIGH-RISE

The guiding rule is hardworking luxury. Built-ins are the byword. Rooms and furnishings must perform overtime for crucial storage and privacy needs. But always follow your heart. Whether you're after an urban farmhouse or a city-slick salon—it can all be done in a high-rise home.

In the wake of a general rehabilitation, the living room of this Manhattan residence was completely redesigned. Architectural furnishings, such as the turn-of-the-century Josef Hoffmann sofa and chairs *(right)*, can provide the kind of exciting detail often missing from white-box spaces.

on't let anyone snow you. Revitalizing a high-rise apartment, even the smallest studio, is one of the toughest renovation jobs going. Why? You start with a host of immutable givens. In a co-op or condo, you can't build out, you can't build up, you can't move the windows—you might even have trouble changing them. The front door remains static. No clever juggling of entrance or exit is allowed. Plumbing and electrical sources are shared, vertically, by dozens of neighbors, which makes relocating the kitchen or bath a lesson in compromise. The access is tricky: how do you get the rubble out of the apartment and into the dumpster at the curb? And how does all that new lumber and those handsome, heavy columns you've set your heart on get from the curb up to the apartment? There's no backyard or garage for temporary storage, so you've got to cover everything you own in the world with plastic drop cloths and still have the grace to live with all that dust. Then, just for breathers, you undoubtedly need to accommodate a slew of co-op or condominium board restrictions. Tough, as we say. Limited options.

Well, that's the bad news. There *is* good news. Unlike the years of landlord-imposed restrictions, the interior is now all yours to do with what you will. And young, innovative designers and architects today have devised daring solutions to demands for space, space, space. Built-in storage has become as cunning as the latest technology. New ideas for partitions, dividers, and interior windows are showing up in high-rise homes everywhere.

The first thing to consider is pulling down the wall between the kitchen and dining room or area. Instantly, you feel a whole lot better. Then tackle the white box. It might need some curves to take the edges off. "I've been able to transform a lot of mundane spaces with just a few gestures," says minimalist designer Joe D'Urso. But that's not the only solution. Original or reproduction architectural detail—moldings, wainscoting, medallions, faux finishes, textured wall treatments—are now available in abundance. The idea is to add intricate places for light and your eyes to rove over—to install a feeling of history in those boxy, machine-made spaces.

Patience and a good architect are prime concerns in any rehabilitation. For a high-rise home, make that lots of determination and an imaginative, thoughtful, really good architect. Interview several. Find one you have a real, conversational rapport with, someone whose sense of humor you like, someone who sees the same movies you do —and then trust him or her.

# THE STREAMLINED CONDO

**VOICE OF EXPERIENCE:** New ceilings provide an opportunity for versatile track lighting. The same track system will take a variety of fixtures, from floods to projection lamps. But for individual control, separate wiring must be installed to connect the track to different wall switches.

"This was a tight and badly laid-out apartment," says New York architect David Estreich, "with bedrooms off the entryway and in the back too. We ripped out everything, even the closets, so that we could re-organize the rooms. Now, all the bedrooms are in the back and the space works."

"The kitchen was a dark, narrow galley," says architect Estreich, "and we opened it up by taking in some of the living room space and installing the glass block" (above). New custom-designed laminate cabinets and Italian ceramic tile on the floor also enlightened the kitchen. Carefully chosen hanging lamps in both the kitchen and the dining room (top) lend sculptural shapes, a softness of form that's in keeping with the curvy architecture and furnishings.

You've seen this place before. Before, that is, the startling and exciting transformation. Space like this exists in every high-rise in every city across the country—1,200 square feet of white-box rooms and not an architectural detail in sight. Just your basic rectangle, in this case and in so many others, divided so inefficiently that the small quarters feel even smaller. What's impressive here is the new sweep of that limited space and the newly installed interior architecture.

"Once we had gutted the apartment and taken down the walls," Estreich explains, "we found supporting beams in the ceiling and along the sides. So we added extra ones to regularize the rooms and covered them with drywall, painted to look the same." The results are the recessed storage units and latticed ceiling in the dining room *(left, above)* and the coffered ceiling in the kitchen *(left, below)*. The small, square entryway turned into a not-too-grand rotunda with a curved ceiling that also provides soft lighting *(opposite)*. Glass block dividers also work as major architectural elements that strengthen both interest and light. All these decorative details, although subtle, add a feeling of being in a house.

With the built-in pattern writ so large, the rest of the surfaces remain sleek, for contrast. Accessories are kept to a minimum in the small space. Fresh flowers, fruit, two high-impact hanging lights, and a few casual objects chosen for shape let the strong surfaces of glass and laminate show off. Estreich sums it up best: "It's a little jewel of an apartment now."

# THE ENGINEERED
# APARTMENT

**VOICE OF EXPERIENCE:** Before any high-rise renovation work, plan the access for materials and furnishings. Check that the freight elevator is available when the lumber truck arrives. Make sure the one-piece, fiberglass tub and shower enslosure will fit through the smallest door en route to the bath.

"Decorated spaces can live without people," says New York designer Joe D'Urso, who is the master of the stripped-down place. "Mine cannot." D'Urso's work is committed to the architectural use of interior space, as the elegant monasticism in this co-op clearly shows. Not everyone can live this way. A strong sense of self is essential for survival in a D'Urso environment. But his clients are a special breed who seek him out, looking for the D'Urso brand of minimalism.

"I'm trying to execute the role of the designer as objectively as possible," D'Urso explains. "That seems new because somewhere along the line, something else got in there which has confused the whole issue. And that is the idea of superficial individuality. We're overconcerned with individuality. Everybody wants to have something different from everybody else. Well, that is a waste of time and an unreality."

In this case, high above Manhattan, D'Urso's carpeted platforms become furniture and the lone Mackintosh chair turns into sculptural art. Pink warms the room and the green plays off a weathered copper roof of a nearby building. In such simple surroundings, the view becomes the focus of the room—a three-dimensional poster. "When I get bored," says the owner in all sincerity, "I go out and buy a new flower."

Early on, designer D'Urso would use only white and black, but he's taken to pastels recently. And red. "There's something so basic, so universal about red," he says. "It's practically neutral."

# THE NEWS IN DETAIL

Architect Wheelwright replaced the lost interior detail in the front foyer *(below)* with contemporary equivalents: rich marble tile, mahogany trim, and a dramatically recessed coffered light.

**VOICE OF EXPERIENCE:** Pocket doors are a good space-saving feature for apartments or small houses. They slide in line with the opening instead of swinging into the room. True pocket doors literally tuck into the wall cavity. Since they use up space in the wall normally reserved for framing, the framing around the pocket tends to be a bit rickety, and needs extra bracing. A similar effect can be achieved by installing shoji-screen doors with sliding track hardware (the type used in closets with bypassing doors). The aluminum track can be buried beneath a piece of trim to match the doors.

Old high-rise apartments offer the best of both worlds: a convenient, urban location and the generous space and comforting feel of a house—with emotional details and gracious living built right in. But what happens when the rich architectural detail that's supposed to come with the territory can't be resurrected?

That was the hitch in this 3,600-square-foot New York apartment. The wonderful details were in such a sorry state that repair was impossible. The result? Architect Peter Wheelwright's imaginative addition of luxurious, new details to doors, walls, moldings, and floors that use very rich but very contemporary ideas and materials. Wheelwright's fresh design and even fresher thinking emphasize a striking point for would-be renovators. You don't necessarily need original or period details to create an apartment with drama and personality. The sensual details here reproduce the mood —but certainly not the look—of the original architecture. "Virtually everything came out," says Wheelwright. "And we did a lot of built-in work." An airy, free-flowing layout makes the most of the new details while resolving the usual apartment problem of squandered space.

The main hall *(right)* once contained a second passage that led to the servants' quarters. Removing it let the hall take a straighter and wider course to the second foyer, where light pours in. The left wall takes a graceful curve as it approaches the foyer.

The second foyer *(right)* was moved out of its dark recess, closer to the living room's entrance. Mahogany trim on the baseboard and framing the mirror provides rich texture and warmth. The upper portion of the wall is outfitted with mirrors to help amplify light. Notice the latticed ceiling.

Built in the early 1900s, this huge New York apartment was up to its crumbling crown moldings in maid's rooms and hallways—most of it the legacy of an outmoded life-style.

"The owners like American Federalist architecture and lots of detail," says Peter Wheelwright. "I translated their interest into marble-tiled floors, mahogany moldings, brass hardware, and patterned interior windows and doors. Now they have detail—but it's contemporary."

While the apartment mostly needed to have several tiny rooms opened up, the dining and living rooms—connected by the usual arch—suffered from too much stark space. Architect Wheelwright's ingenious solution was this "nonwall wall"—a windowed partition that adds the touch of mystery each room was lacking. Subtly beautiful and simply constructed of metal studs and drywall, then upholstered in silk, the partition is a sculptural presence. It allows light and sight lines to flow around both sides and through the mahogany-trimmed window.

**ON JAPANESE STYLE:** The Japanese way with color and form is finding its way into American homes and is particularly evident here. "My interests do lie in that area," acknowledges Wheelwright. In the apartment, his interpretation of shoji screens turns into sandblasted wire-mesh glass pocket doors with mahogany trim and brass pulls. "I like the spareness, the natural materials, and the composition of Japanese design," says Wheelwright. At the heart of Japan's influence is the integrity of materials—pattern and color are organic, not added on.

Above the fireplace, the ornate mantel was replaced by a single mahogany board. And marble tile—instead of pilasters—makes a contemporary frame for the firebox. Note how the tile extends like a baseboard from the hearth, tying fireplace and room together.

With the massings and setbacks of a classic skyscraper, the entire rear wall has been sculpted to cover up old plumbing and cleverly designed to solve real-life problems. The wall becomes a giant headboard solid enough to lean against, and the built-in lighting is the perfect answer to the needs of bedtime readers. The Eliel Saarinen armchair just to the left of the bed echoes the room's architectural design and comfort. This is minimalism without an undernourished look—a fine place to rest a weary head.

**ON DECORATIVE DETAILS:** Nothing else so quickly offers a sense of home and feeling to white-box rooms. Details are back with a vengeance —and a difference. The new details are rich, simple, and unpretentious, just the opposite of white-painted plaster moldings, which would have weighed heavily upon this renovation's easygoing elegance. Here, the choice of mahogany wood trim throughout was an inspired one. In rooms as architectural as a T-square, the woody details add warmth.

Adjacent to the bedroom, the bathroom was a small feat of engineering and expense. Carved out of a former maid's room, the necessary pipes had to be run from a bath at the front of the apartment. It's now finely tailored with Italian tiled walls and pink marble floor.

# PRIVATE PENTHOUSE

**VOICE OF EXPERIENCE:** While replacing old, somewhat leaky windows high above the ground may be impractical, most of the benefits offered by new units can be achieved by adding storm windows. Rigid plastic sheeting in minimal frames can be set tightly against molding inside the existing window to cut drafts and save heat. Also, tightly fitted storms cut noise transmission by roughly 50 percent—a little-known benefit that's a particular blessing in cities.

n the shoulder-to-shoulder squeeze of big-city life, often the only place to go is up. And this New York rooftop aerie, converted from nearly raw warehouse space, is the just reward of that inventive search. It captures the practical romance that's always been at the heart of urban living.

Confronted with a yawning vertical space, architects Douglas Peix and William Crawford imaginatively decided to split the space horizontally —and the owners agreed. Originally, it was 28 feet high from the peak of the skylight to the 24-foot-by-40-foot main floor. The new floor created a dramatic living room under glass, and it liberated space below for two bedrooms and a kitchen and living area.

High-powered design in the compact kitchen/dining space *(below)* makes cooking and entertaining efficient. An illusion of more space is created by the placement of columns that punctuate the kitchen, while a similar postmodern framing appears opposite, alongside the dining table.

Since there are windows only in the bedrooms on the first floor, the stairway to the living room was strategically placed to let natural light brighten the dining and kitchen space. Underscaled furnishings were a conscious choice to avoid overwhelming the small space.

Each area assumes its own identity without the need of walls. Peix and Crawford executed a complete, though compact, kitchen, leaving room for Toshiyuki Kita's artfully mismatched ice-cream-colored chairs and a sleek Eurostyle table.

**Housed in its own pavilion *(below)*, the kitchen, small and tidy, works hard. A stainless steel sink, gooseneck faucet, and black tile counter contrast with the warmth of wooden cabinets *(above)*. Black enamel handles unify the counter and cabinets.**

**ROOMS WITH A VIEW:**
The steel structure of
this skylight came with
the territory—a raw
room with little floor
space and a fabulous
but inaccessible roof-
top view. Dividing the
space horizontally, to
make two floors, and
reglazing the skylight
brought the sky-
scrapers into view.
Very often in urban
apartments, raising or
lowering the floor level
lets the view become
part of the design.

**THE PRICE:** Completed
in 1983, this cost-con-
scious renovation,
says New York archi-
tect Douglas Peix, cost
a civilized $55,000.

O n the new upstairs level, the
living room is open to a
sweeping panorama both night
and day. The entryway and
steps at left were spliced into the latticework to provide access to the
deck, which will eventually include a
garden. Otherwise, the skylight
remains intact, though it was reglazed
with new custom-cut glass frosted at
eye level for privacy.

Cleverly placed track lighting
brightens the room at night without
detracting from the main event. Similarly, the witty, carved-wood coffee
table and colorfully edged French
modular seating are hardly background, but the easy colors keep the
view in focus.

All that glass, of course, means things
heat up considerably during the day,
which is partially cured by a hard-
working overhead fan. In the evening,
when the owners really use the space,
the room cools rapidly. Steam heat,
piped in from downstairs, and the
unusual city choice of an old-fashioned
stove provide wintertime warmth.

**Informal and inviting furnishings, plus
the warmth of the pine handrails and
stairs, ensures that the steel skylight
and stony cityscape don't overpower
the room. The living room, here, is very
much at ease.**

**VOICE OF EXPERIENCE:** While single-thickness stove-pipe is fine between the stove and wall, a special fitting, called a thimble (usually three layers of pipe with insulation in between), makes the transition between the pipe inside and the pipe outside. Always check local codes first. Some metropolitan areas do not allow certain types of auxiliary heaters. And using them may also jeopardize fire insurance.

# THE NEW CLASSICS

**VOICE OF EXPERIENCE:** The cost per square foot is only a rough yardstick for both new construction and renovation work, because the bottom line has too many variables. For instance, large, open spaces, even when elaborately detailed, are usually much less expensive per square foot than very small kitchens and baths. Areas that require concentrated mechanical work (heating, cooling, plumbing, and electrical) are the most costly.

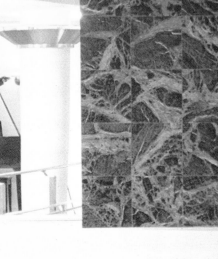

**"W**e couldn't change the windows," says New York architect Peter Shelton, "which is a common problem in high-rises. But we did want as much light as possible, and we wanted to see the view from everywhere in the room. So we designed the curved mezzanine level."

**T**his style is pure New York high-rise, vintage 1980s. Both the structure and the furnishings carry a custom-look label that's clearly a slice of our time. It pulls together the furnishings and shapes of the twentieth century's modern masters, but the roots are really in the Hollywood sets and grand ocean-liner scale of the 1930s and 1940s. In all, it's a lush and impressive home.

"What the owner wanted was a party place, but he also wanted a home where his children could visit and feel comfortable," says architect Peter Shelton, who completed this opulent renovation along with his architect partner, Lee Mindel. "The interesting thing," Shelton continues, "is that the owner first came to us because he admired a discotheque we had worked on. He liked the lighting and the railings, the curves and the polished surfaces."

Located on New York's East Side, with part of a bridge and river for a view, this co-op was originally two apartments—a studio and a one-bedroom—that the owner purchased so that he could turn them into one. With just under 2,000 square feet overall, the architects took out all the walls except one in the bedroom, and then put in a mezzanine level for the master bedroom, study/guest room, second bath, dining area, and kitchen.

Glamorous materials set the mood. A Grand Hotel staircase, which the architects designed to connect the wide-open living room to the second level, is made of marble and brass. The same imported marble, plus another, creates the dramatic two-dimensional mantel. And three shades of dress-for-success gray on the carpet and the furniture subtly define the different areas.

On the staircase **(above)** and mezzanine **(left)**, railings are made of steel with inset brass to further the 1930s ocean-liner mood. A lavish use of marble on floors and the staircase sets the appropriately rich background. And contemporary Angelo Donghia chairs echo the dressiness of the deco era.

Two windows look as if they flank the fireplace **(opposite)**, but cleverly, only one is real. On the left is a mirror that reflects the piano on the mezzanine opposite. On the right, a sliding panel opens from the bedroom for an owner's-eye view of the living room.

The walls of the master bedroom remained intact, but architects Shelton and Mindel punched a hole in the wall behind the bed to permit another interior window, this one from the bathroom. Just below the open panel *(right, above)* is a whirlpool bath, and when the panel is open, a fire in the opposite fireplace can be enjoyed while soaking. Stock molding on the wall, painted the same creamy beige as the rest of the room, sets up the suggestion of a headboard and also provides a unified frame for the window.

Looking from the dining area through the passageway into the kitchen and the bedroom beyond *(right, below)*, you can see the architects' attention to livable details: "The hallway is set at an oblique angle to the window wall in the living room, again so you can see the bridge view as you come from the kitchen," says Shelton. "But its curving path also creates an ease of circulation. It encourages people to wander around—which is just what you want them to do at a party."

**In this bed-sitting room, the bed itself is a little building, a piece of architecture. Summer-crisp linens and little bedside lamps *(above)* are streamlined frills. The pairing of objects around the fireplace gives focus and structure to the room, while uplighting sconces and down-lighting spots *(left)* help mold and gentle the slick surfaces. The mantel *(opposite)* is a cleaned and painted urban artifact—the luck of a salvage find.**

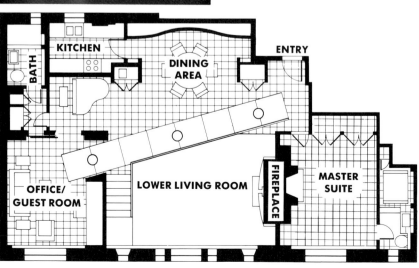

**THE PRICE:** "Completed in 1984, this renovation took about a year," says architect Shelton, "and cost about $130 a square foot." It also won an award for architectural distinction.

# THE GREAT VICTORIANS
## TOWN HOUSES, BROWNSTONES, AND PAINTED LADIES

From sprawling mansions to urban row houses, from Back Bay Boston to Capitol Hill Seattle, Victorians offer gracious rooms with a view of the nineteenth century. Scrub down the shell, remake the marrow, and you have an extraordinary renovation: a new-old house of unabashed sentiment.

For the right-thinking Victorian, more was more. No house was complete without conspicuous visual display, like this peacock wall frieze stenciled by present-day craftsmen in a Brooklyn brownstone, or *(opposite)*, the vintage fretwork of a San Francisco Queen Anne.

t's one of those amazing but true tales. The rise and fall and rise again of Victoriana. From 1860 to 1910—some would add a few years on either side—the style of Victoria's era reigned in America. Beginning about 1920 until 1960 or so, the Modernist movement, encouraged by the early Arts and Crafts designers, banished everything even remotely Victorian—and made us all feel relieved. Today, no one seems to be able to get enough, much like the Victorians themselves.

Our legacy runs the gamut: houses with dormers and turrets, fretwork and cupolas, back stairs and front porches; coy lighting through fringes and pleated silk shades, leaded and stained-glass chandeliers; heavy furniture with ornate carving, burls, and trick curves; upholstery with richly detailed patterns that were a mere backdrop for more lushly patterned plump cushions. Anything worth doing, the Victorians declared, was worth doing to excess.

The original Victorian houses were dark and stuffy, filled with tunnel-like hallways and rabbit-warren rooms heated by fireplaces. At the time they were being built, the idea of the middle-class home, the sanctuary of the family, was taking hold, so the houses often have a front parlor (which evolved into the living room); servants' quarters (including the closed-off kitchen, pantry, and maid's room); and an upstairs master bedroom suite, complete with lady-of-the-house boudoir (the original bathroom). But nothing's certain with a Victorian floor plan.

The architectural style covers a stunning range of space and shape, from the relative simplicity of Greek Revival to the more fanciful Queen Anne houses. Brick row houses in Baltimore are Victorian and so are Italianate villas in Galveston. Carpenter Gothic cottages qualify and so do Mansard town houses, with double sloped roofs. All sorts of regional variations were constructed as America moved west and then returned east. The odd thing, though, despite all this flux and flow, is that you absolutely know a Victorian when you see one. And the ornamentation, inside and out, is the key.

Your task in rehabilitating a Victorian, more than with most houses, is to select, to discriminate, to find reproductions or original trim, to plan the interior that works for your needs. Don't be afraid to renovate rather than restore, to have the guts to knock down a wall or two and let a little twentieth-century light into those dusty rooms.

Says Clem Labine, publisher of *The Old-House Journal* and the unofficial voice of the ad hoc preservation movement in the U.S., "When looking at a Victorian house for the first time, don't get carried away by decorative detailing, which is very easy to do. Instead, make sure there are no budget-busting structural or mechanical problems." And more advice: "Beware of turning over major decisions to a contractor until he or she has demonstrated a sensitivity to Victorian buildings."

# THE LIGHT-FILLED GINGERBREAD

nside the gem of a San Francisco painted lady *(page 161)* is the surprise of contemporary space and light. The owners took a middle-of-the-road approach to their Victorian, with changes that are neither a swagged-out re-creation nor a gut job that ignores its nineteenth-century heritage. "We kept the best of the living room's Victorian details," says owner Paula Fracchia, "without sacrificing the goal of our renovation: simplicity." The winning ways of the opened-up house include the general spareness of the interior in a house that was built for excess, as well as the unexpected mix of white-lacquered Josef Hoffmann dining chairs and pedestal table within the vintage architecture.

# STATE-OF-THE-ART TOWN HOUSE

**VOICE OF EXPERIENCE:** The least exciting problem of a major renovation is the cleanup—how to get rid of the mounds of debris. An economical solution is to rent a roll-off dumpster: a large, rectangular container. When you're done filling it, a special truck picks up the huge metal box and tows it away.

Preservation is important, but nothing is sacrosanct. "No single strategy," says New York architect Henry Smith-Miller, "no single style can accommodate today's situation." Young architects now mine the past for ideas and sources, but the results are rooted in the new age.

However sleek and up to date this condominium looks, the balance between old and new is present everywhere, accomplished by the fine architectural hand of Henry Smith-Miller. This approach reorganizes the interior of the house without stripping the envelope of its integrity. Fine old details like window frames and the graceful hall staircase work as contrast—and inspiration—for the opened-up floor plan and additions. If your desire is for contemporary space, there's no need to wipe the slate squeaky clean.

The first floor has access to the outside, but, says Smith-Miller, "it is four feet below the walkway. It isn't terrific to look out the window." His solution was to raise the floor and remove the walls of an upstairs second bedroom (above the tree, *opposite*) and to install an intermediate platform level. Now light floods the open space, and the view upstairs is worth the effort.

At the end of the gallery *(right)*, two paths diverge at the corner chair. Turn left and you walk out onto the waist-high platform "overlook," with a short stairway down to the living room *(opposite)*. The platform is a sculptural presence, a new shape in the old, boxy plan, carefully linked by plank, railing, and curves to the gallery/dining areas. The living room, sunken in the original scheme, appears now to be a side trip off the main pathway, marked by the tubular railing.

The original arched window in the living room is a reminder of the house's roots, part of the old envelope that surrounds this renovation. The upper portion is purposely left bare to fix the room in time, while the lower section is covered with narrow blinds (colored the same sea green as the painted trim) to screen the unappetizing view.

The living room furnishings underscore the changes in the structure. All the furniture is completely traditional —wingback chairs, the standard sixties straight-lined sofa. What's new is the architectural wrapping. It makes the forms look contemporary. Modern classic Alvar Aalto webbed chairs, on the side, and the Aalto stool on the rug, plus the architect-designed lamps all act as timely middlemen in the bold transition.

In a completely reorganized town house on New York's Upper East Side, the center has been refocused on a daylighted gallery *(below)*, but the flowing stairway and the discreet spaces of the original house are mercifully intact. The gallery provides a showcase for the collectible Mackintosh chairs.

The wrecking ball was swung judiciously here, clearing the way for today's airier materials of glass block, tubular railing, and overhead recessed lighting.

**THE TWELVE-MONTH RULE:** It took one year to complete this town house's renovation. Says architect Smith-Miller, "I always say nine months, whether it's a kitchen or an entire house, and it always runs longer. In 1980, the cost was $280,000."

A mirror on the far wall opposes another, inset to the right of the open window that looks into the dining area. The effect is an infinitely repeating vista of Queen Anne chairs and rubrum lilies. And yes, that is a toucan on the chair—the household's pet.

The town house's turning point: Seen from below, the entryway gallery ends as a stairway into the living room and as the crossroad for walking toward the dining partition and room.

Called a "duplex" in Manhattan, this two-story town-house apartment has 5,000 square feet and five bedrooms, including the curved master suite.

Given the long stretch of the gallery and the broad vista of the living room, it's surprising to turn toward the dining room (*left, below,* and *opposite*) and come face to face with a wall. Well, almost a wall. It doesn't quite reach the ceiling and it's open at both ends. Architect Smith-Miller calls it a "metaphysical wall."

Its center is a small window (*left, top*) that looks into the dining room. The wall marks off the dining area as a separate space, but the unconnected wall is a reminder of the open plan. From the living room, you can see into the dining area, but the only way to get a seat at the table is to follow the architectural path set out by the metal railings—around the interrupting wall. It's theater; it's illusion; and it makes the dining area a great deal more intimate.

On the table side of the metaphysial wall, the coy view opens up into a gracious, open space that's comfortable for dining (*opposite*). Both the mirror and the small still life in the cutout are now obvious. The special details and craftsmanship of the renovation become just as obvious. An architectural frame around the window echoes the original building lines but looks wholly contemporary. The straight edges of the dining wall divider offset the old-fashioned multi-paned windows. Metal pipe railing, borrowed from industrial spaces, marks the limit of the new gallery path, but it also contrasts with the furnishings and architecture. And in lovely counterpoint, the solid, dark table and Queen Anne chairs fill out the bare bones of the white space. In all, it's judicious and continuing contrast that makes this room special, and yet everything in it is kept to a spare minimum.

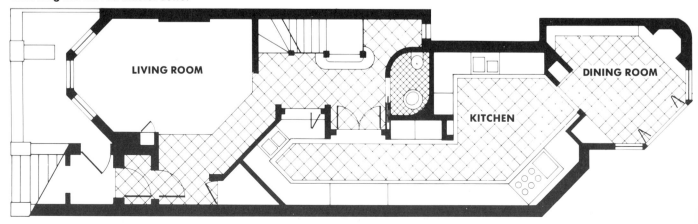

LIVING ROOM

KITCHEN

DINING ROOM

**VOICE OF EXPERIENCE:** Where joints between different building materials in different planes may be difficult to keep closed, consider an architectural detail called a reveal. This term describes a recess (sometimes called a shadow line) that makes a purposeful break between the materials. Note the joint between the white divider wall and the floor (below), where the wall surface never meets the floor, and seems almost to float.

# PERFECT RETROFIT

An overhanging front porch once blocked light in this 1905 Chicago town house. The solution? Remove the porch roof but retain the architectural lines with the illusion of a veranda.

Neither irreverent nor dogmatic, the rehabilitation of this turn-of-the-century Victorian town house harmonizes yesterday's space with today's tempo. A major job on the inside—the interior was completely gutted—outside, the façade was simply cleaned up. Grain broker-turned-architect Sidney Weinberg wanted to keep as many remnants of the past as possible while still adding much-needed light and contemporary comforts.

When most of the front porch was removed, the lower part of the brick was a totally different color from that of the upper section. Minimal sand-blasting (which Weinberg now regrets for the pitting it caused) and an acid wash somewhat revitalized the brick-work and the carved lintels of stone. White paint refreshed the brackets, cornice moldings, dentils, and other wood flourishes.

Inside, a grim, warrenlike collection of rooms was decompartmentalized. Beams, light, and partitions organize the now nearly wall-less space. Living quarters occupy the second and attic floors with bedrooms below, except for a lofty one that makes a partial third level.

**"T**his was a typical little dark Victorian house," says architect Sidney Weinberg, "with a typical Victorian layout. In a thirty-foot-wide building, there was a row of ten-foot-square bedrooms and a narrow hallway dividing them from the living room. I needed to open it up."

Crisp and clean, the gutted interior is a contemporary construction in a snug old structure retrofitted with fresh mechanics. Light now spills into the two-story living area from new windows set into niches. The serpentine fireplace enclosure *(opposite* and *page 169)* eases traffic and deemphasizes the mass of a load-bearing wall. Cutouts lighten everything still more, visually expanding the volume of space and helping to disperse the daylight. Oak floors and touches warm up an essentially cubist plan.

Meaningless accessories are banned here, so that each and every element counts, from the thin-slat blinds for open-and-shut privacy to the decorative beam above the dining table, which Weinberg calls a "light trough." One dramatic landscape painting, Frederick McDuff's *Cabins du Bain in Brittany,* breaks up the overall white-on-whiteness while serving as a surrogate window vista. Its frame echoes the welting on the curved partition alongside. Every detail here is careful and complete.

Across the floor from the dining area, the open, geometric kitchen is equally frill-free. A curved serving/eating ledge counterpoints the focal fireplace wall in the adjoining living area. Architectural interest is aroused by a light well from the loft bedroom above and by another structurally superfluous beam set above the refrigerator. Combining open-shelf and enclosed storage space, the laminated cabinets allow both the display of cooking equipment and plenty of pantry hiding places, too. An outlet strip for barebulb under-cupboard lighting and the recessed ceiling spots are up to any culinary task, while surfaces remain clear.

A resourceful accommodation to building codes that required two routes to the top floor, a new back stairway with a wood-capped diagonal railing leads the eye upward and also provides a perch for sideline chefs.

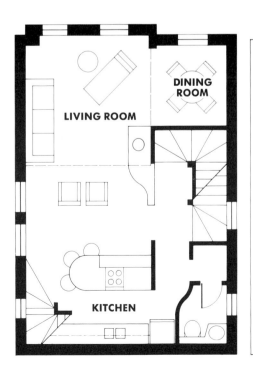

Sound planning and a no-holds-barred rearrangement of rooms turned 1,800 square feet of outmoded space into a contemporary home.

**THE PRICE:** "When it was done in 1980," says architect Weinberg, "this renovation cost about $50 or $60 a square foot. Today, it would cost about $100."

"Originally," says architect Weinberg, "the attic space was unfinished and completely unlivable." Now tucked under the roof, the loft bedroom dou- bles nicely as an office. Little in the way of real furniture is required, as the architecture and built-ins do most of the work.

A plastic laminate shelf fills one corner as an additional bedside table or a desk. The box of a closet takes up a minimum of space. That way, the sky- light can flood the room with sunshine that reaches the lower-level kitchen as well as the bathroom behind the partition that turns into a headboard.

As open as can be, the half-wall sur- rounding the loft is overscored with metal piping and wood, restating the themes of the oak flooring as well as the bath and closet doors.

# THE VICTORIAN IMPULSE

**Being true to the period can actually outclass the house. Owner Clem Labine chose the highest style of the time for his 1883 Brooklyn brownstone, "as if it had been done by the best designer of the day, not some tract-house contractor." The richly woodworked hall** *(opposite)* **is embellished with painstakingly applied wall stenciling.**

I wanted my house to be a museum," says Clem Labine, who lovingly re-created this Victorian fantasy over a period of several years. "I get my kicks from interpretative restoration."

Not everyone could live with gilded art nouveau peacocks strutting along the picture rail or with the lush hallway on the right. And, as Labine affably admits, not everyone should. But for the publisher of *The Old-House Journal,* a newsletter that's a fountainhead of precise, detailed information on how to pull off a restoration that would fool Prince Albert, that richness and the authentic re-creations are his whole life.

In 1968, Clem Labine and his wife, Claire, were collared at a cocktail party and talked into buying their brownstone by a Park Slope, Brooklyn, homesteader who appealed to them on a very basic level: "You can get this big house really cheap." "That I could understand," Labine says now. "Aesthetics were not a major part of the decision."

Then came the psychic horrors by now familiar to tens of thousands of rehabbers: "It was the first rooming-house brownstone in Park Slope to sell for as much as $25,000. Everyone thought we were nuts. We had nightmares about getting in over our heads. We were next door to a really rowdy rooming house. We worried about what we were doing to our kids." Early on, Labine made up his mind that his three children were going to have to live with it.

His very first impulsive act in rehabilitating the house was to tear the plaster from brick and beams on the lower floor. That was before he knew better. He now regrets the decision, calling it "the bare-brick mistake, naïve and degrading to the building." Party brick walls, he explains, were done hastily and sloppily by masons awaiting immediate coverage by careful plasterers.

Those were the days when only George-Washington-slept-here was deemed worthy of preserving, and people in Victorian or turn-of-the-century homes were still hellbent on modernizing, allowing fast-buck contractors to cover clapboard with aluminum siding, to rip off front porches, and to replace wainscoting with Formica. But Labine's early trials and errors became a galvanizing experience.

In the course of converting from abused rooming house to one-family elegance, the Labines discovered a glaring information gap. The work on the house spawned his now successful publishing venture, and in October 1973 the first issue of *The Old-House Journal* was distributed at a local flea market. Labine quit his job as a technical editor at McGraw-Hill and devoted himself full-time to the house and the newsletter—each project informing the other.

A lot of people now credit Clem Labine with putting an end to the modern travesties and praise the patient, persistent lobbying of *The Old-House Journal* for raising the old-house consciousness of America. But Labine, with characteristic modesty, takes only partial credit for the shift. "Obviously we had an influence, but we didn't invent the phenomenon."

Restorers interested in perfect re-creations and renovators who want only a few Victorian details both owe a debt to Clem Labine, whose early interest has now spawned a multi-million-dollar industry of restoration products and services.

"There has been a growing disenchantment with modern design and construction," says Clem Labine. "The old less-is-more trick can be played only so often before people realize that, in most cases, less is, in fact, less. Most people like a certain visual richness and entertainment."

One of a long row of 1880s brownstones, Labine's home is an obsessive Victorian vision—an artful deception, really, for Labine is more concerned with the spirit than the letter of the nineteenth century. The house, says Labine, "was the Levitt house of its day, an outstanding example of mediocre 1880s taste." To be true to the house's roots, he would have ended up with pedestrian, middle-class Victoriana, and he didn't want that. Instead, present-day craftsmen executed reproductions of the very best of the Victorian period, including the walnut wainscoting in the front hall, the glowing cabinetry in the dining room, the stained-glass panel over the front door, and the elaborate stencil designs painted in lieu of wallpaper. None of these were originally found in the house.

As their guiding spirit, the Labines chose Christopher Dresser, a leading English designer of the era. They consulted original lithographs of Dresser's work to select colors and designs for ceilings, walls, dadoes, and friezes.

A dramatic peacock frieze travels around all four walls. Labine chose the repeating pattern from a late-Victorian "idea" book by designer Christopher Dresser.

**LABINE'S FIVE TOUGH QUESTIONS FOR CONTRACTORS:**
1. Is every effort being made to retain original parts of the house?
2. Is the work merely concealing deterioration or solving fundamental problems?
3. When cleaning the exterior, is the gentlest method being used?
4. How will the appearance of the building be altered?
5. What evidence is there that new materials will perform as advertised?

Clem Labine's professional and personal lives are now fused into "one seamless whole"—everybody's fantasy. His home, his hobby, his livelihood, his cause are all focused on a single mission: to prevent further "remuddling" of the architectural heritage of the nineteenth century.

Two Golden Rules of Rehabilitation were formulated by Clem Labine as he worked on this house, and he then set them in concrete for *The Old-House Journal.* First, Don't Destroy Good Old Work: repair rather than replace old-house parts whenever possible. And, To Thine Own Style Be True: don't replace six-over-six windows on a Greek Revival structure with mock-Tudor crosshatched versions. The results, on these pages, vividly speak for themselves.

When original moldings, doors, balusters, and the like are already missing, Labine has "no problem with reproductions." But he's got rules about that, too. "Three components—design, workmanship, and materials—need to be as fine as one hundred years ago." He claims that workmanship is less a problem than material. "Even if you can find a master carpenter to make you a set of rolling doors, you can't get the American walnut used for the originals."

The rules are useful and valid, well worth weighing every time you contemplate modifying a house. At *Metropolitan Home,* our view is that a rule grows up because there's a good reason for it, learned through experience. Some pioneer was there before you. But our view is also that rules are made to be broken and that strict methods may lead to madness. You're the keeper of your castle.

Historical restoration, clearly, is both a demanding and a rewarding process. Should you embark on it, be prepared to deal with the problems of refinishing wide-plank floors, mending iron fences, supporting listing staircases, finding replacements for any absent details, and bearing up bravely against harrowing problems of old-building pathology like rot, termites, and sagging floors. Clem Labine, along with his unimpeachable newsletter, has done a great deal to reeducate the "well-meaning restorers who can do more damage to a house in two weeks than can two decades of neglect." And if you do take on a restoration, Labine and his *Journal* will be there to support your sagging spirits.

**Although we think of stenciling as Colonial decoration, it was popular well into the twentieth century, rendered as elaborate pattern-on-pattern display. It may look like wallpaper *(top),* but the grid of flowers on the dining room ceiling was applied one rosette at a time. The "folded ribbon" parquet floor border *(center)* is original, though Labine will use reproductions when they're good enough. Silk-screened on paper by a local artist, the dining room frieze *(bottom)* even has a personal touch. Labine substituted sunflowers, the symbol of the aesthetic movement, for the standard art nouveau iris.**

**VOICE OF EXPERIENCE:** Few contractors have the experience to recreate elaborate wood and plaster moldings found in many older homes. While there is no good substitute for wood (an architectural salvage supply house may provide a piece approximating what you need), fiberglass reproductions of plaster molding blend in well. Pieces from classic Corinthian columns to decorative Victorian ceiling medallions can be nailed or glued in place, then spackled to hide seams. A prime and finish coat of paint completes the invisible connection between old and new.

# TOWN HOUSE WITH A SECRET

**Behind this early-1900s, ivy-vined façade is the surprise of a thoroughly postmodern home. It's a Victorian with lofty aspirations.**

**H**ere's where renovation comes full circle to describe an entirely new shape. The owners of this Chicago town house are veteran urban pioneers, having cut their teeth on the wide-open spaces. "We had lived in a loft," says Jeanette Jordano, "and I loved all three thousand square feet of it. I was afraid of a twenty-foot-wide building."

With the owners' clear-sighted goal in mind, architects George Pappageorge and David Haymes recast the interior space and raised the roof to fit it all in. They opened up the main floor and replaced several small rooms with a single, massive, T-shaped wall gentled by curved forms. In front of the wall is the living room *(opposite)*. Behind it, the dining room has a recessed light cove above a Le Corbusier table and chairs to give off a romantic glow. Beyond the dining

room is the kitchen *(bottom)*. A quarry tile floor unifies the separate areas.

"The architects made us feel as if we still lived in a loft," exults Jordano. So the lessons and the style of factory chic come home to roost in the nest of a late-Victorian house.

**A result of misguided updating rather than remodeling, this typical turn-of-the-century two-flat was a labyrinth of dark, featureless, small rooms (like the former kitchen, *above*) until Chicago architects Pappageorge and Haymes literally blew the lid off. In the considerably brightened new kitchen *(left)*, quarry tile follows the loft level's diagonal lead. Factory windows bring the back porch indoors for breakfast. Vertical blinds allow for privacy and a choice of sunlit space without breaking up the lines of the new design.**

**VOICE OF EXPERIENCE:** Perimeter electrical wiring works when all the furniture is arranged against the walls. But to bring power to islands or furniture created when partition walls are removed, electric lines must be run in the floor to a flush-floor outlet. These receptacles have a brass cover that can be screwed into place when the outlets are not needed. The covers avoid the cluttered look and potential danger of using extension cords.

In contrast to the home's original, stingy floor plan, the new design yields space—and light—galore. After opening up the main level, architects Pappageorge and Haymes raised the pitched attic roof an additional six feet above the living area to create room for a loft space. They then devised a smaller, open second floor and "dropped" it into the rest of the plan at an angle, leaving the living room with two-story height. Now there's light at the top of the pipe-railed stairs, cascading down from the loft/roof deck and flowing in from the sunroom that's sequestered just behind a prefab fireplace *(opposite).*

Upstairs, part of the loft-level suite, is a new high-and-mighty, splashproof bath *(below).* The open shower with a two-inch raised border has a sloped floor for drainage. Above the brand-new bathtub that's open to the rest of the room, a skylight in the roof allows for solar—or stellar—soaks.

**An overview of the reconstructed town house (right) shows how the loft capsule is set at an angle into the main level.**

**LIGHT AT THE TOP:** A skylight in the sun-room's ceiling, just behind the fireplace *(below),* makes the room deserve its name. Recessed detailing allows for good looks, reflected light, and maximum effect even when the blinds on the tall windows are closed.

# THE POSSIBLE DREAM HOUSE

At its best, remodeling is revisionist architecture, retaining the flavor of the original house but also adding the spice of innovation. In this very fresh wrap of an 1890s Victorian in the Chicago suburbs, the designs of the nineteenth and twentieth centuries mingle freely, teaming up to make a whole new package.

The new amendments are not the usual additions of a dormer here or a skylight there. Instead, a sweeping curve that brackets the existing quarters in both body and spirit adds a study annex at the front that's an extension of the squared-off porch and roof line, a dining area on the side, and a new lowered living room at the back.

The Victorian mood is retained in the wraparound porch, and care has been taken to relate the new windows, in size and placement, to the old. Seen from the street, their standard, double-hung dimensions relate them to the windows of the second and third stories, even though the new ones are fixed-pane and double-glazed. On the inside looking out, the squares recombine into big-four blocks, trading in the nineteenth century for a more contemporary air. Some past mistakes of the house were even repeated to avoid radical departures: the new additions are faced with aluminum siding too.

The revitalized residence reads like a primer in remodeling—without a cliché in sight.

**THE PRICE:** Architect Bob Lubotsky, part of the partnership that accomplished this sinuous addition in the mid-1970s, estimates the cost at "between $110,000 and $120,000, which included renovating the kitchen, although it would be considerably more today." The extra space adds up to 12 feet by 15 feet for the side corridor of study and dining area and 600 square feet for the new room at the back of the house that added a generous living room.

**VOICE OF EXPERIENCE:** Double-glazing is a good investment for large areas of glass, whether operating windows or fixed glass (windows that don't open). The two layers of glass sandwich a thin layer of dead air, which saves heating and cooling costs, and prevents condensation. Surrounding structural frames must be exceptionally rigid so that heavy loads, from accumulated snow on the roof, for example, will not put pressure on the glass.

THE MOVE TO THE BACK: More and more, when an old house is updated, the living room marches to the rear. Everyone now wants a private retreat —a far cry from the front parlor. Here, "as is typical with Victorians," says architect Lubotsky, "the house was built four feet above the ground. The new living room is lower, to make it adjacent to the outside deck."

EXPECT THE UNEXPECTED: "When we ripped off the aluminum siding in the back," says architect Lubotsky, "we found that the structural wood had rotted. It simply didn't show with the aluminum covering. We had another job just to replace the timbers before we even started to work on the addition."

Focused on an overscaled fireplace, the living room addition gains headroom and legroom by first dropping down from the old floor level and then angling subtly out of bounds into the side yard. Around the room, high windows float the ceiling, directing the room's sight lines up and away from neighboring houses. Rising undulations of the new fireplace/stereo niche second the sight lines. A fine example of the plasterer's art, the shelving is made the old way, with lathing over a wooden frame.

Subdued and natural materials throughout the room work very well with the strong, new architectural elements. Billowy navy blue sofas set upon the sanded and refinished glossy wood floors fit right in with ceramic and terra-cotta accessories, which have been scattered around with a careful hand. Even that big wooden decoy blends in. All the furnishings sit in easy harmony with the new curves of the fireplace/stereo wall. Yet the architecture remains the dominant focus. Note too that the mix of styles here is an easy combination of new and old—just like the house.

The key to the living room addition, which seems to have poured out of the rear corner of the house and filled the backyard, is a steel I-beam a foot deep. It supports the house's upper stories and replaces the rear wall, spanning the entire opening above the steps and white railing (above). The depth of the I-beam is also the depth of the new vaulted ceiling that arches over the elevated breakfast area and tunnel-shaped kitchen opposite. The arch was preshaped by stacking a dozen pieces of 12-foot-long wallboard on a bowed form and allowing them to bend into the proper shape with their own weight. Each span was then lifted into place.

Both high and wide, the living room looks from the nineteenth century into the twentieth. Subdued materials—oak floors, plaster-white walls, and raised tile hearth—don't compete with the strongly architectural fireplace wall.

# THE GREENHOUSE EFFECT

D on't judge this vintage Victorian by its well-preserved facade. It is, of course, authentic turn-of-the-century Chicago architecture, right down to its signature bay windows. But that's only the cover story. When the owners purchased it, the house resembled a war-zone ruin. "In the process of gutting and renovating," says owner Yvette Cusack, "we saved nothing, because nothing was worth saving—no moldings, no staircases, nothing but the shell." By not reproducing or restoring, architect Kenneth Schroeder bent not only the rules but the walls too. He worked particular magic in the back of the house, which now reads like a Cinderella saga of enlightened renovation.

And that's where both the drama and the family live. The new glass wall is really a prefabricated greenhouse appended to the back of the building. The greenhouse comes in a kit that's put together on site. It measures 8 feet by 18 feet. It cost a third less than a carpenter-built addition—about $4,500 for the greenhouse and $2,500 for the labor—yet it added light-loving space to the kitchen. A structural steel lintel was added at the top of the greenhouse, where it meets the house, to replace the load-bearing wall that was removed. And a new heating/cooling unit was installed in the floor, just inside. "You can't slap on a new, glass wall and expect the

old heating system to do all the work," says Schroeder. "You need some extra help." Upstairs, new, generously proportioned windows open up the second floor and a clean-lined balcony brightens up the third.

Precisely engineered, the house has all sorts of delicious details. Cutouts, crannies, overlooks, and curvy surfaces more than compensate for the absent cornices, carved balustrades, and ceiling medallions of the original architecture. The new glass more than compensates for the lost details, as well. "All the rooms have natural light," says Cusack. "Even on cloudy days the house is cheerful."

**Spiral stairs connect the kitchen with the rooms above and below without eating up physical or visual space (opposite). The wedge-shaped kitchen island—a back-saving 38 inches high instead of the standard 36—mimics the shape of the cutout above. The mezzanine-level opening was created to allow light from the second-story windows to illuminate both an upstairs family room and the kitchen below.**

# THE URBAN VILLA

**HOW TO AVOID RENOVATOR'S REMORSE:** It's those ideas you get in the middle of the night that cause trouble. Is it a good one? Designer Lloyd's advice: "Think and think, then think some more. When you see the same idea coming around for the third time, you will know it's right."

Located in a pioneer neighborhood just over the bridge from Manhattan, this 1860s Brooklyn row house has tenants in the upper two stories. The owner lives on the parlor and below-street levels, with access to the backyard.

There was a time when single-family brownstones ripe for renewal could be picked up for a song. Not even so very long ago. The early 1970s still offered plenty of inexpensive choices in city neighborhoods up and down the East Coast. A fury of renovation fever soon hit, of course, and today, the melody's nearly gone. A smart way to afford one nowadays, though you'll probably need to hunt for a while, is to purchase a seedy two-family brownstone in a run-down neighborhood and wait for things to change while you update the house. Our advice is to find one with an apartment in decent enough shape to rent out immediately. That way, the monthly income helps improve your part of the house. By the time your own space is completed, you'll undoubtedly be able to add amenities upstairs that can command a higher rental and to find the tenants who'll pay it. The assumption is that the neighborhood has been moving up all the while—so choose carefully.

That was exactly the process for this Brooklyn row house. "The owner has just redone the tenant's apartment," says *Metropolitan Home* design editor Ben Lloyd, who accomplished the owner's two-floor rehabilitation, "and the neighborhood is now ready for a higher rental."

Renovation in the owner's space is a sly bow to the past and a welcome home to the present. Changes have been considerate of the old house, but not to a fault. The front parlor's good fittings—Egyptian Revival window frames, marble fireplace mantel, and the several levels of ceiling molding—didn't need work at all. The impulse to paint everything white in brownstones ended with the 1970s, and here contrasting color was cleverly used to emphasize the architectural details. The rich cream walls, too, are a surprise—glossy, saturated, sunshiny, and a long way from eggshell. At midpoint, the cream is overcombed with white to create an inexpensive, folksy wainscoting.

Before work began, the front parlor was in good shape. The pine floor was already stripped, though not sanded, and the walls needed only spackling and sanding for painting.

**THE RIPPLE EFFECT:**
The wainscoting below was achieved by "combing," a decorative technique for suggesting wood grain. White latex paint, rolled on over the dry cream wall color, is combed wet with a notched cardboard "brush."

Updating the traditional gateleg, designer Lloyd built up the base with stock lumber and used X-shaped stretchers for support. The top has green marble inset into the painted wood.

**ON SANDING:** Floor refinishing is a task best left to professionals, whose standard job is sanding, applying one coat of moisture cure, then a few coats of polyurethane.

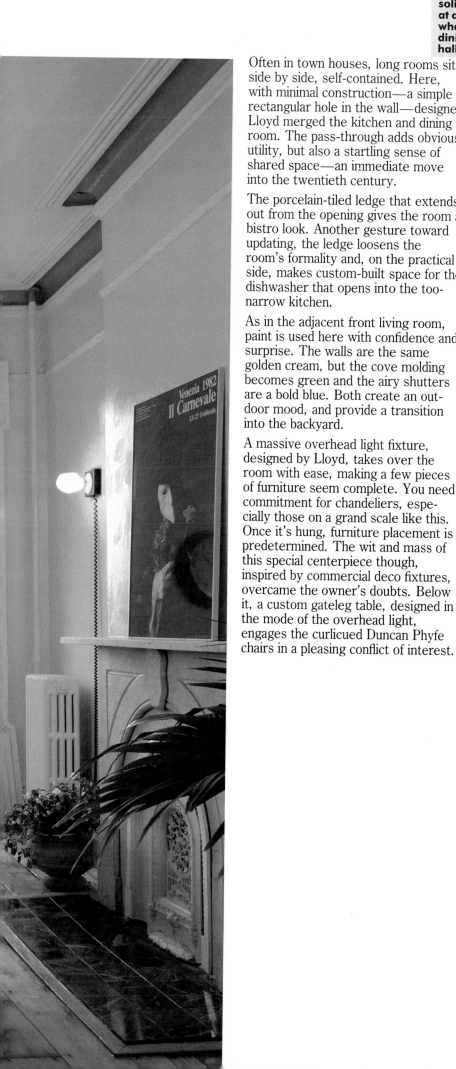

VOICE OF EXPERIENCE: Louver doors offer an efficient compromise between solid doors and none at all. For instance, where a kitchen or dining room adjoins a hall or greenhouse, the louvers' adjustable slats can deflect harsh sunlight without giving up light or a desired sense of space.

Often in town houses, long rooms sit side by side, self-contained. Here, with minimal construction—a simple rectangular hole in the wall—designer Lloyd merged the kitchen and dining room. The pass-through adds obvious utility, but also a startling sense of shared space—an immediate move into the twentieth century.

The porcelain-tiled ledge that extends out from the opening gives the room a bistro look. Another gesture toward updating, the ledge loosens the room's formality and, on the practical side, makes custom-built space for the dishwasher that opens into the too-narrow kitchen.

As in the adjacent front living room, paint is used here with confidence and surprise. The walls are the same golden cream, but the cove molding becomes green and the airy shutters are a bold blue. Both create an out-door mood, and provide a transition into the backyard.

A massive overhead light fixture, designed by Lloyd, takes over the room with ease, making a few pieces of furniture seem complete. You need commitment for chandeliers, especially those on a grand scale like this. Once it's hung, furniture placement is predetermined. The wit and mass of this special centerpiece though, inspired by commercial deco fixtures, overcame the owner's doubts. Below it, a custom gateleg table, designed in the mode of the overhead light, engages the curlicued Duncan Phyfe chairs in a pleasing conflict of interest.

A view from the back of the house, toward the front living room, shows the Victorian scale and deco styling of the refurbished dining room, along with stripped pocket doors that can close off the living room.

Tidied up for the photograph, this in-the-throes dining room *(below)* shows that replastering has begun on the pass-through opening from the kitchen. Though it seems an awful scar, no trace of the gash shows later *(opposite)*. Note the color of the old floors before the refinishing.

**ON TRACK:** Track lighting can be a modern cliché unless there's some point to aiming those individual pools of light. Surprisingly, kitchen work and counter areas benefit most from this on-target application, and especially in a galley kitchen.

With the addition of the pass-through counter, the old boxcar kitchen was transformed into a working, narrow galley. The serviceable breakthrough opens up and modernizes the kitchen. The apparent shortcomings can also be blessings. That tight squeeze makes an enjoyable workspace, where a quick turn takes the cook from cutting board to stove.

The unused right wall was reclaimed by glass-doored cabinets *(right),* framed in clear pine and custom built for the space, even though they have the look and feel of the period. A pine bar-type glass rack provides much-needed storage plus intriguing display. The new dishwasher, flush with the right-wall counters, extends under the new pass-through, covered by the wall from the dining side.

Although the glamour of exposed brick has faded with the novelty, remnants of the fad remain. Tiling on the wall replaces the insulation of the missing plaster coat *(opposite).* Paint reseals the wounds and wire baker's shelves lighten the bare brick. The same beautifully practical ceramic tile covers the counters, backboard walls —even the floor.

**Black and white tiles—on the walls, floors, and counters (opposite)—make crisp work of the kitchen changes. A two-inch-thick poured-in-place concrete slab and a thin coat of mortar-based adhesive give proper support to the ceramic tile floor, a checkerboard, placed on end. Shutter doors lead to the new greenhouse.**

**Dark, disheartening, and dingy, the former kitchen area was little more than a narrow hotplate. Using the neglected right wall turned it into more efficient space.**

"Solarium kits have a tendency to leak when it rains," says designer Lloyd. "The more complicated the design, with movable louvers or whatever, the more you're likely to have crannies and cracks that can spring leaks. This kit is the simplest model, with all the glass fixed, except for the door." Double-glazed for winter efficiency, the solarium collects and distributes the sun's warmth to the two adjoining rooms.

I n any renovation, there's bound to be a place where fixing and mending won't do. Sometimes the best answer to an old problem will mean a fresh start. The rickety, "modernized" sunroom at the back of the house actually blocked light *(below, left)*. It was out of keeping with the rest of the architecture. It's our case in point: it had to go.

Designer Lloyd decided to tear off the lean-to and replace it with a modern counterpart—a glass and aluminum structure that comes in a kit. An outside, wooden stairway was built to lead from the new solarium into the backyard *(near right)*. Under the solarium, on the lower level, is the bath and bedroom, with a door from the room that leads directly out to the patio.

Banishing the dark lean-to gained not only a light-filled living room but another room—the sunlit solarium. It's like a terrace on a grand hotel overlooking a garden, except with the option of immediate shade and privacy as soon as you unfurl the pleated drape overhead.

**Trading in the dark structure** *(below, left),* **for the light-beamed, glass-filled frame** *(below, right)* **is almost magical— from night to day. The kit includes glass end walls.**

# A LABOR OF LOVE

ONE MAN'S VIEW: "The architect must control the process, while the client controls the project," says New Yorker Ralph Gillis, who designs both corporate and residential renovations. "It's the expert who must manage the ongoing work."

Located on Manhattan's Upper West Side, this brownstone was built in 1890 by Clarence True, who built many ornate homes on nearby Riverside Drive. The exterior is of Indiana limestone.

It's not so much what came out of this row house that makes it so wonderful. It's the care, labor, love, and patience with which everything went in. "I don't like to say this house was gutted," explains architect Ralph Gillis, "because that implies we lost the details." The conversion of this 20-foot-wide, 55-foot-long, four-story brownstone clearly hasn't lost a thing. Yet in fusing Victorian details with contemporary design, Gillis did make a great many changes.

"We took out everything but the floors, and then we stockpiled everything, from the doors to the trim to the cabinetry. We installed completely new plumbing, moving all the bathrooms. We also put in a very powerful electrical system, three hundred fifty amps with five circuit breakers, so we'd be safe for future needs. There's a new, hundred-gallon water heater and a new gas burner that circulates hot water in winter and chilled water in summer. We did a lot more. Eventually, we re-used all the trim that was removed—even the cabinetry."

On the main floor, at street level, the divided living room and hall were opened up by removing a wall and three accordion glass doors. The lighter, flowing space now works as one, wide-open room. Freed from its dark stairhall, however, the gem of a staircase was sagging, top to bottom, about three inches. Because he wanted to use the original materials, Gillis took apart the risers and treads and rebuilt it, raising the stringers (the side members). During the original construction, the walls had been poorly supported—"Lucky for us they don't build them like they used to," says Gillis. So he supported the stair landing with now invisible steel tie rods attached to the masonry. Finally, he replaced the "modernized" square spindles (installed by a previous owner) with custom-made turned spindles—to the tune of 125 of them. And that's just the staircase.

In all, says Gillis, construction took twenty months, with six months of planning before that—"but it was all worth it."

The view toward the front door (left) shows off the town house's patiently refinished mahogany trim, parquet flooring, and the new, open floor plan. A wall used to stand where the columns do now. Although the fireplace in the living room (right) is original, it needed a new firebox, flue, and relined chimney. The upper mirror was added after the house was built— "probably in the 1920s," says Gillis— and the mantel came from another house of the same period.

**VOICE OF EXPERIENCE:** Usually, wood floors are sanded in the direction of the grain. Since that's impossible on parquet floors, it's important to finish with an extremely fine sandpaper. For best results, some boards may benefit from hand sanding, particularly when the pattern uses contrasting woods. After thorough patching and cleaning (and careful vacuuming to remove sawdust), two coats of polyurethane (three on new, raw wood) provides a durable finish.

A spacious, sparsely furnished dining room and a corridor kitchen have been carved from a mess of hallways and tiny rooms on the main floor. The kitchen—angled, efficient, and utterly inventive—actually has three separate areas. A main 15-foot-by-16-foot corridor *(below)* leads to a small pantry and then out to the backyard through a greenhouse. As you enter the kitchen, there's another 9-foot-by-7-foot area for food storage and the refrigerator/freezer.

A new, stamped-tin ceiling was installed, but the pattern was carefully matched to the original and was manufactured by the same company. "The tin," says architect Gillis, "comes in two-foot-by-four-foot sheets. We ran them diagonally to match the shape of the kitchen and to pick up the pattern on the tiled floor." A restaurant stove stands in for the Victorian hearth, and wire shelving offers a techy contrast to the butcher block.

**Forty hours of an architect's time went into planning this tiled floor and, especially, its border *(left)*, so that when it was laid on this odd-shaped kitchen floor, none of the tile had to be cut. Although a small detail, it's typical of the work throughout the house. And it reads first class.**

**Several areas work in the kitchen for a family of several cooks. Here, extra butcher blocks extend the freestanding center one. Note the one-hand faucet controls.**

In the dining room, the main attractions, of course, are the impressive mahogany-frame windows. "You can't just hire a company to come and install new windows in frames like these," notes Gillis wryly. "It's a painstaking, long, minutely detailed job. We added new, doubled-glazed windows, but we were careful not to destroy the five-inch-wide trim or the inset shutter pockets." Below the windows, panels were taken off to remove the old radiators. Fan units for air-circulated heating/cooling were then installed and the panels were replaced. It was an ingenious way of getting up-to-date technology to look like the old house.

# CHARM AND HOW TO GET IT
## COTTAGES AND BUNGALOWS

What matters here is what you put into a house. It's the wisdom to settle for a structure and pull out all the stops on the inside. There's a jolt of sensuality in the rooms and more than a little enchantment. In every case, the confidence and romance of the owner translates into a unique version of home—each charming in a different way.

Going country doesn't mean going quaint. A tour of English country homes inspired this owner, costume designer Theadora Van Runkle, to redesign her 1920 Laurel Canyon cabin in the Hollywood Hills *(opposite and above)*. The message here is honest and the feeling says loving touch. "It is possible to turn a house that has nothing going for it into a dream," she says now.

Charm, says Webster's, is a practice of magic and enchantment. We are attracted almost against our will, compelled. We are under a spell. Charm, says the real estate ad, trying to invoke the sorcerer's art, and we know, odds-on, that someone's running a con. But you have to see it, don't you?

Our point? No definition for charm can satisfy—except the one you invest in. You write the ticket and you weave the magic.

A fieldstone farmhouse, circa 1735, could add up to what one contented owner calls "the kind of house that's forever. It's not just shelter." That declaration came amid a host of the usual renovation woes: a sagging roof; walls out of plumb; some tacky "improvements" such as an original, wide-plank kitchen floor disfigured by asphalt tile. In the case of charm, it's not really how much work is needed that makes for a buy or a pass, though you must, by all means, inspect everything.

The real motivation is attitude—whether you have the time and the taste for a house to come together piece by piece; whether you're enchanted enough to accumulate layer upon layer for the slow build-up of love and care and living with a warm, deep gloss. Provenance and type of structure count least of all. We don't bother defining charm as an old, historical landmark. You can take that country cottage air and breeze it right into a fifties Colonial and we'd applaud. You need vision, of course. You need some clear thinking about the kind of architecture you're taking on. There's nothing worse, says Milwaukee architect Joseph Valerio, than "making the 1980s look like the 1920s. Additions should be compatible, not identical. It's just as wrong to take a 1920s farmhouse and stick on a Marcel Breuer/Richard Meier–style addition. You have to look at the entire building." Yes. Except charm is also the confidence to ignore the rules and to do it your own way after all.

You also have to avoid the urge to kitsch out with wagon-wheel chandeliers, decoupaged milk cans, and yards and yards of calico. Charm doesn't suffer cliché. If it's the country mood you're after, one look at the revamped barn in this chapter will tell you that the simplest, most personal solutions work best. If you're seeking the reassuring comfort of the English, then look no further than the flair of the living room opposite.

Perhaps more than any other style, charm is quirky and individual. The more your very personal style is stamped on the space, the more magic in the house.

Snuggled up against a hillside in Hollywood, this blooming cottage was "a rats' nest when I moved in—just a canyon shack," says owner Theadora Van Runkle, whose expertise in movie costume design was called into service for the chintz-and-charm mood of her redone house. This very filled-up living and dining room could have been overwhelming, but the new skylights, French doors and windows, white paint and stripped woods keep it light. Muted romantic floral patterns set a rich stage for Van Runkle's lovingly gathered antiques and collectibles.

**VOICE OF EXPERIENCE:** To expose roof beams and wood sheathing nailed to them, and still have an energy-efficient house, add rigid styrene panel insulation above the sheathing. The lightweight material provides an R-value (a figure used to describe a material's resistance to heat transmission) of approximately 6.0, significantly higher than fiberglass or cellulose. Tongue-and-groove panels (typically in lightweight two-foot-by-eight-foot sheets) can be covered by finished roofing.

**ADMONITIONS ON OLD LACE:** Mixing and matching patterns, as on the bed and table below, work fine. But worn linens, unlike finely worn carpets, merely look old and discarded. Antique and collected linens need to be pristine. You can find them, often in mint condition, at auctions and flea markets.

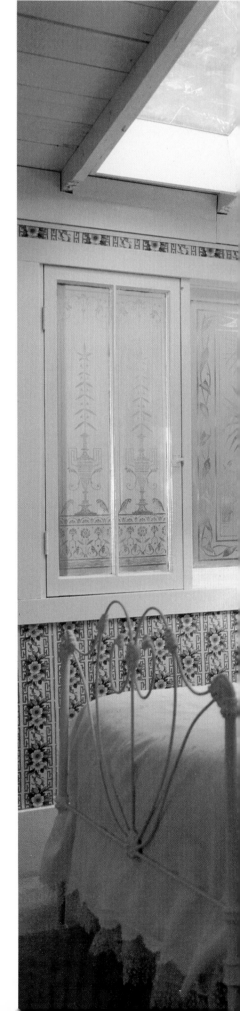

 espite its Victorian air, Van Runkle's reincarnated home blends yesterday's history and today's reality with a style that teases, confuses, recalls, and appreciates. The results are sublimely cozy. New floral fabrics on ornately carved old furniture, old lace hankies pressed under bright, clear glass—there's no embarrassment here about reusing the past in a delightfully stylish mishmash, restored or not.

Three months went into renovating and redecorating the former cabin. "The house was falling down," Van Runkle says. "The inside was the color of a sycamore leaf. It was a very dusty, dirty little house."

She began with the structure, making "a great many changes." The living room, once illuminated by just one small window, is now practically all French doors. Skylights in a foyer, bedroom, and bath add refreshing daylight. Dismantling an acoustical tile ceiling, she found an inner flat ceiling

"I did the whole redesign and dealt with the carpenters myself," says Van Runkle. She's especially proud of her accomplishment for reasons beyond aesthetics. "A lot of women hesitate to do it and for good reason, because carpenters can be very difficult. But women should take charge."

and removed that, too, in order to follow the line of the peaked roof.

She then took on the walls and eventually worked her way through the furniture, stripping wood and not refinishing it, changing dark velvet upholstery to bright floral patterns on a light background.

Reversing the expected turns a cliché into style. In the bedroom (above and right), the windows remain bare while the bed and table take the decoration— flounces of clean, white linen. Cozy, but not cute.

Two skylights, newly installed in the peaked roof above the bed, bring in light, allowing the etched glass in the windows to provide privacy and atmosphere.

In the same fashion that Van Runkle is a "method" costume designer, which she describes as "thinking a lot about an assignment and working it out that way," she spent time planning the look of her home. "The house works in a circle, which is very nice for a party," she explains. "I got the idea from reading about Stanford White. He designed his houses so the morning sun hit the breakfast room, the midmorning sun hit the morning room, the midday sun hit the sitting room, and the afternoon sun hit the porch."

Van Runkle's thought-out care in the flow and light in the rooms makes the house seem special, but there's another secret. The element that keeps her eclectic collection from reading leftover 1960s is simple: white. That idea came from a trip to England. "I'm an Anglophile," she says, "and as I toured the houses and gardens, I was fantasizing and writing

**Instead of rustic simplicity, Van Runkle has opted for disciplined excess, as on the dining area wall (above) and throughout the house. The paired set of candleholders here adds a bit of formal symmetry that's a restful change in the freewheeling mix.**

in my journal about what I wanted to do with this house. I realized in England that I wanted the walls white," she recalls. "I was so sick of clutter. I've always been just entranced with the nineteenth century, always lived in immense, over-done Victorians. Suddenly I wanted to make everything as plain as possible." That's relatively speaking, of course.

**In the cottage's small front sun porch (right), a new, unblemished wood floor and standard French windows set off the simple lines of white-painted panel-ing and straight ladder-back chairs. But hanging china platters, ornate and gilt lighting, and lush flowers display the Van Runkle decorative signature.**

**AN OUTDOOR OPTION:** Not everyone wants to weed and water, though most want a yard for outdoor living. A subscriber to this low-maintenance school of dealing with the out-of-doors, Van Runkle tore out the gardens while the house renovation was progressing and trucked in pea gravel for a serene, uncluttered yard. A side benefit was a cleaner house. ''The gravel keeps down the dust to the point where you don't even have to dust inside,'' she says.

# INSTANT HERITAGE FOR A NEW HOUSE

**CHARM COMES FROM THE UNEXPECTED MIX:** Looking at the outside of this just-built cedar shell, one would never suspect the vintage interior. "The house is like a Fabergé egg," says designer-owner Holt. "It looks like a standard new house on the outside, but inside, it's a surprise."

VOICE OF EXPERIENCE: A growing number of firms now specialize in architectural artifacts salvaged from deteriorating buildings prior to demolition. Inventories in some of the larger supply houses include everything from Victorian tubs with claw and ball feet to newel posts with dentil block carving. Salvage firms are a rich resource for renovators, although as more people realize the value of older, handcrafted building parts, real bargains are getting much harder to find.

"When I began looking for a home to purchase on a modest income in the mountain community of Missoula, Montana," says antiques dealer and interior designer Gary Holt, "I ran into a problem—especially since I wanted that 'starter' house to be something other than a plastic box or a house-on-wheels. Add to that the fact that I have strong opinions about what makes a house a home and an always growing collection of antiques, and the problem seemed insurmountable.

"Rehabbing an old house appeared to be the obvious choice, but when I added renovation expenses to the constraints of old floor plans, each new prospect fell short of my demands." Here's where a sharp eye and Holt's refusal to compromise turned an absolutely ordinary house into one that glows with the special charm of the past.

He lucked into a contractor's distress sale. "I found a developer who was forced to sell a new, cedar-frame shell which resembled a Montana shed barn," says Holt. "It struck me that the new structure was the solution. Rehabbing in this case meant carefully adding salvaged materials to the latest technology in wiring, plumbing, and insulation. I used turn-of-the-century materials to reconstruct the house— pine lumber from an 1880 gold mill became the new floors, ceiling, and beams. Other materials came from a Grange Hall and from Craftsman-style 1890s schools and homes."

"It's just what I wanted," says owner Holt of his new/old home, "an old house with none of the old-house problems."

# THE CITY-SLICK BARN

This kind of barn razing is a far cry from the efforts of pioneer settlers, but it does get the job done. The original 1890 barn was built in northern New York State *(opposite, left)*, dismantled, and moved to Connecticut, which is where the current, visionary owners discovered it. Then the frame was chopped down to size at the knees *(middle)* so that the barn's first level of horizontal side bracing became the new ground floor. Add new sheathing, new windows, a new wing—and the old barn is really raised into a second home *(far right)*.

olidly established in New York City's high-pressure fashion world, John and Janet Jay live in a Manhattan high-rise—"a very typical, one-bedroom East Side apartment" is Janet's description. Like so many fast-track city couples, what they wanted—what they needed—was a country safety valve. Janet found the barn in pieces on a wooded lot in Connecticut, just waiting for a buyer with vision to put it back together again. "I called John in Paris and said, 'I think this place has potential'—and that was it." The idea of recycling a barn wasn't entirely new. They had already discussed it as a way to get the space they craved. "In New York you always have the feeling of tightness, of limitations, but I don't think John appreciated, until recently, what the barn could offer," Janet says with a smile.

A year of renovation later, the whole first floor was masterfully worked into one room, barely divided by the two-faced stone fireplace that warms the dining area as well as the opposite living room *(above and right)*. While the one-piece, 42-foot beams spanning the house are original, the smaller, rough-hewn ceiling joists that support the second-story flooring are new—but weathered to match the older parts.

Confident and sophisticated, owners John and Janet Jay set classics of modern design—such as Le Corbusier's "Grand Comfort" leather love seat and chairs—into the heavily rustic architecture. The resulting contrast makes for a supremely personal room.

Renovation plans are made to be refined. And that was true for the Jays. Urban claustrophobia momentarily clouded their better judgment, and they devised an initial plan that would glory in all that two-story space. Then, they remembered.

They'd need closets, bathrooms, private spaces. So they opted for a compromise. A two-story opening over the fireplace keeps the downstairs glorious. The upstairs "attic" space has the master bedroom, guest and dressing rooms, two baths, and a floating bridge to join the two sides. At one end of the downstairs room, a staircase made of painted metal railings and wood goes up to the second split-level.

The straight-lined country kitchen is housed in a newly constructed "L," built from the recycled beams and siding of local barns. The "L" also includes a breakfast room and a garage.

The Jays' version of country is hardly down-home. Folk art and antique toys are used with studied and dramatic effect to play off the rough shell and techy interior: three children's chairs on the stair landing *(near right),* a wooden sled under the stairs *(far right),* and a welcoming wagon in the kitchen *(above)* are placed with a discerning eye.

**VOICE OF EXPERIENCE:** Too often, an energy retrofit saves heating and cooling dollars at the expense of historic architectural detail. Stress skin panels solve this problem in timber-frame buildings. The prefabricated panels (available through many prefab home manufacturers) include interior wallboard, an insulating core, and exterior siding, all sandwiched together at the factory and ready for installation. Energy is conserved, and so is the handcrafted framework.

In the upstairs master bedroom, there's not an alarm clock in sight—or, for that matter, a fourth wall. The near monkish simplicity of the bedroom is the very thing that lends charm. All but the barest necessities have been banished from this attic-shaped space except, of course, the extraordinary nineteenth-century Swedish Gustavian bed made of painted pine.

And although it may look as if the rain could pour in through the chink-riddled, but atmospheric, pine boards of the original barn ceiling, there's a heavy layer of insulation above them—as well as a new roof.

**A bow to Bauhaus design, the painted metal railing is the only metal construction in the house. Other ideas that were not born in a barn: exposed-transformer track lighting that sits above the great beams instead of hanging below them, and the little round window that punctuates the gable.**

**A colorist in the cosmetics business, Janet Jay had no trouble using her color sense in subtle ways throughout the house. She developed the pale pastel enamels for the pair of Adirondack chairs on the rear deck. The chairs came unpainted in a mail-order kit.**

"We feel the escape the minute we get here," says Janet Jay, who, along with husband John, masterminded the design that turned this Connecticut barn into a high-style home. "It's a real personal house. Not a party house, not a show-off house. It's just for us."

# SHAKER CHIC

Set on a small city lot in Freeport, Illinois, this **Dutch Colonial** *(right)* was remodeled on the inside to feel like an old-fashioned midwestern farmhouse —an unusual trick for an ordinary house.

Outside, owners **Tait and Phil Weigel** provided privacy with lattice sheets on the porch.

With appealing restraint, the Weigels' style is a combination of seventies minimalism and country primitive. They prize original paint, Shaker simplicity, and ruthless editing. "My home reflects what is going on in my life," says Tait Weigel. "I'm weeding out, simplifying." Most people raise the ceilings, but, here, those on the first floor were lowered to a cozier level. Original narrow oak flooring was covered with six-inch-wide tongue-in-groove pine "boxcar" siding, either stained cherry and sealed with polyurethane (in the dining room, *below*) or painted white (in the kitchen, *below, opposite*). Built-ins throughout conceal the clutter of modern appliances.

Upstairs in the master bedroom, the pine floor was painted a high-gloss white, while the owners added pine boards to the walls, also painted white. "Shaker plain country antiques in original paint are the focal point for our sparsely furnished home. White walls, woodwork in grays and orangey-reds make a crisp background for our antiques—all found in the Midwest," says Tait Weigel. The spare arrangement lends a contemporary mood.

The reason this bed-room is so appealing is its very scrubbed-down look. Each piece stands out, dramatic. A red-painted, cannon-ball bed (minus the balls), a country Hep-plewhite stand (possi-bly Shaker), and a six-board blanket chest need no accessories.

**ON SHAKER FURNITURE:** The modernist's choice in antiques for their plain lines, sim-ple finishes, and hon-est function, Shaker antiques are found both painted and unpainted, with origi-nal paint being the more expensive. And prices have been climbing with the demand in recent years.

# THE APPEAL OF HANDCRAFTING

This winsome 1915 bungalow tweaked the T-square of Houston architect Val Glitsch. Along with her husband, Paul Hester, she spent a year and a half of Sundays (plus many Tuesday and Wednesday nights) making it right. They fleshed out the home's latent charm by using their own inexperienced carpentry skills. The result is newly fashioned trim work and a fresh layout that's rife with personal detail.

Before the couple moved in and began work themselves, they hired a contractor to complete some major changes. The plumbing of the old bungalow was rusty and weak, without nearly enough pressure for modern-day needs. Similarly, the electrical system had never been updated to the kind of power needed to run today's house. As an architect, of course, Glitsch had a head start on most homeowners, but it's still possible to hire experts for the rough stuff and to accomplish the interior details yourself.

Once living in the house, Glitsch and Hester moved almost every door to untangle the home's space-crunching layout. That included shunting the front door to the left two and a half feet. Better sight lines now give the illusion of more space and show off the new and restored details. Although all the windows on the downstairs living room level are original to the house, they were shuffled for better light and looks. The reason the windows in the living room are two different sizes *(opposite),* says Glitsch, is that "the house is very close to the property line. Nobody wanted to emphasize the side views. The front view is the important one." The only problem with the front view was a porch, original to the house, that blocked not only the vista but most of the light. "We ripped off the porch across the facade," says Glitsch, "and that helped make the new entrance more important. It also brought in the light."

Aside from the oak and cypress stair rail *(below),* all the trim work on the windows, ceiling, and door moldings was fashioned by the owners from precut fir pieces. The trim was then stained with natural oils.

**"The staircase is original to the house," says architect Val Glitsch," "but we added the trim and the column at the bottom."**

**RECYCLING THE SUN- SHINE:** The two new windows upstairs provide light for a former attic space that was reclaimed as a guest bedroom. But the windows on the main floor are original to this house *(below)*. They were simply moved around to make sure of getting the best natural light inside. You don't, necessarily, have to throw everything out to get the light you want.

**TRY TECH: The fastest way to change and update the look of a vintage room, no matter the size, is by using contemporary industrial lighting. Not high wattage, mind you, high-tech. It will con-** **trast with the woods and architecture of the house and enliven the room; it will add excitement. That's just the way the lighting works in the kitchen here, from the cheerful round over the sink to**

**Although Glitsch and Hester did a good deal of the carpentry work themselves, the tall, pantrylike cabinets at the end of the sink counter (*above* and *opposite*) were custom made for them to provide ingenious storage. Notice the top is flush with the cabinet line beside them.**

In 1946, about thirty years after the house was originally built, two additions were patched on. The downstairs bath was the first one and, at the back, a shed was attached to the old kitchen. Hester and Glitsch used the old shed as part of their new, expanded kitchen, adding a closet and a laundry area.

They started from the floor and worked their way up. Lifting off a linoleum travesty in the kitchen revealed the glorious, six-inch-board, heart-of-pine beauty, which they oiled to a glossy finish.

The squarely charming cabinets were constructed from birch plywood and hardware-store windows. The glass panels were then sandblasted to make them opaque, and the cabinets were painted in a country mood of gray-green. The trim in the kitchen—both the wall molding (*opposite*) and the crowning pediment over the window (*above*)—were all put together by Hester and Glitsch from pieces of pine and fir, including quarter-inch and half-inch round molding, then painted the same chalky lilac as the rest of the redone kitchen.

**A mix of appliances and materials makes this kitchen so appealing: charcoal gray mosaic ceramic tile surrounds the stainless steel double sink and makes a sharp contrast with the cottage colors and cabinetry. A very up-to-date dishwasher is housed under the sink and to the left. And the wonderful white stove (*opposite*) is an old model. "We found it at a salvage yard and had it refurbished," says Glitsch.**

the rippled, black-
glass hanging lamp.
Both provide charming
counterpoint.

oing it yourself doesn't mean doing it all. "Paul and I served as eighty-five percent of the labor force," says architect Val Glitsch, but even with her special skills, they left some areas to the experts. Major electrical and plumbing jobs were subcontracted—wisely, we might add.

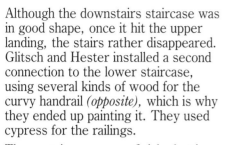

**VOICE OF EXPERIENCE:** When it is impractical to conceal new heating ducts or pipes in existing spaces, they can be incorporated into an extension of the building frame, creating an offset between ceiling and walls. It's a basic skill of renovation: turning a mechanical problem into an architectural advantage.

Although the downstairs staircase was in good shape, once it hit the upper landing, the stairs rather disappeared. Glitsch and Hester installed a second connection to the lower staircase, using several kinds of wood for the curvy handrail *(opposite)*, which is why they ended up painting it. They used cypress for the railings.

The upstairs was an unfinished attic space that had never been used. The couple added several walls, made of drywall, to create a tiny guest bedroom and Glitsch's studio workroom. Now, bathed in the glow of a movable-glass skylight *(opposite)*, a new pediment and column frame the entrance to the studio. Note the interior window and subtle paint colors, chosen to complement the soft light that filters through the trees outside.

Simple and spare, most of the effect in the bedroom comes from using a few colors and materials quite judiciously. Two oak washstands and brass reading lights offer formal symmetry on either side of the bed. Also, their warm wood breaks up the plain blue room. Sheers at the windows let the architectural lines speak for themselves.

The downstairs bedroom's distinctive ceiling isn't just for show. New air-conditioning and heating ductwork needed a crossover from one side of the house to the other, so the ceiling got the job. The result is a handsome, sculptured effect, created by sheathing the hardware with plasterboard.

# THE SUNSHINE STATE

Installing personal style doesn't necessarily mean a great many changes. In this floor-through apartment in a San Francisco town house, the owners, with strong taste and clear vision, have opted for an easy-going approach that uses the town-house architecture as a background for the warmth of wood, natural materials, and welcoming colors.

Brick walls have been painted white to highlight the artwork and furnishings. Narrow oak flooring was sanded, bleached, rubbed with yellow paint, and then sealed with polyurethane. Materials are honest and unimproved—a stone garden seat, a bamboo table, a skin throw, a rough-textured urn. The pleasing shapes and tactile materials take over for strong architectural features. And work just as well. The result is a sunlit and utterly hospitable room.

Across from the seating area, the owners removed a wall, leaving the supports, to turn the railroad flat into a loftlike space. Industrial, recessed, and exposed lighting fixtures provide work light in the new kitchen and dramatic spots in the living/dining room. The centerpiece kitchen island was the real stroke of style and luck. Made from an old hardware store counter, the oak piece now supports a luxurious marble slab that once was the wainscoting on a public building. The marble backsplash and counter on the kitchen's cooking side complement the island. A floor-to-ceiling grid of white shelving was built in for storage behind the dining table. The warm wood, of course, unifies the one-room plan: pale golden brown or beige, it's all of a piece.

**VOICE OF EXPERIENCE:** Metal-frame casement windows can be a chronic maintenance problem. In winter, the metal frames are as cold inside as out, causing condensation. They also require regular repainting. To remove the old layers of paint, use a heat gun and scraper, then finish by sanding. A wire brush wheel on a power drill works well on stubborn patches. Before repainting, apply a rust-inhibiting primer. It will safeguard all the hard work.

# THE THINKING COOK'S KITCHEN

With cooking the new indoor sport and with the mania for equipment at a high-pitched frenzy, brainstorming an up-to-date kitchen design is both agonizing and exciting. Take the time to figure out how you really *use* a kitchen, your wants versus your needs. And then, go for the warmth.

The kitchen of a rambling San Francisco town house, 1920s vintage, displays the kind of new ideas that clever renovation solutions can bring: bold green marble and stainless steel are a recipe for functional elegance; the pull-out drawer below the cooktop *(above)* holds outsize pots and pans.

We have a saying at *Metropolitan Home* that the kitchen is the new living room. But a kitchen must also be Shipping and Receiving—furiously functional, planned, precise. The ideal, of course, is hearth and honed, combining sense and sensibility in one tall order. Good design is as important as performance.

There's an abundance of received wisdom about kitchen plans. Some of it's useful. For instance, knowing how to coordinate all the steps that, in sequence, produce a glorious new kitchen can save you a packet of money and many sleepless nights. In a kitchen renovation, more than in any other room, everything depends on every other thing. You must, in concert with a designer, come up with a plan that specifies each detail and plots every square inch several months before you actually get to see your choices. You can't begin to think about major appliances until you've located the plumbing and electricity sources. You can't do that until you've figured out which stove and refrigerator and dishwasher and compactor and, maybe, washer/dryer you want, how much space all that needs, and what the water and power demands will be. And do you want another conventional oven and/or a microwave? You can't order cabinets until you've worked out the needs and trade-offs for storage and the materials and colors of flooring and walls and, then, countertops. Every tiny decision works back to the major ones.

What about the textbook requirement of four feet between major appliances—what we call "the eternal triangle"? Sometimes it works. It saves steps. But suppose you want a kitchen island with a second sink. And, supposing some more, you want a second cooktop atop that island. And, finally, how many feet away is the sofa on which your guest is lolling while you cook and chat? Designer Charles Morris Mount, who's based in New York and noted for stellar kitchen renovations, prefers "the exploded kitchen concept, which has overlapping work triangles, multiple triangles, several areas. Cleanup work, with a second sink, can be in another room or separate area."

Watch out for the rules. They're only as good as the last kitchen in which they worked. Some are as dated as the notion of only one cook in the family—that female. Any design you're considering must take account of who really hangs out in the kitchen. As we see it, that usually includes all the friends who've come to dinner. Be absolutely true to the way the room called "the kitchen" really works in your house. Labels don't produce innovative design; living does.

A word about the budget for redoing a kitchen: as Washington, D.C., architect Michael Holt says, "A ten-by-ten kitchen costs $20,000 while a ten-by-ten bedroom costs $2,000. And within the kitchen itself, you can use a $55 stove or a $3,000 stove. It's hard to generalize." Your possibilities range widely and so do the dollars. Whatever amount you have to spend, remember, it will be exactly enough for a dazzling, revamped kitchen.

# INSTALLING THE KITCHEN SYNC

With cool beauty and a rather sophisticated mix of materials, this San Francisco kitchen's hyperfunctional design not only looks good but also works hard.

A center island, with its distinctive green marble top, is strategically surrounded by the other kitchen areas: opposite the island is the profession-ally sanctioned cooktop; just adjacent is ample counter and storage space. The whole makes for arm's-length convenience and heavy duty.

The attention to style, the feeling of interior architecture, is what makes this town-house kitchen so special. The elegant materials underscore the fact that the kitchen today is much more open to display. The marble's strong color and texture and the understated glitter of the brass hardware are reminders that the kitchen's a room, too, not just a work station.

Storage needs are met by simple cabinetry that varies in size. And though looking built-in, the refrigerator/freezer's snug housing has extra space at the back to allow for the circulation of air. Warm wood flooring is echoed by the detailing on the center island and the butcher-block counter under the generous cabinets.

A Eurostyle black laminate table and a couple of Mallet-Stevens chairs (top) provide a casual breakfast area, a place for cook's company, and an extra work counter—whichever's needed.

**ON MARBLE:** As kitchens are transformed into rooms for living, into places where friends visit and cook together, marble—decidedly a living room material—has moved into kitchen design in a big way. Whites, pinks, greens, and grays are prized on counters, dining tables, and center islands. Marble is basically a fragile material and quite porous, which makes it vulnerable to stain from oil and acidic liquids. But it's a natural material and so ages beautifully. Good protective polishes are now widely available. A two-foot-by-six-foot slab of green or pink marble goes for about $500, but the cost depends more on cutting and finishing choices than the rock itself. Marble tile, as in the kitchen below, is a comparatively inexpensive alternative.

an Francisco architect Dan Phipps raised the ceilings and realized the potential of this kitchen, opening it to light and space. For the stacked-to-the-ceiling storage, Phipps mixed in glass-fronted doors and natural pine shelving with the solid doors to break up the mass of white cabinets along one wall. All the cabinets were custom built, designed by the architect.

However handsome, the all-important center island is strictly business, housing a compactor, double stainless steel sink, and dishwasher *(below)*. Catty-corner from the cooktop, microwave and conventional ovens are stacked and flush-mounted to promote even more space *(right)*. From there, it's still only a quick step to the sink and cooktop.

For all the up-to-date appliances, equipment, and hardware, the mood here is easy and reminiscent of the welcoming charm of a big country kitchen. The architect was clever enough to allow elements of the home's vintage to stand out against all the new gleaming function. The rich wood door and the refinished oak floor blend comfortably with brass handles and marble counters. Similarly, the butcher-block worktop and the marble's butcher-block frame warm the

hard-working room. An unusual detail, and one worth remembering for other kitchens, is the mix of solid and glass-door cabinets. Dishes sit on unfinished pine shelving (again, the warmth of wood) while a slightly tinted green glass picks up the green marble tiles.

Even with black glass appliances alongside and a television below, it's just those glass-fronted cabinets that provide the country hearth mood.

**Installing new windows in the kitchen, after the ceiling was raised, allowed for much more light. Notice the two different window widths.**

**VOICE OF EXPERIENCE:** To add heat in kitchens where it will be most appreciated (at your feet, right by the counter) without using up precious storage space, use low-profile electric units made to fit into the kickspace recess between lower cabinets and the floor.

# AN OLD-TIME KITCHEN THAT COOKS

VOICE OF EXPERIENCE: Solid hardwood paneling and molding used in older homes is now considered "exotic" wood—and the prices are equally exotic. Often, hardwood veneers are used instead—thin skins of select hardwood, factory-glued to plywood. But refinishing veneer paneling (or furniture) requires a light touch, since too much sanding exposes

"I knew the house was old by the roof lines," says New Orleans owner Clancy Dupépé. He wanted a "pure house with most of its original features." But when he found his historical possibility, only the four front rooms of the original house remained. They had the open spaces and 12-foot ceilings Dupépé craved, though, so he added a living room wing, converted the attic into four bedrooms and two baths, and then added this country-fresh kitchen wing.

The new kitchen owes its old-time ambience to beams and floorboards recycled from demolished buildings, new millwork made from old timbers, and a custom chandelier with folk art overtones. Dupépé really took the trouble to graft the new structure onto the old without showing any of the new seams.

Open shelves, a refrigerator with a stainless steel face, and a professional cooktop give the room a casually collected charm. It's functional, but not slick, like the backstairs of a kitchen in a great country house. A soft sea-green paint color also evokes the muted atmosphere of slower times.

The kitchen gets its European mood from the barstools, which are local copies of a French chair. Other gestures support the European Country style: Louis XV–style doors hide the ovens; a new brass and iron hood over the cooktop has the working air of rough metal; and the open hearth beneath the cooktop is used to store pots.

Two completely different styles of sink emphasize the breezy charm of this kitchen's design. The main blue porcelain one, standard size, is under the window. A second, small sink is rounded and made of stainless steel with a gooseneck faucet. Used for food preparation, it's a nice counterpoint to the old-fashioned tiles atop the counter.

he plywood beneath
he veneer. You need
b be careful.

The elegant spiral
staircase in the main
hallway, adjacent to
the kitchen, is made of
heart-of-pine and
iron. It adds flair and
saves space.

# A CONTEMPORARY WAY WITH WOOD

In the race to get the kitchen all decked out with professional equipment, sometimes the feeling of hearth-and-hominess becomes eclipsed. The owners of this Portland, Oregon, kitchen were determined not to lose the feeling of warmth. Through the work of architect David Jenkins, the problem was solved by an up-to-the-minute design that uses materials full of tactile textures and welcoming colors.

The blond wood and ivory-colored marble countertops rein in the professional range and remind all the silvery metal surfaces that there's a living room right next door. All the fir cabinetry is clean, but not clinical, and certainly fulfills the owners' desires.

Organization here follows the newest plans, with two separate working triangles, one for cooking and the other for cleanup. Two chefs can easily cook in the kitchen without spoiling each other's broth.

Given the kitchen's proximity to the living area, the giant venting hood is both functional and decorative, work-

ing as a structural divider between the two spaces. Faced in galvanized metal to match the hood, the built-in refrigerator is counter-deep and a real space saver. Notice that the motor is on top (not behind), which permits the refrigerator to be flush with the wall. Under the glass-doored cabinets, a battery of countertop appliances hide behind roll-up tambour doors. The doors, like those on old-fashioned roll-top desks, keep the lines of the room clean and yet still add a bit of old-timey flavor.

Terra-cotta tile on the floor provides a rich background for the pale wood.

**The commercial gas cooktop is set into the marble-capped center island. A six-burner unit here, it can be ordered with one to eight burners. It also provides the best of restaurant-stove durability and function—minus the hard-to-clean oven.**

**VOICE OF EXPERIENCE:** Taking out most, but not all, of a common partition wall will bring light from one room into another, and make traffic between a kitchen and dining room or area much more efficient. A large opening may require adding a header (the horizontal beam across the top of the opening) and one or two support columns, while a smaller pass-through can be made without removing any timbers.

# THE CHEF'S SPECIAL

**A**s anyone who's whirled a whisk in a commercial kitchen can tell you, there's simply no comparing that arm's-length-away convenience to the standard home on the range. On the other hand, all that stainless steel and industrial green can get a bit grim. Enter, then, this balanced medium in a Manhattan high-rise, designed by architect Martin E. Rich. A royal-blue counter, Modernist stools, and warm Mexican tile floors are proof enough you're home. The same goes for the brick-size white tiles on the wall and the cheerfully evocative deco ceramics.

For the rough stuff—the working core—the rest of this kitchen simmers with pragmatism. The cabinets are original to the apartment but had been covered with years of paint. Now stripped, as wood might have been, to expose the steel, they gleam like professional showcases. Both the cabinets and a diner's six-burner stove *(top)* appear just as they would in the restaurant kitchen—unadorned and ready to work. For counterpoint, there's cabinetry with hidden options to make use of every bit of space *(above)*. This is a handy, handsome use of a 15-foot-square space.

**ON DISPLAY:** Besides the streamlined cabinets and counters that make this kitchen work so well, there's a great deal of cookware, utensils, appliances, and serving dishes that just hang out—without, however, cluttering the room. That's avoided because tools and pots are grouped and organized for both the eye and the cooking hand. The result of the display is right-at-hand convenience, plus the charm of a working kitchen, which makes its own theater. Note, as examples, the knife rack set into wood molding on the windowsill and also the hanging pots over the center island *(opposite, top)*.

# BUILDING ON YOUR DREAM

**W**hen no amount of renovation will transform the kitchen you have into the kitchen you want, the solution is to add a wing. And though you obviously won't build for light alone, no room deserves it more. Accomplished by *Metropolitan Home* design editor Donna Warner, this generous 800-square-foot addition in Fairfield County, Connecticut, has a many-windowed peak *(opposite, above)* that scoops up light and delivers it into the central work area. Over-the-counter storage, which ate up window space in the old kitchen, has been banished in favor of generous side windows. "I love this room," says Warner. "It's visually understandable but it is also very exciting."

With so many windows, and so much of the wall and ceiling in glass, the addition demanded extra insulation. Besides ample fiberglass batting insulation below the roof, a dense, aluminum-foil-faced urethane sheathing provides an additional barrier to heat loss and also helps keep the addition cool in the summer. Even the concrete floor is an insulated slab.

By design, this kitchen moves gradually toward the light, starting in the narrow pantry, expanding into the peaked-roof center, then soaring into the window-walled dining area at the front. "Light changes it," says designer Warner, "and that's how it was planned to be. It's not the same depending on where you sit or work in the room." Enhancing the light changes, the semigloss wall and ceiling colors progress too: mustard in the hall, lighter yellow in the kitchen, cream in the dining area. An off-center island *(opposite, below)* encourages foot traffic on the cleanup side of the kitchen, away from the hard-working cooking area.

This is the kind of kitchen the whole family enjoys—a far cry from just a place to cook.

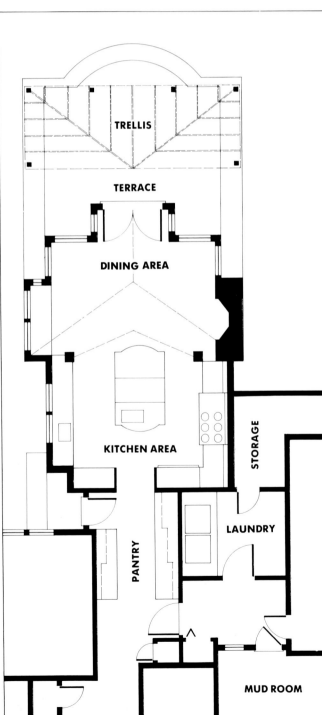

**Narrow where it joins the house so it won't block a guest-room window, the addition then widens in a series of steps—a ziggurat—to use the available space. As shown in the floor plan, the space gradually unfolds from the tight pantry/hallway to the expansive terrace.**

**A bracketed arch is used as a design theme throughout the addition. The shape is clearly seen in the marble atop the island, on the terrace, on the wall above the fireplace, and in the central arch above the island *(opposite)*. "It's a graceful, comforting curve," says designer Warner, "that evokes the feeling of a hearth."**

The low pantry end of the kitchen fits under the existing roof line, while the kitchen/dining room area flares into the light. The façade's redwood ship-lap siding *(right)* was painted yellow.

Looking from the front of the addition toward the old house, architecture and light work together to keep the design lively—part of the pleasure of being in this kitchen. The semigloss-painted, multifaceted ceiling changes moment to moment with the play of light, making exciting use of the sunlight coming from the glass-filled end gables. Even the kitchen sink window on the east side has its own little channel to funnel the morning sun into the room.

**THE FINE DETAILS:** Ten-dollar swivel-base spotlights *(far left)* dramatize the glossy ceiling from atop the capital molding that finishes off and camouflages a structural column. And a built-in refrigerator leaves room to inset a high-tech microwave *(left)* alongside the restaurant stove.

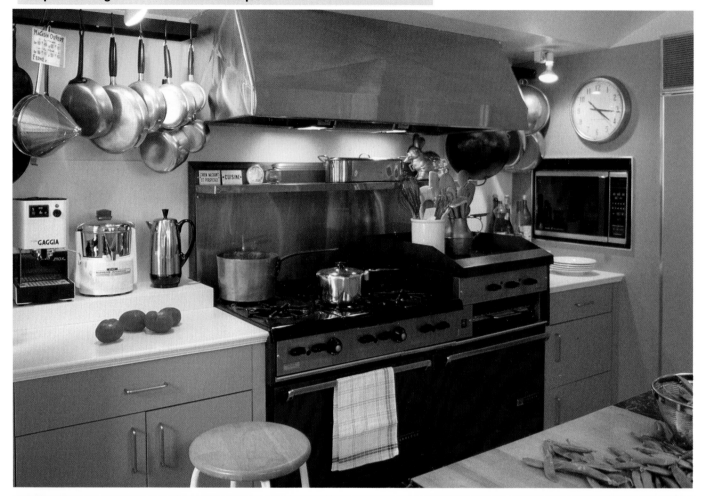

**VOICE OF EXPERIENCE:** When renovating the facade of a hearth, don't forget to check the chimney, too. Before the final cleanup, call in a chimney sweep, who should be able to assess the flue tile and other components. Some firms now offer a high-tech solution to chimney inspection. They lower a mini video camera down the flue to check every nook and cranny. You and the inspector watch the show on a closed-circuit TV.

On the narrow-aisled cooking side of the kitchen, everything is planned to be a short step or a long reach away, even in such a big room. Working at the chopping block section of the marble-topped island *(opposite, above),* the cook is never out of touch, turning around only to reach the custom-sized pot rack, the built-in microwave, or the commercial refrigerator and restaurant stove.

In the pantry *(opposite, below),* stepped overhead cabinets and curved entry portals compress the space before expanding into the big room. The result is to make the explosion of light at the end of the room come as a welcome surprise. Used emotionally this way, light and architecture become a contemporary alternative to conventional kitchen decoration.

Storage throughout the addition was designed and considered down to every square inch. Floor-to-ceiling cupboards *(above, left)* were designed into the "dead," interior walls, almost taking the dishes right out of the washer and capable of racking up layers of provisions. Under the island *(above, middle),* partitioned spice and cutlery drawers team up with roll-out crockery bins, standard options from cabinetmakers. And, in the pantry/hallway *(above, right),* over-the-counter cabinets step out as they approach the doorway into the kitchen—part of the visual squeeze play. "There's an enormous variety in cabinet options being manufactured today," says designer Warner. "You can almost always find exactly the kind you need for efficient storage without resorting to custom designs."

The kitchen's social areas—the center island with stools and the dining space—are efficiently warmed by a fireplace whose tall, shallow design throws heat into the room, not up the chimney. Instead of being enclosed, the beautiful Belgian block and green slate chimney has been framed by a painted plasterboard apron and now floats in the wall. The plan is eventually to outline the arch in neon lighting.

# THE NEW POWER LOOK

**THE LATEST BIG CHILL:** Once strictly professional, refrigerator/ freezers with glass-fronted doors, like the one below, are starting to make inroads into the made-for-home market. It's like having a Mercedes in your kitchen. To save space and cut down on noise, this one's outsize condenser motor is stowed out of sight in the garage. However glamorous the look, the need for that

I f we were to freeze a moment in contemporary kitchen design, this one on the parlor level of a New York row house would be it. Every element here is up-to-the-minute kitchen style: French windows (not sliding glass doors), bistro chairs (not bentwood), stainless steel sinks (not porcelain), a marble counter (not butcher block), a professional restaurant stove *and* refrigerator *and* wood-burning grill

At the center of things is a space-cleaving work island covered with that cool marble. It's an at-home version of the multipurpose counter running through most professional kitchens that separates cooking space from cleaning and preparation areas. And it's just as efficient. Along both long sides of the island, beneath the marble, is a strip with conveniently spaced electrical outlets. A hinged chopping block counter (in the foreground and folded down here) extends the marble island and swings out of the way when not needed. Porcelain-knobbed oak cabinets and a polished cherry floor contrast with the industrial-strength cookware.

large, space-eating condenser is an important factor when you consider installing a professional refrigerator.

**VOICE OF EXPERIENCE:** Heavy-duty commercial refrigerators, stoves, mixers, and other kitchen appliances may work on normal household wiring only if you run them one at a time. Even consumer electric stoves that require a 220-volt line may be mismatched to your home's electrical system. Before buying commercial equipment, ask a licensed electrician about the combined electrical load and cost of adding commercial-duty wiring and additional safe circuits.

# A KITCHEN TO LIVE IN

**THE UPWARDLY MOBILE FIXTURE:** Fluted or sleek, plaster or plastic, wall-hugging sconces are coming up in the world. They throw a wash of soft, dramatic light and provide instant archi-tecture in any room. The sconces in the kitchen here quickly set the mood of salon and, stylistically, move the room miles beyond the old white lab.

A far cry from harvest gold, the pale palette in this kitchen includes soft yellow, lavender, and blue—chosen for their identical intensities. Notice that one cabinet door and drawer (above) are accented in lavender laminate.

Kitchens, of course, are no longer chained to a hot stove. The old cooking/breakfast area/dining room formula is often giving way to a loft's openness, fleshed out with furnishings and detail once found in every room *but* the kitchen. Now, front-parlor warmth and space are as welcome—and important—as making dinner. And this room, with its superefficient work and storage areas awash in peaceful pastels, is like a gracious salon come home to the kitchen.

Although seeming every inch a studio loft with vintage architecture, this kitchen was, in fact, created from bare, white-walled space. Those moldings are added-on reproductions; the neo-classic mantel is also a plaster reproduction. The glossy hardwood floor is brand-new, nailed-down planking, while the French windows and appealing half-moon are actually all-American energy savers. An Indian dhurrie rug and chubby armchair covered in painted fabric remind you this room isn't just for cooking. The point here is that straight-edged, white box space doesn't need to stay that way—whether you're contemplating a kitchen, a living room, or both.

Although this kitchen/studio is spread out over a rather commodious 15 feet by 15 feet, the real action takes place in an efficiently planned galley that could easily be incorporated into far less room. This is a concept that can shrink to fit an apartment or expand into a loft.

A closeup of the cooking galley shows the working lineup. On the wall, the kitchen's major appliances are arranged for easy access without slighting the room's airy appeal. The black refrigerator/freezer and ovens are placed at either end of the cooktop, and plentiful cabinets provide visual bookends for the center aisle. Across the way, the marble-topped island houses sink, built-in mixer, and dishwasher. The island can double as an eating counter, just as the dining table can fill in as a work space.

**Here's the old idea of a work triangle transformed into a trapezoid—and the geometry works just as well. A stainless steel sink is centered in the island, with the cooktop opposite. Refrigerator and ovens flank the cooktop.**

The details of high-intensity storage and state-of-the-art appliances set the scene for this functional kitchen to work beautifully:

An induction cooktop *(top row, left),* which heats by magnetic friction, stays cool enough to accommodate a strip of handy chopping block without warping the wood. Drawers under the cooktop are specially sized to take large appliances and overscaled pots and pans.

A conventional oven and a microwave oven *(top row, middle)* provide the best of both worlds. They also stack to fit and feature glossy black-glass faces.

Utensils and silverware are quick-to-hand and easy to fit in drawers *(top row, right)* that are not too big and not too small, adjacent to the refrigerator.

Hidden conveniences *(bottom row, left):* A pull-out, pop-up mixer and trash bin free work space on the marble top of the center island and free the counters of clutter. Note the clever storage of outsize and varying drawers in the island.

Many manufacturers of laminate cabinetry offer the option of a crafty flip-out trough *(bottom row, middle)* that can be installed beneath the sink as a catchall space for sponges and soaps.

Pull-out pantry *(bottom row, right):* is a nifty solution for tight spaces. These shelving units pull out of the cabinet and will take a double row of stacked cans and packages.

# LIMITED ADDITION

The front of the house *(left)* didn't change at all, but the architects did maintain the continuity of the architecture by using the same red detailing on the new bay window *(opposite)* as on the front door and living room French windows. New additions shouldn't jar.

From the outside, the bay window that was added on to the rear of the house looks completely natural. A rectangular transom above the new window helps throw light into the kitchen.

Squeezed into the aft of a 1920s-built bungalow in Washington, D.C., this kitchen was so small, its stove had to be in the basement. Not exactly efficient. And the house is situated on a small lot, which made adding on impossible.

The imaginative solution was provided by D.C. architects Stephen Banigan and Jerry Harpole. They bumped out the back wall just a little, installing a new, cantilevered bay window to add three precious feet and sorely needed light. Then they took advantage of the room's nine-foot ceiling height and used it to maximum effect. Three tiers of brand-new, efficient cabinetry, custom designed, make the kitchen space feel ample. And they managed to fit a full range of appliances, plus a dining area, into the nine-foot-by-eight-foot space.

The new mosaic tile floor has the look of the house's era and keeps the tight space opened up and light. And the unexpected color of shiny blue-gray cabinets with accents of wood counters—unusual for a kitchen—lends a sophisticated mood.

Finally, though, it's the bold lines of the bay window, the architectural grid, that draws the eye and turns the narrow corridor into a real kitchen.

In the triple-tier stack of cabinets, it's the small, square, second level that makes this design. Inset to be out of the way of cooking work, the cabinets' glass doors add charm and break up what would otherwise be a solid mass.

# THE MODULE PLAN

Located in a suburban Seattle house, this kitchen was originally a room that was walled off from the living areas, making it dark and cramped. Partially opening the walls, to make pass-throughs on two sides, created a new, "little house" module that sets off the kitchen without entirely giving up the private work area the owners wanted. Very thoughtfully designed, it now includes first-class materials, efficient storage, and commercial equipment in a pleasing open-air space where every square inch has been put to work.

**VOICE OF EXPERIENCE:** Warm water and soap should be enough to handle cleaning tasks on stainless steel sinks and fixtures—with a dash of ammonia to increase the surface luster (only a teaspoonful to about a quart of soapy water). Avoid abrasives other than an extremely fine polishing pumice (used in some proprietary cleaners). It is wise to test even this pastelike abrasive on a small spot to be sure it won't cause graining and dull the finish.

S een from the outside, the new kitchen module sets up its own little "house," creating a room within a room. Yet it's still open to natural light and to the sociability of the living and dining areas.

Cleverly, and without using a great deal of floor space, every angle and surface has been planned to make this module work much bigger than it looks. Counters are covered in either butcher block or tile squares, grouted in a contrasting black, and edged with pine. Most small appliances are tucked away in drawers and cabinets to keep the surfaces clear. The cut-out wall opposite the living room *(above)* has a taller counter that acts as a pass-through and server, covered in a honey-colored laminate. Just beneath it is the stainless steel sink with the faucet of choice these days— a gooseneck. The arched gooseneck moves up and out of harm's way to fill a large pot or a watering can. It also lends a bit of gracious curve to a straight-lined sink. Dishes get tucked away in a charmingly recessed shelf that's the hollow part of the pass-through counter.

**The range in new-made cabinetry has seen the return of the breadbox drawer *(below)*, here in a cottage style, painted white.**

**VOICE OF EXPERIENCE:** Maple or birch butcher-block countertops are heavy and costly, but they add warmth to the kitchen. The drawback to wood counters is that you can't use them the way they are supposed to be used. True butcher's blocks are thick slabs of hardwood. When they become gouged, stained, grooved, and generally disfigured, the butcher calls in a resurfacer who lops off the uppermost few inches. Then the carving continues. Don't expect a wood counter to maintain that kind of professional appearance or to clean easily after long use.

All the major appliances here take cooking seriously indeed. A trio of ovens—convection, conventional, and microwave, plus a pull-out warming drawer—has black glass fronts and is housed in a stacked unit opposite the sink *(above)*. A large refrigerator and separate freezer are set into the module wall, next to the ovens. The rugged restaurant stove includes a griddle alongside the large cooktop and, overhead, takes massive ventilation from a gleaming overscaled range hood. An industrial fixture within the hood throws light on whatever's cooking on the stove.

Storage throughout the kitchen is capacious and detailed. A combination of ready-made and custom-designed cabinets, painted white, embrace everything a devoted cook wants without the need of a pantry. On drawers, no handles appear to fuss up the clean lines. Instead, the handholds double as curvy eye-pleasers. A gray-green strip beneath the counters and at the baseboards provides both contrast and unity. As does the black-grouted tile floor, which echoes the countertops.

**Other options in closed storage offer drawers *(below)* that easily hold racks of spice jars or hard-to-fit baking pans.**

Big kitchens are as tough to plan as small ones. Put the focus on separate areas that work alone but still connect to the overall room. In this dream of a kitchen—18 feet by 20 feet—four distinct areas fit together. On the left side, there's luxury: compartment storage, a second cooktop, a wine cooler, and an ice maker. The cooktop has an exchangeable griddle, two burners, rotisserie, and grill. The right side is the core of the working kitchen. Appliances are top-of-the-line performers from the venting hood to the complex microwave/ conventional oven unit. Almond counter- tops, backsplashes, and end panels are made of Corian. Cabi- nets are laminated in a warm glow of rose- pink, then finished with contoured ash strips. Italian tile cov- ers the floor in a time- less checkerboard. And lighting is built in for the unobtrusive clarity—down onto the counter, up into the cabinets.

# BUILDING INTO THE BACKYARD

I n the 1950s, or even the '60s and early '70s, the standard backyard addition was the family den. Today, it's the new family room—a group participation kitchen, like this one in a suburban Chicago house.

Originally built as a one-story cottage, the house got its second story several decades later *(above)*. But it's the new kitchen/family room, completed about five years ago, that transforms the house's personality and just about doubles its space *(below)*. Expanding

into the backyard, the addition is cunningly spliced to the back of the house, leaving the façade unaltered. The moral of this soaring two-story, designed by architects Stuart Cohen and Anders Nereim, is that boring architecture needn't stay that way.

Three ascending gables—"Papa Bear, Mama Bear, and Baby Bear," as Stuart Cohen calls them—were inspired by the garage's original roof line. The addition is anchored, visually and actually, by the wit of a simple column. Beneath the middle gable's skylight and lattice-board ceiling, the new, loftlike kitchen takes advantage of the backyard with a door to the terrace and windows that are generous in number and scale.

The working area of the kitchen is a U-shaped space, bordered on the left wall by storage cabinets, ovens, and laminate counter. In the middle is the double stainless steel sink. The other arm of the U is formed by a long island that has an inset cooktop and griddle. Several details of planning and design are worth noticing here. A mir-

ror makes an unusual backsplash for the counter, next to the ovens; it opens up the narrow galley and throws natural light into the closed-in cooking area. Notice too that another working and/or serving counter can be pulled up along the island to complement the dining table. An electrical outlet at the end of the island allows for easy use of countertop appliances. And finally, the clever detail of the one downward-turned factory lamp means the drama of the skylight and two-story space isn't diminished—but there's still overhead lighting to keep the table surface clear.

**Here, as in so many suburban houses lately, the new addition has shifted the focus of the home from the front to the back. Shingled siding keeps the new façade in the context of the old, but look how much the windows vary—and it works fine because of their very careful placement.**

**VOICE OF EXPERIENCE:** In combination with a conventional door, large double-hung windows offer an interesting alternative to sliding patio doors. Since windowsills (as opposed to doorsills) generally cannot stand up to rain splatters and accumulations of snow resting against the sash, this detail should be used only in combination with a liberal roof overhang or, as in this addition, as part of an entry wall recessed from the exterior wall of the building.

# OPENING UP THE GALLEY

**BISTRO BURNERS:** Want a restaurant stove but don't have room for the bulk? Manufacturers are now offering commercial-duty cooktops, four- and six-burner, that can fit right into a countertop. That way, you get the performance without the huge stove. The one below is set into the marble island counter.

**VOICE OF EXPERIENCE:** Marble is an elegant but somewhat unpredictable building material and should not be installed to be self-supporting. Typically, it is glued to three-quarter-inch plywood (recessed a bit so as not to compete with the smooth marble edge). Even then, substantial overhangs must be supported against flexing with legs or brackets.

As soon as a renter becomes an owner, the first thing to go is the wall between the kitchen and living room. Every high-rise kitchen is ripe for this kind of renovation. With that wall gone, immediately the apartment seems larger. A wider aisle, an extended countertop, efficient double-deck cabinets, and the new marble bar/buffet overhang on two sides of the central island all add up to newfound work spaces. The metal cabinets with glass shelves are lit from below, so everything looks beautiful from the living room. And the elegance of the 11-foot-by-3½-foot slab of *rojo alicante* marble feels good in the living room and positively right in the kitchen.

**L-hooks screwed into lath strips create a kitchen tool rack that will keep the chicken scissors distinct from the potato masher.**

**This deep garbage bin drawer makes a clean sweep of cooking cleanups. It's an option for under-the-counter cabinets.**

# PINK AND BLACK IS COMING BACK

**VOICE OF EXPERIENCE:** A galley kitchen will seem roomier without clunky upper cabinets. (The bottom shelf is usually the only one well used anyway.) In a narrow space, a floor-to-ceiling mini-pantry at one end may be more efficient. Revolving and pull-out hardware can also double the cabinet space.

In this Chicago loft, thinking small adds up to big style. A T-shaped island within the space *(right)* balances functional appointments and terrific impact. Elegant black tile, counters, and cabinets are a bold choice. A six-foot-high wooden pantry is secured flush to the walls, and a half-size refrigerator fits under a counter. Hanging racks free the counter-tops for appliances.

# THE WARMTH OF WOOD

If you crave a crisp kitchen without the hard edges of tech, a large dose of natural materials will do the trick. Here, sleek lines and warm materials meld the traditional to the modern. Flush birch cabinets fill the long, narrow space in a way metal simply cannot. Overscaled round molding injects a country mood. And the stepped-back design and pale color of the urethane-sealed wood keep the room light. A cooktop sits atop a cabinet.

# THE SURPRISE OF CONCRETE

Seattle architect James Olson calls his condominium apartment a "cross between a Florentine villa and a parking garage." Using stainless steel and poured concrete, Olson housed cabinets, cooktop, oven, and microwave in a concrete counter that looks grainy and right next to the soaring skylight and greenery in the living room. A cast-iron pot rack keeps cookware handy, and the large gray hood provides ventilation.

# THE NEO-FIFTIES KITCHEN

**A window slices through a kitchen cabinet in a visual pun, one of the unexpected twists of design that mark this renovation as being of our own time.**

With an easy commute to downtown Los Angeles, the couple who owns this postwar house liked their location but not their matchbox structure. Architect Eric Moss was hired to turn the double-gabled bungalow into a more spacious home, and this added-on kitchen wing is part of that result. The wit and wonder of the revamped house is Moss's dramatic use of mundane materials, which kept the renovation cost-conscious and within budget. Moss relied on craftsmanship and high-impact design to provide a different definition of elegance. Here, the retro look—a pointed and playful evocation of the 1950s—takes over the kitchen, yet it still works for the present.

The new face of high-tech shows up in corrugated white plastic, one of the standard finishes for these European cabinets that are available here. Moss used the same plastic to cover the dishwasher, giving a unified, under-the-counter look to the long, working wall. A porcelain double sink—a choice both fifties and contemporary—fits under the window. And the window itself, covered with narrow blinds, is straight out of postwar housing. Ceramic tile on the floor, counter, and backsplash are all in the same kind.

A skylight, framed in plywood, lights up the kitchen in a way that the 1950s never did. And the red accents of phone and accessories read right out of the present.

**Combining simple materials and haute couture workmanship is a trademark of the West Coast's young architects and is evidenced in the witty work of Eric Moss.**

# THE SEMI-PROFESSIONAL KITCHEN

The heightened sophistication of home cooking nowadays means everything from steak and eggs to grilled quail. Many want the restaurant experience at home, right down to the tools the professionals use. Space strategies, materials, and equipment from the commercial kitchen are now widely available for home use. And all of it will fit into the live-in country kitchen or the techno-whizzy galley.

These three kitchens, all in suburban homes, illustrate the point. All borrow freely from restaurant design and wares, yet all three are obviously comfortable rooms. If you're contemplating installing a restaurant range, here's what you need to know.

The first qualification is a love of cooking. Otherwise, the money's not worth it. After that, there's a tremendous variation in prices of commercial stoves—not particularly from brand to brand but "from parts of the country to other parts—dealers within the same area," says Charles Augusto, president of New York's Kaplan Bros. Some dealers sell at full list price, whereas others discount as much as

In a Connecticut kitchen *(left)*, bold purple and bullnose molding soften the industrial edges. *New York Times* food writer Craig Claiborne uses the marble-topped counter as a desk and the warmth of wood to break up stainless steel fittings *(below)*. And, in Washington, D.C., bright copper and red tile do the same trick *(opposite)*.

50 percent. A basic range—a unit with six burners and one oven in standard black enamel—will cost betwen $950 (discounted) and $1,500 (list price), compared with about $500 for a good, four-burner domestic stove.

Virtually all ranges by the name manufacturers are created equal. What you can get on the basic stove is from two to a dozen burners on top and one or

two huge ovens below. Options depend on what you like to cook and eat: griddle surfaces, salamander broilers, or "hot tops" for big-pot stews and sauces.

And remember this: restaurant stoves will not fit through every doorway. Remember to check the dimensions before you purchase the stove.

# THE PERSONAL SPA
## BATHS AND DRESSING ROOMS

The bath is now open to a world of inspiration. Rules about what's proper have been indefinitely suspended. Bathrooms have become restorative suites with saunas and hot tubs. Old fixtures, often antiques, live happily next to state-of-the-art whirlpools and private exercise centers. The upshot? A real room where comfort and luxury are both at home.

The blue powder room (above) in a sprawling Colonial house near Washington, D.C., got its color from five coats of flat white paint, each sanded, then three spongings of blue glaze and three final varnish glazings, all supervised by owner Dorothy Slover, an instructor in the art of painting faux finishes. The luxurious bath/dressing room on the right is part of a second-floor bedroom suite in a town house on New York's Upper West Side. The all-wet room is new-scaled but old-time tiled. A generous brass shower head is flanked by cast-bronze reproduction ship lights.

No room in the house has been so transformed in the last five or so years as the bathroom. Pampering has become a serious business, a reward for all our hard work. We want a room that satisfies our fantasies as well as our needs. We want the size and the sizzle of the spa—everyday amenities for weary eyes and bodies. "The new bathroom is like an easy chair, something relaxing to come home to," says New York designer Eric Bernard, who has made baths his specialty. Today, as often as not, the motivation for planning a bumpout or adding a wing starts with finding a cramped and crowded water closet or a hard-edged white lab when you move in.

The Japanese and European tradition of luxury in the bath has spilled over into America in a big way: deep soaking tubs and hand-held showers; whirlpools and saunas; real furniture and sculptural fixtures; smooth finishes and rich, solid colors in faucets, sinks, hardware, and handles. Double sinks for the two-career family. Brass and marble, brushed chrome and stainless steel, unexpected combinations of columns and sconces, warm woods and techy black tile, the comfort and grace of grand old hotel baths—all of it is being retrofitted into new and existing floor plans.

The bottom line on what's possible for your bathroom lies beneath the floor, down there with the plumbing. Tubs and sinks can't be moved too far without incurring a costly rerouting of plumbing. Even when fixtures stay put, there may be other problems. Says Houston contractor Burke Windham, "You have to consider that when you add new equipment to existing plumbing, the tolerances may be too slim." Which means the waste pipe on that fabulous new whirlpool bath may not quite fit the corresponding pipe in your home's plumbing. A good plumber can deal with such things, but they add to costs.

Think about all those choices ahead of time. And think, too, about how long you can manage without a bathroom while the renovation is underway. Whatever estimate of time you're given by the contractor, add 25 percent—at least. One ambitious owner of an 1830s Greek Revival ruin (with major potential, naturally) lived for months with "piles of rubble and BX cable dangling through sections of wall that had been hacked away by the plumbers. I started smoking again," she says. "I went into therapy and spent every Wednesday talking about the house, the house."

There's cause for caution here, absolutely. But "if you're doing a complete renovation, don't skimp on the bathroom," warns contractor Windham. "Buyers now demand whirlpool tubs and separate showers." You might, in other words, lose your mind for a bit, but this is one place you'll get it back in resale value.

# THE MASTERFUL BATH

Divided by snazzy blinds from the rest of the master bedroom, this renovated bath in a Minneapolis bungalow has a new pedestal sink, tweedy fabric on the wall, and a custom-designed whirl-pool/tub that was constructed from a wooden frame and then armored with hand-laid tile.

# THE WET ROOM

**"W**e turned this four-thousand-square-foot loft into the biggest studio apartment in New York," says designer Kevin Walz, who executed the renovation. "It was a former baseball cap factory, and all we had were some leftover storage racks and a lot of head forms." What fashion designer Adri wanted was a loft that encompassed every part of her life, including a city-dweller's dream: a pool of one's own.

Besides installing a kitchen, a workshop space, and an exercise area *(below)*, Walz fulfilled Adri's fantasy by designing the loft's center attraction: a ten-foot-square, white-tiled whirlpool/ tub. Now gleaming and sybaritic, the tub is three and a half feet deep to accommodate total soaking. The surrounding platform provides extra seating and then craftily turns into a kitchen counter on one side and a dressing room vanity on the other—at the conventional height of 36 inches *(inset above)*.

**HEAVY CONSIDERA-TIONS:** "We had the minimum needed to support the tub and all that water—one hundred fifty pounds per square foot," says Walz, "but because the industrial building was eighty years old, we added a number of structural two-foot-by-ten-foot joists under the whirlpool to help spread out the weight."

**THE PRICE:** "The entire project of four thousand square feet would cost about $150 to $160 per square foot today," says designer Kevin Walz. "And if you were putting in only the whirlpool and platform, it would run about $15,000."

# THE NEW RETREAT

**D**esign in a ranch house tends to ignore both bathrooms and closets. Originally, builders were hell-bent on fitting in all the tidy, labeled spaces without much regard for size. So ranches have squirrely little closets and cramped little baths. Joining the old bath and a closet to make a totally new, spacious room, as was done in this fifties ranch, makes much more sense.

Despite all the architectural disadvantages, one benefit of ranches is that they tend to have poured concrete floors. That means the floor can take the weight of the biggest whirlpool tub you can find. This one is top-of-the-line, equipped with six adjustable jets for blissful soaking. The earth-toned ceramic squares here help anchor the yellow, blue, and lavender palette.

Like most ranch baths, upstairs or down, this one was shy of windows. Since it doesn't compromise privacy, an overhead skylight does a better job than larger windows would. But there's no need for a huge one. A two-foot-square skylight is more than sufficient.

**Unexpected detail: Clear and patterned glass blocks set into the wall form a charming "window" *(above)* and a crosshatched pattern of light tile contrasts with a darker blue border in the roomy shower *(below).***

# A JAPANESE BATHHOUSE

**VOICE OF EXPERIENCE:** For extra protection against leaks in tiled shower enclosures, spread a bead of flexible butyl or silicone caulk in critical corners before setting and grouting the tile. Clear silicone is the most effective caulk for making surface repairs should the grout spring a leak. It adheres well, and is flexible enough to shift with the tile during changes in temperature and humidity. And it dries clear.

The Japanese view of the bath as a restorative and a ritual finds full expression in this ten-foot-square bathhouse. A tumbledown former garden shed, the new bathhouse now sits alongside an 1890s Seattle cottage and is reached by a path from the main house *(above)*. Both structures were completely reworked inside and out.

Accomplished by a team of architect Tom Hoffman and designer Susan Okamoto, the shed was opened up with wraparound paned doors and windows and, as in Japan, was then painted a muted gray-green to be in harmony with its natural setting. New plumbing was installed. Inside, there's a traditional open floor plan, a complete lack of clutter, and a feeling of peace and relaxation. The whirlpool tub is 22 inches deep and the platform, including the deck, is 8 feet by 16 feet. Handmade California ceramic tile covers the decking and the inside of the tub, while mass-produced tile, in a darker tone, covers the floor. The platform is close to two feet off the floor.

The Japanese use the design possibilities of wood like no other culture, relying on the intrinsic beauty of wood as its own decoration in spare and minimal rooms. Traditionally, highly figured woods are finely finished but left unvarnished, so the pattern of the grain will show. The same technique was used here, with vertical-grain fir on the floors, paneling, facing, and walls. "Structural construction in the Northwest area," says designer Okamoto, "usually uses fir. We just left it unfinished, without the drywall." Instead of wax or finish, the wood was treated with Benite oil, which stains it slightly darker, but maintains its natural texture. The effect is elegant, going far beyond ski-lodge rustic.

**A study in contrast: Oak floors in the main house provide a rich background for the lighter fir pillars. And tatami mats, edged in a contemporary black border, set off the rich woods.**

**In the main house, the Oriental spirit is influenced by a Westerner's idea of comfort. Susan Okamoto banished futons in favor of plump and inviting chaises, which she designed herself.**

**THE PRICE:** Carved out of a garden shed in 1984, this ten-foot-by-ten-foot bathhouse cost about $20,000 to complete, including a new sound system designed to be moistureproof.

**VOICE OF EXPERIENCE:** The extra expense of an operator skylight pays for itself by reducing mold and mildew problems common in baths and spas. Signs of quality include double bubbles (the skylight version of double glazing to eliminate condensation) and copper flashing built into the skylight frame.

# BATH, WITH A CITY VIEW

**A** knockout vista of San Francisco dictated the design here, with the drama exploited by naked floor-to-ceiling windows and a cunningly placed glass rectangle at one end. If your taste doesn't lean toward bare-bath windows, the skylight above the tub would alone solve the need for light.

Italian ceramic tile on the walls and Italian vinyl tile on the floor and bath platform add convenience and warm color. The deep soaking tub and the hand-held shower make a shower curtain an optional choice.

**ON SOAKING TUBS:** Wider and deeper than old-style bathtubs, equipped with nerve-soothing whirlpool jets, the soaking tub is showing up more and more. Finishes come in procelain, cast iron, fiberglass, and marble. When installing, a wraparound deck helps hide the plumbing. Heights of the deck will vary, depending on the tub's depth, the floor support, and the pipes.

The overhead lights put a bit of drama in the room and are a particularly exciting touch when one is bathing at night. Recessed ceiling light, of course, needs to be planned at an early stage of the renovation—before the clean wallboard and paint are applied. If you're thinking about such details in the bath, remember to get them into the blueprints—and into the budget—before the work begins.

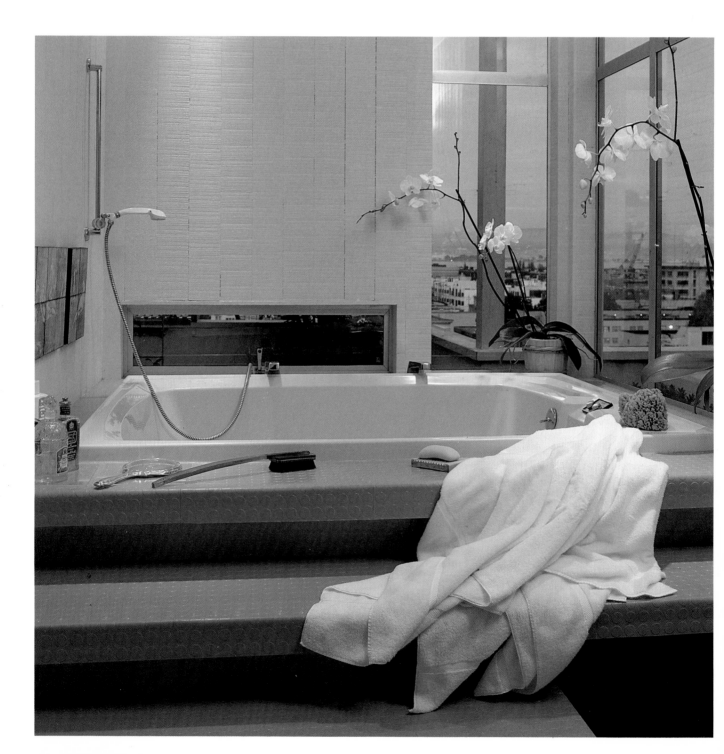

# BATH, WITH A CANYON VIEW

**VOICE OF EXPERIENCE:** Protect against the hazards of electrical shock in the bath (or kitchen) with quick-tripping circuit breakers, called Ground Fault Circuit Interrupters (GFCIs).

Should a problem develop, these devices cut off power very fast. The extra cost (above conventional circuit breakers) is worth it.

"This bath disappeared and came back," says the Los Angeles owner. "We took it down to the subfloor and framing" (without moving the plumbing sources, however), then expanded it into a master bath. New floor-to-ceiling windows were installed for the view of a Hollywood canyon.

Cream-colored tile defines the ingenious shower and tub area, which was custom designed. The tile is grouted in a contrasting gray (grouting comes in a wide range of colors). An unusual pale purple-gray on the walls sets off the cream tile. The owner liked the stainless steel lab sink for its minimalist lines.

Glass doors lead from the bath to a newly installed deck. The result is the option of bathing al fresco while still retaining the requisite privacy.

# THE GLAMOUR BATH

**VOICE OF EXPERIENCE:** On new bath (or kitchen or laundry) walls, use gypsum wallboard with a "W/R" rating—meaning Water Resistant. Treated with chemicals that leave a light green color and available in conventional thicknesses, this special board can be primed and painted, wallpapered, or tiled.

Throwing out old conventions yields new solutions: towel racks on wheeled carts roam with you; dual vanities back-to-back work much better than side by side; real lamps, not wall fluorescents, shine when the sun doesn't; an intriguing palette of creamy tile and nature's pastel colors brightens the room. Overhead, a white-glass skylit ceiling provides natural light.

A bath addition or combining closets and cubbyhole bathrooms needn't end up like a large locker room. All that space can be tricked into compartments. Here, shoji-style pine partitions with opaque milk glass and wide-swinging doors divide the room but don't close in the space. The result turns this bath into a spa without diminishing the glorious light. Fixtures and colors were chosen with an equally discerning eye for drama and function: sculptural black sinks set into coral laminate counters are placed opposite one another —for an efficient change—and a surprising new tub in an old style—with exposed chrome plumbing and showy ball feet—sits at the back bathing area.

# THE FRENCH LINE

**URBAN ARCHAEOLOGY AND THE UPSCALE REPRODUCTION:** If this is the look you love, a treasure hunt in France isn't the only answer. Many of the fixtures here are the plunder from the wreckage and auction sales of old buildings and hotels. A little creative scrounging could net a similar catch. Then too, Howard Kaplan, among others, perfectly reproduces most of these furnishings and fittings. They're now widely available of good quality.

Re-creating the old hotel bath is a fantasy come true here. This bath was designed around gilded antique French fixtures by French-furnishings importer Howard Kaplan, owner of the French Country Store in New York. Yet there was no sacrifice of amenities; they're as modern as the Concorde. The delight—and the surprise—of this bath is that it's tucked into a loft, a recycled printing plant in lower Manhattan, thus proving once more that any style you fancy can be installed in most any kind of space.

The step-up whirlpool tub and shower fairly drips with an array of gleaming brass. A little poetic license lets loose a lead garden pig to root on the tile step and allows a brass-edged tilting mirror to double as a towel rack.

An art nouveau armoire *(opposite)* adds its swooping, sinuous lines and painstakingly matched woods to the space by the tub, while Tiffany-style hanging lamps and an antique porcelain sink recall the elegance of a suite at the George V. Oriental carpets and an etched-glass door emphasize the old-style elegance.

**Along with the other high-quality fixtures and fittings in this richly ornamented bath, the brass faucets and drain lock are thoroughly French, as the *chaud* and *froid* proclaim.**

**VOICE OF EXPERIENCE:** Moving supply pipes to a new sink location is generally not a problem since the water is supplied under pressure. The pipes could turn a corner, even run up- and downhill past obstructions, without altering the flow. Moving drain lines, however, is another matter. Since drains work by gravity, they must flow downhill. Adding twists, turns, and nearly flat sections of pipe can lead to sluggish drains that are easily clogged.

# THE BEDSIDE SPA

**VOICE OF EXPERIENCE:** To protect living materials in damp environments, install a vent fan to evacuate moisture. Use double glazing on windows and doors to reduce the condensation. Treat wood with a prime coat and two finish coats of polyurethane.

With just 16 feet by 16 feet of new addition, architect Victor Belcic created this flamboyant bedroom extension of a suburban New York ranch house *(right)*. At the edge of the room, the floor drops 2 feet, while the ceiling (8 feet in the old section) starts a dramatic 30-degree climb, ending at 24 feet. The pine deck, enclosing the hot tub, is sealed with several coats of polyurethane.

# A SOLUTION IN BOLD STROKES

**SINK OPTIONS:** You can mount a sink in three ways: on a pedestal, wall-hung, or set in a counter. If counter-mounted, you have more decisions: on the surface, where the lip rests on the counter; recessed, so the counter overhangs the dropped-in sink; or cast-in, which means the sink and the counter are made of the same material (such as marble or Corian).

**On the opposite side of the room, the shower is enclosed by opaque glass doors and, beyond, the toilet has a sliding door for privacy.**

"I've always been influenced more by film, especially Fellini, than by other designers," says David James, who created this bath/bedroom suite for himself in a Los Angeles bungalow. "And really, interior design isn't that different from other art forms." James's style preferences seem particularly appropriate here, since the house, built in 1925, was originally a live-in work space for Warner Bros. set designers.

After knocking out the wall between the tiny upstairs bedroom and the bathroom, designer James divided the sleeping area from the bath with a Jean-Harlow-meets-Eurostyle vanity and a thirties-looking mirror and light, which he designed himself. A high, narrow shelf above the bed provides extra storage, and a movable floor light changes the mood depending on where it lands. This certainly isn't design by the book, but, as James says, "Everything comes out of my own head."

# A SOLUTION IN OLD-FASHIONED FANTASY

The old sink has a new Corian surround that its century-old originators never imagined. Painted and set in the open, the old tub looks like sculpture.

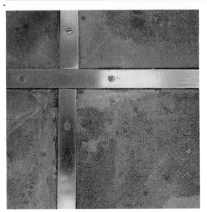

**LOCKER-ROOM LUXE: The slab concrete floor was poured, sealed with epoxy, and embellished with flush brass strips.**

**B**ecause the bathroom is usually small, it's the most likely room for a complete renovation. In this to-the-studs renewal, the charm of the bath was determined by the necessity of invention—all the existing plumbing was left in place. Reversing the usual process, the banal, semi-modern fixtures were discarded in favor of old ones. An antique tub was put into service with new paint, and the old zinc sink was updated with a contemporary gooseneck faucet. Then the room's envelope was refitted.

Waterproof plastic laminate covers the wallboard, with the seams finely masked by decorative strips of hand-fitted half round. You know that the window columns conceal the pipes, but the gesture is appreciated. And the new concrete floor, epoxy-sealed and centrally drained, is enriched with brass strips, echoing the walls.

Accessories continue the playful, old-fashioned motif: a Victorian oval mirror, brass lamp, wooden column, and a salvaged hunk of curved molding is hung over the tub for the joy of it.

# ROSES AND THE RETRO LOOK

"I like the tightrope a little," says fashion designer Betsey Johnson, about both her lifestyle and her home. Johnson's imagination is engaged by the high comedy and powerful expressiveness of pop culture, by the mix of exaggeration and simplification that turns a look into a logo. She likes artificiality. She likes mass production. She likes things that are tough, cheap, easy to use. She mixes, matches, overdoes, and underplays disparate pieces of visual culture, creating things that have surreal chic. This is, after all, the designer who gave us the high-heeled sneaker.

The bath in her Manhattan condominium loft displays the same collagist sensibility. The bold "tile" wall is actually four-foot-by-eight-foot Masonite sheets, with painted black lines. An opaque glass-block wall (below) lets light in from the bedroom and puts the real thing next to the imitation. The mosaic tile floor was original, but could well have been added. Johnson chose porcelain antique fixtures instead of modern ones, throwing curves into the very crisp lines of the room. And she then added color and soft texture: a nostalgic shower curtain, complete with old-style shower ring, and semi-precious jars and jewels from another era both provide judicious contrast.

The sweet roses-on-graph-paper romanticism here comes from an interplay of techy walls and floors with the curves of an antique sink. (opposite) These sinks are hard to find and very pricey, but the charm makes them worth it.

**VOICE OF EXPERIENCE:** Don't jump at antique or reproduction fixtures without a plan for matching them to reproduction fittings. Several plumbing and renovation supply firms sell individual hot and cold faucets that can be matched to three-hole basins by an experienced plumber. Single-tap, single-lever fittings can be used, while the holes for hot and cold taps are covered with blanks (typically, thin, stainless steel wafers tightened down onto caulking with a butterfly-type molly that grips the edges of the opening from beneath the sink).

# CALIFORNIA, COUNTRY STYLE

Leave it to young, innovative Californians—like architect Andrew Batey and designer Hope Batey—to turn this former Wells Fargo station into the villa of everyone's dreams. What makes it work? French doors thrown open to the California sun. Mexican tile that evokes a courtyard's private pleasures. And the luxury of a room to house one's very own custom-built soaking tub. The tub is two and a half feet deep and is lined with well-caulked Saltillo tile. The same tile covers the floor.

This is California Country—a continent away from Early American rustic.

# JAPAN, CONTEMPORARY STYLE

Created by the design team of Bromley/Jacobsen, this bath is clearly under the Japanese design influence. The keys are the plain yet slick geometry, strong architectural forms, and the deft use of texture and material.

The startling part of this bath is the gray concrete—who would have guessed it could look so futuristic, so serene? A freestanding vanity of cast concrete has the architectural look of a model skyscraper and houses a stainless steel round sink with an enameled faucet. And the plumbing is openly displayed, merely painted. Square concrete blocks also make the floor.

But it's the shower design that sets up the quiet drama in the room. The shower is lined with metallic lacquer and a leaded glass door fits snugly into the opening. Within the cool, pristine palette, the burnished metal of the lining, the door, and the sink becomes warm color and texture. Little, tailored details count for a lot here.

Like the subtle colors, light is natural rather than applied, coming from an overhead skylight.

# THE RENOVATOR'S SOURCE BOOK

Like genius itself, renovation is 10 percent inspiration and 90 percent perspiration. Even if you turn over the entire project to an architect or a general contractor, you'll still have to make choices. Skylights to sconces, faucets to flooring, doorknobs to porch posts—just making decisions is a labor-intensive process fraught with anxiety. This chapter carefully surveys the rich renovation product market, separating the best from the rest in 24 wall-to-wall and floor-to-ceiling categories, everything from major appliances to minor—but vital—details. You'll find products, prices, and practical advice, along with techniques, trade-offs, and inspiring ideas. All of it is designed to help transform your vision into the reality you can live with and love.

# APPLIANCES

Like sound systems, you can now buy combination units or individual components. Evaluate appliances for efficiency and convenience certainly, but also assess how well they fit—both physically and aesthetically—into your overall renovation scheme.

## COOKTOPS

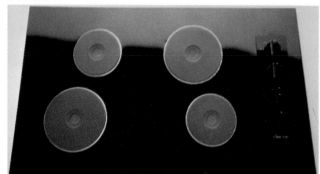

**Sleek Eurostyling for made-in-America cooktops.**

Divorced from the all-in-one kitchen range, cooktops ($200 to $800) permit far greater design flexibility. Most are 29 to 36 inches wide, 19 to 22 inches deep, and 3 to 6 inches thick. If under-the-counter storage is at a premium, choose the shallower types and tuck in drawers or shelves below. The newest cooktops come with interchangeable cartridges so you can take out a burner and put in a grill or a griddle. You'll pay more for a cooktop with a built-in, down-draft exhaust system (the duct-work goes under the counter), but then you won't have to install an overhead hood.

## WASHERS/DRYERS

So you won't have to tote baskets of laundry up and down the stairs or from one part of the house to another, try to locate a laundry room near the bedrooms. Stackable or twin washers and dryers ($250 to $600) come in full-size or scaled-down versions (designed to fit into standard-size closets). Side-by-side units ($200 to $400 each) can be tucked under a standard kitchen counter. With flexible duct pipe, any location is possible, but putting a washer and dryer against an outside wall will make plumbing and venting easier and cheaper.

**Stacked units fit small spaces.**

## RANGES

**For tight spaces: range, oven, and dishwasher.**

Freestanding or built-in, standard ranges are 30 inches wide. But there are 24- and even 21-inch models available. For really tight quarters, Modern Maid offers a 30-inch range with a dishwasher below and an oven above. Depending on the features you can't live without—self-cleaning oven, microchip control, black glass doors, lights, timers—prices range from $400 to $1,200. If you can find one, a gas stove from the '30s or '40s is a charm-laden

**Chef's choice: an all-in-one restaurant range.**

**Still cooking: a 1930s gas kitchen stove.**

alternative at $200 to $400. For serious cooks who can spare the space, restaurant ranges offer more precise cooking. Prices start at about $1,500 for one-oven units and go up to $2,500 for models with six burners, two ovens, broiler, griddle, and grill. An alternative: restaurant cooktops ($600 to $800). Most offer four to six burners and a griddle/grill. They stand on short legs, so the countertop supporting the cooktop must be lowered to make them flush with surrounding counters.

## REFRIGERATORS

**In-the-door water and ice dispensers cut energy loss.**

One reason commercial refrigerators ($2,000 and up) are finding their way into homes is that they're only 24 inches deep and can be installed flush with most kitchen counters. Residential side-by-side models, 28 to 32 inches deep with a freezer on one side, refrigerator on the other, start at about $800 for basic white and go up to $1,800. Widths and heights vary. Make sure any new refrigerator will fit in the old space. You can update an old fridge with a "designer style" kit that will hold any one-quarter-inch material, usually a colored laminate.

---

## DISHWASHERS

Digital readouts are fine, but choose a dishwasher ($300 to $600) for efficiency first: energy- and water-saving features, adjustable racks, and a timer to turn the machine on when electric rates are lowest. Customize the front with optional black glass or painted panels.

**Black glass front panels add tuxedo class.**

## WALL OVENS

**Stacked ovens save counter and cabinet space.**

They're easier to use—less stooping—and they make the most of vertical space. Self-cleaning single ovens cost about $600 to $800. Stacked units with a microwave on top run $1,600 to $1,800. Locate against an outside wall for easy access to utility lines.

## EXHAUST FANS

Tempted to do without? Don't. Exhaust fans remove not only kitchen grease and heat, but also the moisture that reduces the effectiveness of home insulation. The newest models, built into over-the-range cabinets ($200 to $300) are practically invisible. Where venting to the outside is impossible, ductless fans ($75 to $150) will filter grease-laden air but won't remove heat or moisture from the kitchen. Restaurant ranges require bigger hoods and more powerful fans.

**Match the hood and fan motor size to range size.**

# CABINETS

Look for functional engineering, easy-reach access, and high-volume storage that makes the most of every cubic inch.

**Under-the-sink "drawer."**

**Lazy susan corner storage.**

**Vintage option: build in an old corner cabinet.**

**Mobile trolley extends counter space, storage.**

Kitchen cabinet dealers would rather sell you new cabinets, of course, but they do stock and sell standard-size accessories that will fit into most mass-produced cabinets.

If you want new cabinets, buy the best you can afford. Invest in sturdy, well-made units precisely engineered for efficiency and convenience, ones that can be customized from the start with the accessories you need.

In order of popularity and price, there are three types of kitchen cabinets:

• Mass-produced stock cabinets from kitchen cabinet dealers come in standard sizes that range from 9 to 48 inches in width. To make stock cabinets fit into the space available, you may need to use "fillers," panels of various widths that close the gaps between individual cabinets. Available from cabinet dealers, the fillers are painted, stained, or laminated to match the finish on the cabinets.

• Special-order cabinets, also from kitchen cabinet dealers, are usually the same size but may offer more and better finishes, superior construction and

**Pull-out wastebasket.**

The sad truth is that most kitchens in older homes are woefully inadequate and inherently inefficient. But resist the impulse to gut and start from scratch, at least until you've analyzed the problems and considered the options.

In many cases, it may be smarter to invest in well-engineered cabinets than in costly demolition and reconstruction.

Making it work may mean only retrofitting existing cabinets with readily available adjustable shelves and slide-out bins, baskets, racks, and lazy susans.

hardware, and more accessory options.

• Custom cabinets are made by local cabinetmakers according to specifications from you, your architect, or designer.

Regardless of style, cabinet quality is a function of good materials and sound construction.

**Quick access: custom, open shelving of painted pine.**

Cabinet interiors are usually made of particleboard, plywood, or a combination of the two. Both are good, but plywood is stronger and more expensive. Frequently, particleboard is used as a filler between wood veneers or layers of plastic laminate on doors and sides. Face frames, even if surfaced with veneer or laminate, should be made of solid wood.

For drawer sides and backs, look for solid wood or plywood, reinforced bottoms, and dovetail joints or mortise-and-tenon corners.

And remember, if you skimp on hardware, you'll

**Oak bullnose trim conceals under-the-cabinet fluorescent lighting fixtures.**

be reminded every time you open a drawer. Steer clear of plastic glides or guides stapled to the sides or bottoms of drawers. Plastic hardware is durable, but it should be screwed on. Best bet: metal glides and guides.

Drawer fronts and doors may be made of solid wood or veneered or laminate-surfaced plywood or particleboard. All are suitable. But because particleboard is prone to crumbling or fracturing under impact, all the edges of drawers and doors should be veneered or laminated too.

Materials and construction aside, cabinets should be designed to provide the easiest access possible as

well as versatile high-volume storage—especially for equipment like big stewpots, small appliances, mixing bowls, platters, and baking sheets. The best ones make use of dead space in front of sinks and cooktops, and in corners. Tilt-out bins, pivoting "turnaround" corner shelves, slide-out racks and shelves, pop-up appliance platforms, oversize and extra-deep drawers, pull-out cutting boards, and adjustable wire baskets put all the contents within easy reach. Cabinets with self-closing doors equipped with concealed spring-loaded hinges work best.

As for price, expect to pay about $7,500 to $15,000 for new, good-quality cabi-

**Antique furniture can work in the kitchen.**

**Slide-out pantry.**

nets, installed by a contractor in an average-size kitchen. Fortunately, a well-renovated kitchen will return from 80 to 120 percent of your investment when you sell the house.

If all you really want is a facelift, however, there are companies that specialize in refinishing cabinets. They also provide replacement doors and drawer fronts, if necessary. Either of these routes will cost about $2,000 to $5,000 for a typical kitchen.

Manufacturers of kitchen cabinets are not the only resources, though. Vintage kitchen cabinets, hutches, buffets, corner cabinets, chests, and general-store counters can be found at salvage outlets or antique shops and can add drama and surprise to any kitchen renovation.

**Canny choices: pop-up mixer, deep drawers, and slide-out shelves.**

# COLUMNS

Whether structural or decorative, grand or streamlined, columns warm rooms with human scale and history. Classic marble versions are showing up again, but new wood materials work just as well.

No single element has so dominated the renovation marketplace over the last decade as the column, an icon of postmodern architecture. Alone or in multiples, freestanding as sculpture or cast in a bona fide supporting role, topped by an elaborate capital or unadorned, stationed indoors or out, the column in a home instantly adds character.

Widely available at salvage outlets and wrecking companies, most vintage columns are made of wood and topped with carved wood or cast plaster capitals. Simple porch-post designs can be found for as little as $50. More elaborate columns, rescued perhaps from grand old houses, range from a low of about $200 to as much as $1,500. Much rarer stone or marble versions can cost from $2,000 to $5,000, depending on size and condition.

Newly minted reproduction columns are usually made of wood, although hollow aluminum and fiberglass versions are available.

Prices depend on height, diameter, and whether the capitals and bases are plain or fancy. Typically, though, an eight-foot wood column that is one foot in diameter will cost about $400. An aluminum column of the same dimensions costs about $130.

With a vintage wood column (some are hollow; others solid wood), you'll have to take what you can find and then either build around it or, if possible, alter it to fit. A straight column can simply be cut to length. Shortening a tapered column can be a

**Steel posts: column function, minimalist form.**

**Preserved cast-iron columns in a factory loft.**

**Wooden porch posts move indoors.**

problem because the base or the capital will no longer match the diameter of the post once it's been lopped off. New columns, on the other hand, come in a wide variety of stock sizes. Or you can order columns custom made.

**Tapered wood.**

**Carved stone.**

**Freestanding.**

**Aluminum.**

# COUNTERTOPS

No surface takes more abuse than the countertop. How much you cook, and the budget, should influence your selection. The new range of materials offers the color, pattern, and price to suit your style.

All countertops need not be created equal. Besides giving you a customized look, using two or more materials—such as marble, wood, and laminate—can yield separate countertop areas devoted to specific tasks, such as pastry-making or chopping. And judiciously mixing materials can make your renovation dollars go further. You can splurge on, say, marble for the island and then use plastic laminate for other counters. Your choices include:

• Wood. Factory-made butcher block made of thick, laminated hardwood pieces in standard counter width (25 inches) is sold by the linear foot ($18 to $24), ordinarily in 2- to 12-foot sections. Because it's prone to warping and/or cracking when exposed to moisture, keep it away from the sink. Most stains, scratches, and burns can be sanded out. An alternative is inexpensive construction-grade pine two-by-sixes (at about 55 cents per board foot), but these

**Cottage class: mellow-yellow pine lumber**

need to be professionally glued, clamped, sanded, sealed, and finished, a labor-intensive process that may make them cost more than butcher block.

**Polished or not, marble has rock-of-ages status.**

• Plastic laminate. New-generation laminates (like Formica's Colorcore), are colored all the way through, so those unsightly black seams are no longer a problem. Besides durability and easy maintenance, there's an almost limitless range of colors, patterns, and textures available at $2.50 to $5 a square foot (not including the required plywood, particleboard, or, better yet, moisture-resistant cementboard underlayment). Prelaminated counters in stock sizes (from lumberyards and home improvement stores) are somewhat cheaper, but color choices will be limited.

• Ceramic tile. Glazed tiles resist stains, water, and grease better than the unglazed kind but are more apt to crack from hot pots and pans. Plan on spending $10 to $20 a square foot, including installation.

Ceramic tile itself is practically maintenance-free. But the grout—the porous cementlike substance used to fill the joints between tiles—will absorb grease, stains, and moisture. That doesn't mean you must limit the use of tile to islands or counters away from the stove and the sink. Just seal the grout with liquid silicone or another sealant when the tile's installed and a couple of times a year thereafter.

**Seamless laminates yield solid-color surfaces or layered-edge treatment.**

• Synthetic marble. Du Pont's Corian is the most well known. In a solid color or lightly grained, it looks like white or almond marble but is made of natural minerals and acrylics in half-inch or three-quarter-inch thicknesses. It doesn't require an underlayment but can be installed directly onto base cabinets. Corian is resistant to moisture, and any stains or scratches can be fine-sanded out. The material can be cut and worked like wood using ordinary power saws and routers. For typical 1½ inch thick countertop edges, you'll need to glue a second, thin strip of Corian under the lip of the counter. Cost: $60 to $125 per linear foot.

• Marble, granite, slate. All are subject to staining to some degree, especially by acidic liquids (wine, lemon juice). But what some call stains, others call

charm. Marble is an organic material that ages well. As for price, cutting and finishing runs up the tab more than the cost of the raw material itself. If the plan calls for curves, elaborate edges, and cutouts (around the sink, for example), the cost will go up. Simplify the design if you need to economize. "Honed" is the term to request for marble and granite countertops with soft, matte finishes that disguise scratches and look more earthy than the high polish of high-rise lobbies. If you prefer slate, choose a honed or natural cleft (roughly textured) finish. In two-foot-by-six-foot slabs, marble costs $400 to $500; granite about $500 to $600; and slate, about $200.

**Corian mimics honed marble but costs a lot less.**

# DOORS

Think of them as hinged architecture, able to instantly alter the character of a room or even an entire house. For entry doors, add more visual impact with classic transoms or inventive windows, lots of molding.

## SALVAGED DOORS

**Stripped pine panel doors.**
At $50 to $150, bargains abound at salvage outlets. Professional refinishers will charge another $50 to $100 to strip away layers of old paint and varnish. Make sure the job is done by hand, though. Sandblasting can pit the wood; submersion in caustic chemicals can warp the door. Of course, if you have the time and energy, you can do the job yourself with a gallon of paint remover ($20) and a quart each of stain and varnish.

## SLIDING DOORS

For more light and a better look, choose top factory-made patio doors and top them with a custom-made, to-the-ceiling transom. To cut heat loss, insist on double glazing (two panes of glass). A good pair of sliders, in either aluminum or aluminum-clad wood, will cost $1,000 to $1,800. Installation adds about $250 to $350, depending on how much preparation work is required.

**The see-through wall**

## REPRODUCTIONS

**Victorian reproductions.**
Individual factory-made doors ($250 to $550) or complete custom-made entryways with fanlight transoms and pilasters ($1,500 to $2,000) are

**Prairie style in oak.**
available in a variety of charming reproduction styles. Kiln-dried hardwood is a top-quality choice because it's sturdy and a good insulator.

New components, reproductions of classic architecture elements, re-create a grand eighteenth-century entry.

**Portholes evoke the ocean-liner era.**

**Steel framing *(above, left)*; wood with leaded glass *(above, right)*; wood frame with wood grid *(left)*.**
Glass-paned French doors can replace picture windows or sliding patio doors and are the doors of choice for adding character to a room. The grilles make you feel less exposed than huge expanses of glass. To dramatically change the tone and temper of a room, heighten the doorway and install eight-footers instead of standard six-foot-eight-inch doors. Most factory-mades come in sets of two ($500 to $1,000, depending on material) or three or four, but for a whole wall, you can order individual, fixed units of wood, aluminum-clad wood, or even steel.

# FAUCETS

High style and good design have transformed these fixtures forever. And the prices have risen accordingly. You can cut the plumber's bill by renovating around existing pipes and drains.

For kitchens, spout has a retractable spray hose.

**Swivel-spout sink faucet.**

Eurostyle influences and high-tech engineering have turned plumbing fixtures into design-rich objects of art. The shapes are sculptural and sexy, and baked-enamel colors have

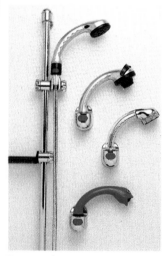

**German imports: rod-and wall-mounted shower heads.**

upstaged chrome. Given the choices, there's no reason to compromise the look of a new sink or tub with locker-room-looking hardware. High-fashion faucets can make an inexpensive sink (or an existing one) look terrific.

Sinks and faucets are sold separately so you don't need to buy both from the same maker. But—and this is important—be sure to buy a faucet that corre-

sponds in size to the pre-drilled holes in the sink, typically 4, 8, or 12 inches apart. Surprisingly, many well-designed and meticulously engineered faucets cost as much or more than sinks themselves. Be prepared to pay $300 to $400 for the best-looking sets on the market.

For both bath and kitchen, single-lever faucets make sense because you can turn them on and adjust both temperature and pressure with one hand (or even an elbow or forearm). Also, single-lever types have fewer parts to wear out over time.

For a kitchen sink, especially one with shallow bowls, do yourself a favor and buy a gooseneck or high-stem faucet. It allows you to easily rinse out stewpots and mixing

**A French Country reproduction faucet in copper.**

**Volume and temperature can be preset—no scalding.**

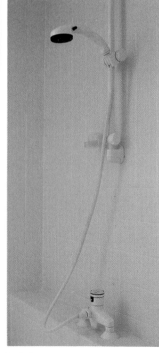

**Height-adjustable "telephone" shower taps into tub's faucet.**

bowls. Naturally, for a double sink, get a faucet with a tap that swivels from side to side. Another worthy feature: retractable spray hose built right into the faucet spout itself.

If you want to turn a bathtub into a shower without tearing out the wall to install new water supply pipes, look for a rod-mounted "telephone" shower assembly ($400 to $500) that connects to the tub's tap with a flexible

**Gooseneck spout in baked-enamel crayon colors.**

hose. Besides saving on the plumber's bill (you can probably make the change yourself), an advantage of this kind of shower fixture is that you can adjust the height by moving the shower head up and down the wall-mounted rod.

# FIREPLACES AND MANTELS

The fireplace is now a warm and comforting luxury and an alternative heat source. New designs combine classic mantels with increased energy efficiency.

## FIREPLACES

**An antique mantel charms a prefabricated fireplace.**

Steel box prefabs cost from $400 for a standard size to $1,200 for one open on both sides. Installation can double the final figure. To keep costs down, choose a "zero clearance" type that can be framed with ordinary stud walls (instead of brick). For efficiency and warmth, choose a heat-circulating type that directs heated air back into the room.

**Painted drywall surrounds brick-lined steel prefab.**

## MANTELS

**A newly minted classic of oak.**

**A marble mantel in a reproduction style.**

**Plaster reproduction.**

Whether or not it frames a firebox, a mantel gives you a terrific opportunity to add architectural charm. Today, we seek highly decorative mantels, including reproductions of classic styles and authentic antiques, to take the edge off stark white rooms.

Among vintage mantels, both wood and marble types are fairly plentiful at architectural salvage companies. Wood will cost from $400 for a mantel on the plain side to $1,200 for intricately carved details. If refinishing is required, don't have it dip stripped or it may warp or cause "carved" details made of plaster to dissolve. As for marble, prices range from a low of about $4,000 (for a no-frills design) to a high of $12,000 for a rare, intricately wrought antique in mint condition.

Reproduction mantels in either wood ($1,000 to $2,000), plaster ($1,500 to $3,000), or marble ($5,000 to $8,000) are made in stock sizes. If you can't find an exact fit, it's often possible to alter the fireplace face to accommodate

**Restored, recycled marble.**

a replacement mantel that's slightly too big, but not one that's too small. Take the dimensions of the firebox opening when you go shopping.

A local mason can build you a mantel of brick or stone ($1,500 to $3,000 depending on size). But before you order, be sure to find out if you'll need to shore up the floor to withstand the mantel's weight.

# FLOORING

From vinyl to recycled heart-of-pine, there are more flooring options than ever. But every covering needs a good, strong foundation—a rock-solid subfloor.

## VINYL

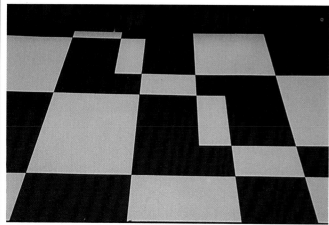

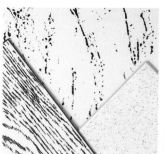

**Vinyl tiles mimic costlier stone and wood.**

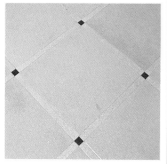

**For a fresh look, install sheet vinyl diagonally.**

**Easy-to-cut tiles permit customized patterns.**

**No-wax sheet flooring.**

For a smooth, strong surface, install vinyl over a plywood or hardboard underlayment. Tiles cost from $1 to $4 per square foot. Installation: $2.50 to $5 per square foot. Sheet flooring costs from $8 to $30 per square yard. Installation: $2.50 to $6 per square yard.

## CONCRETE

A thin layer of concrete over a concrete floor or even a wood one yields the look of stone when divided into "tiles" with metal strips and then sealed with polyurethane. Leave the job to a professional, though. The cost will be determined mostly by the hourly rate charged by local contractors.

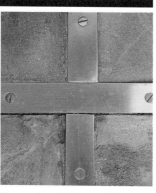

**Concrete with brass inlay.**

## CERAMIC TILE

Ceramic mosaics are factory-made into small sheets glued to a backing ($4 to $12 per square foot), so installation ($3.50 to $6.50 per square foot) is fairly easy. Choose from dozens of colors and patterns and several sizes and shapes: one- or two-inch squares, octagons, hexagons, or rectangles. As for grout, the cementlike filler between tiles, white is the most popular, but you can expand your design options with colored grouts. Glazed or unglazed tiles are both suitable, but glazed types are less prone to stain.

## WOOD

**Refinished pine planks.**

**Tongue-and-groove oak.**

**Parquet border tiles.**

You can have an old wood floor professionally refinished for from $300 to $400 for a 16-foot-by-20-foot room. New strip flooring costs from $4 to $8 per square foot (installation: 60 cents to 85 cents per square foot). Strips are typically 2¼ inches wide; planks, 3 to 8 inches. Parquet ($3 to $5 per square foot) comes in prefabricated foot-square tiles. Installation adds $1.50 to $3 per square foot.

# GLASS BLOCK

The renovator's favorite building block, opaque glass dividers and walls have moved into homes in a big way. Adding light, air, and architectural character, glass block still defines rooms and space.

**Interior windows let in the light, day or night.**

**Serpentine glass block embraces a dining room, masks a poor view, and filters the light.**

**Glass block marries a ziggurat wall.**

**Lighting a stair landing.**

Once reserved for factory windows, glass block is now a bona fide home renovation material and a welcome alternative to the conventional window and the standard stud wall—exterior or interior. Although clear glass block is available, most people choose from a wide range of textured, rippled surfaces that maintain privacy yet let room-enlarging light pass through.

Pattern choices are increasing all the time, and some companies are even offering red-, blue-, and green-tinted glass blocks. Most glass blocks ($22 to $25 per square foot, installed) are 6, 8, and 12 inches square and 4 inches thick, but rectangular block is also available.

As with concrete block or brick, installation requires a skilled mason. But for a straight-run wall you can keep costs down by having three- or four-foot sections preassembled at the factory. Curved walls will have to go up one block at a time. Remember, glass blocks are as heavy or heavier than brick. Make sure sills and floors can stand the weight.

**A translucent and waterproof tub enclosure.**

# GREENHOUSES AND ATRIUMS

A quick and relatively inexpensive room addition, an attached greenhouse weds the indoors with the sunshine, adding space, light, and —need it or not—solar heat.

For about a third of the cost of a carpenter-built room addition, an attached greenhouse or sunroom extends your livable space beyond the exterior walls. Most are manufactured as kits that are shipped in pieces to the site. You can order what you want from catalogs, then hire a local distributor or contractor to put the greenhouse together in a day or two. For a prefabricated small to medium-size lean-to greenhouse, prices range from about $3,000 for an

aluminum-frame kit to $10,000 for one framed in wood (excluding installation). Depending on local building codes, plan on spending another $1,200 to $2,000 for the footing, foundation, and floor. A custom-built atrium will cost two to three times as much as a kit. To keep costs down, incorporate stock windows, doors, and skylights into the design.

A greenhouse makes a great passive solar collector, especially when facing south. Depending upon where you live, it could cut heating bills by 20 to 30 percent. Whether or not you want the passive solar benefits, keep these points in mind:

● Double glazing—two panes of glass with insulating dead air trapped between them—will save energy all year long by keeping warm air in and cold air out during winter months and vice versa during summer months.

● You'll need some sort of shading system to control heat build-up, especially in the summer—interior blinds or shades, or exterior trees or vines.

● Except in small attached greenhouses (say, eight feet by ten feet), you'll probably have to extend heating and air-conditioning ducts into the new room for year-round comfort.

**Mini blinds between glass panes control heat gain.**

**Waterfall profile of an aluminum kit greenhouse is compatible with almost any architectural style.**

**Custom-built sunroom was constructed with ready-made windows and doors.**

# HARDWARE

## More than merely functional, these elements can fine-tune a renovation with high-profile color, style, and ornamental detail.

### DOOR AND DRAWER PULLS

Design and material choices are practically unlimited. New handles can transform the character of existing cabinets for a minimal cash outlay ($1 to $3 each). If you're ordering new cabinets, remember that handles and pulls are ordered separately.

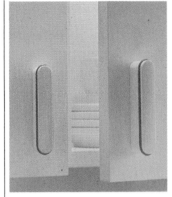

**Rubber rings run color around plastic handles.**

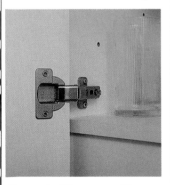

**Contemporary form meets traditional brass.**

### HINGES AND LATCHES

Install touch latches (about $2.50 to $3 each) on cabinet doors and you can eliminate handles and knobs altogether. Pressing on the door automatically trips the latch. One advantage is that you'll never have to clean around cabinet handles again.

Concealed spring-loaded hinges offer the same easy maintenance, plus giving a smoother look to cabinet faces. The spring helps to open and close the door. That's a feature you'll appreciate when both hands are full. Many new cabinets now offer these hinges as standard equipment. To retrofit old cabinets, buy the hinges at hardware stores (about $2 to $3 each).

**Concealed European hinges are now available here.**

### DOORKNOBS

Even new doors do not usually come with hinges, knobs, latches, or locks. You have to order them separately. Whether American-made or imported, all knobs will not fit all doors, so check dimensions.

Knobs usually come in sets of two with latch and striker plates included for from $50 to $125 per set. If it's for an entry door, make sure it has a built-in lock (preferably a dead-bolt type). Although knobs are standard fixtures on American doors, some European models favor levers. U.S. manufacturers are now turning out lever sets in both contemporary and reproduction styles ($100 to $200). Door hinges—in steel, brass, chrome, or wrought iron—are sold separately as well, usually in pairs ($4 to $15).

Spend your money on doorknobs, handles, towel racks, and other up-front details, then feel free to spend less on hinges and other behind-the-scenes hardware.

**The classic brass knob: pure-and-simple beauty.**

**For interior doors, brass knob, skeleton-key plate.**

### BATH HARDWARE

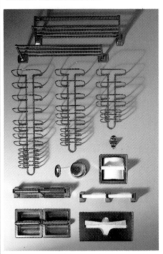

**Grand Hotel accessories are now available for the home.**

Soap dishes, towel bars, toothbrush holders, and tissue dispensers can be ordered from hardware outlets, bathroom dealers, or sink, tub, and tile manufacturers. Because some are designed to be recessed into the wall, have them on hand before renovation begins. Otherwise, you'll have to cut through freshly finished surfaces to install them.

**The French-style lever is an elegant alternative.**

# HEATING AND COOLING

For a made-to-order indoor climate, button up your house against the elements. The money you save can then go toward improvements that show.

## HEATING

If your house is cold, it's probably less the fault of your heating plant than it is of the house itself. Before you buy a new furnace or boiler ($800 to $2,000, depending on size), take the following steps:

● Insulate. If your house is more than 30 years old, it may have no insulation at all. Most homes more than 15 years old don't have enough. Following the recommendations of your local building department can trim heating costs by as much as 20 to 40 percent.

● Weatherstrip around doors and windows. Added together, a multitude of tiny gaps can equal the size of an *open* window.

● Caulk around doors, windows, and foundations to keep air and moisture out. Moisture renders insulation ineffective.

● "Balance" forced-air systems by installing or adjusting dampers in ductwork so rooms heat evenly. In steam or hot water systems, replace worn-out radiator valves and then adjust each one to balance the system.

● Install an energy-saving clock-controlled thermostat that automatically turns the furnace (or air conditioner) off and on to suit your needs through the day.

● Have your furnace cleaned and have the burner's flame adjusted to cut energy costs by 10 percent at least.

● Insulate around hot water, steam pipes, and forced-air ducts that pass through unheated attics, basements, or crawlspaces.

● Add a humidifier. Moist air feels warmer.

## COOLING

You can add an air-conditioner or integrate one into your forced-air system for from $1,000 to $2,500, depending on the size of your house. But you can also make your house easier to cool just by adding an attic fan (to keep hot air from radiating into rooms below) or a "whole house fan" (to vent hot air out of the house, then into and out of the attic).

## HEATING AND COOLING

Except in severe winter regions of the country, a heat pump can be an economical alternative to a conventional furnace and air-conditioner. It efficiently combines the features of both. In winter, it absorbs heat energy from cold outside air and transfers it to the house. In summer, the process is reversed for cooling.

## CEILING FANS

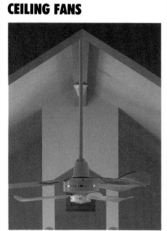

**For lofty spaces, a fan for all seasons.**

Surprise: ceiling fans can help heat your home as well as cool it. And they're particularly valuable for bringing warmed air down in high-ceilinged rooms. To work, however, the fan must have a bidirectional motor (it's the reverse speed that pulls cool air up and bounces warm air off the ceiling). It should also have a variable speed control that works like a dimmer switch, from slow to fast. You can mount a ceiling fan on an existing electrical ceiling box. But if you're hanging one on a sloped ceiling, be sure to ask for a "ball mount." Good-quality fans cost between $150 and $250.

## WOOD STOVES

Wood-burning stoves have all the charm of conventional fireplaces but are much easier to install and more energy-efficient. Check your local building codes before you buy, though. Some areas outlaw them for environmental reasons. Others require specific noncombustible materials below or behind them.

If you covet an antique stove, be absolutely convinced it has been meticulously restored. If it isn't airtight, it won't be efficient. If period charm is what you're after, newly minted reproductions of antique styles abound.

Prices range from about $800 to $1,200 for a cast-iron reproduction to $2,000 for a European import sheathed in ceramic tile.

Take into account the cost of installation, including new flues, chimney, hearth, and roof flashing. And remember, some building codes and insurance companies won't sanction the work unless it has been done by a professional contractor.

**A black iron wood-burner on a high-tech hearth.**

# LIGHTING

Comforting and romantic, welcoming or working, lighting has enormous impact on a room's moods. A whole spectrum of fixtures—new, restored, and reproduction—is now readily available, from sconces to track lights.

# LIGHTING *(cont.)*

The time to think about lighting is early, not later, when you discover that adding an on/off switch means ripping the walls apart. Indirect lighting especially requires early planning, since it is often integrated into walls and ceilings.

## SCONCES

**Nouveau deco: a frosted bowl on a black bracket.**

**White plaster provides light and architecture.**

**New wave: starship shape in frosted acrylic.**

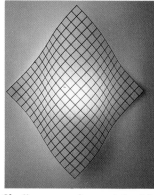

**Shoji-screened: a metal grid and fiberglass "paper" yield a mellow glow.**

**Shallow, sliver-thin metal dish hugs the wall.**

Wall sconces look right when wired directly into an electrical box recessed into the wall (no cord snaking down to an outlet). But that means early planning, when the walls are still open to new wiring. Otherwise, an electrician will have to "fish" new wiring up through the floor and walls to power a new fixture, a time-consuming, messy procedure that can also get expensive.

Sconces can supplement or even replace overhead fixtures and table and floor lamps. But think about more than shape and color. What kind of illumination do you need and where do you want the light to go? Some sconces will provide only up-lighting. Others have frosted bowls that

**A frosted glass funnel banded with a glossy white metal lip.**

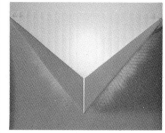

**Sculpted light: perforated vee creates its own aura.**

aim light out as well as up; still others shine up and down but not out. Up-lighted sconces best emphasize architectural details—cove ceilings, beams, cornices, columns, and archways. For more general illumination, choose sconces with light-emitting fronts and/or

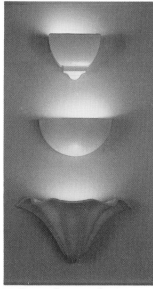

**Wall art: shapes of your choice in plaster.**

sides. Very few sconces come with built-in on/off switches. Consequently, you must also plan for the installation and placement of wall switches. Ask the electrician to provide two or more switches that will control all the wall- or ceiling-mounted fixtures in one room, especially in big rooms with two or more entrances. Also, specify rheostats (dimmers) on all switches so you can precisely adjust the level of light.

Sconces cost as little as $25 for simple, quarter-moon types with incandescent bulbs, and as much as $800 for Italian imports outfitted with tiny halogen bulbs. Halogen bulbs, by the way, last up to seven times longer than the conventional kind and use half the power and produce half the heat. The size of a halogen bulb—about 2¼ inches long and ¼ inch wide—allows for very slim, wall-hugging lighting designs.

There's no hard and fast rule for how high to mount a wall sconce, as long as the bulb or interior is not visible. But remember: sconces will protrude 4 to 12 inches from the wall. In traffic areas, make sure you avoid collisions with heads and shoulders.

# CEILING FIXTURES

**Domesticated factory lights.**

**Halogen ceiling fixtures, mini spotlights under the shelf.**

If you're tight for space, or want to avoid decorative fixtures, think about installing recessed lighting into the ceiling, especially if you're replacing a ceiling and can easily run new wiring. These light sources ($35 to $90 per fixture) are all but invisible and can illuminate entire walls, which will then reflect light throughout the room.

Glass-globed factory lights ($80 to $120) are excellent for kitchen task-lighting as well as general illumination, because the bowls diffuse the light.

You can install a series of ceiling fixtures even without tearing out the ceiling. An electrician will drill a series of holes in the ceiling and the rafters and "fish" the wires up through a wall—it takes time but it's possible. After that, of course, the ceiling will need a lot of patching.

## SPOTS

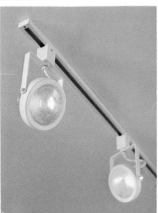

**Low-voltage track lights yield precise beams.**

**Wall-mounted halogen lamp for reading in bed.**

floods) if you can keep them somewhat hidden— they do tend to glare.

**A collar around a column all but conceals a $10 fixture.**

The beauty of track lights (besides being able to aim them) is that you can use a room's single existing ceiling outlet to electrify the track (available in two-, four-, and eight-foot sections). Fixtures (wide-beam floods or narrow-beam, low-voltage spotlights) go for from $35 to $120 each.

For up-lighting high ceilings, columns, and archways, you may be able to get by with inexpensive fixtures (either spots or

# MOLDINGS

Quick to dress up a room, moldings work as applied architecture. Painted wood, polymers, or other composition materials look every bit as good as plaster.

**A staircase restored with stock spindles and rails.**

**Vintage details, made of synthetics, yield the look of plaster.**

**A custom cornice made from stacked pine strips.**

Architectural details made of synthetic plaster come in an enormous range of shapes and styles—some brand-new, others authentic reproductions. With the new choices, adding ornamental detail becomes not only easy but irresistible. Options include ceiling medallions, cornices, garlands, capitals, and corbels. Of course, stock milled wood moldings are still appropriate, still plentiful, and still affordable at the local lumberyard. If you need to match vintage wood molding, a local millwright can make a "knife"

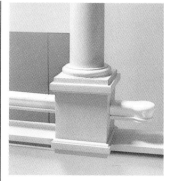

**Lumberyard remnants are cleverly combined.**

that will cut the same pattern as the original for from $75 to $100.

**Faux plaster moldings create an inviting entry.**

## CEILINGS

Ornamental details aren't limited to walls, of course. Try thinking of the ceiling as a fifth wall that can add new dimension and detail to a room. Among your choices are tin ceilings ($14 to $20 per two-foot-by-four-foot panel) and cornice moldings ($7 to $14 per four-foot section) in either authentic reproduction patterns or brand-new designs. They go up with screws and can be finished with a clear sealer (to prevent rust) or painted.

A less expensive but no less dramatic alternative is to use ordinary gypsum wallboard ($7 to $10 per

**Layered gypsum wallboard dramatically outlines a ceiling.**

four-foot-by-eight-foot sheet), cut, layered, and painted to create an on-

**Tin ceiling panels and cornices, made today.**

the-ceiling molding. Because gypsum crumbles when cut, use metal J-channels. The channels fit over the cut edges and disappear under two or three coats of drywall compound sanded smooth.

# NEW MATERIALS

Space-age synthetics and Old World staples hit the renovation marketplace every day. Many that were once reserved for historic mansions or sleek airports are now, thankfully, homebound.

Rich-and-thin slate for walls, floors, or counters.

Synthetic terra-cotta is the newest "stone" available.

The antidote for monotonous rooms is a rich and varied mix of surface and finishing materials. To meet renovators' unceasing demands for variety and problem-solving alternatives, manufacturers have invented some brand-new materials and adapted some old favorites for home use. Among them:

● Slate, granite, and marble. Once available only by the slab, they're now made in thinly sliced tiles ($8 to $15 per square foot) that can be used just like ceramic tiles—on floors, walls, and countertops. An even more affordable alternative is counterfeit stone. Some synthetics are made of real crushed stone reconstituted in an acrylic base and pressed in tiles. These are indistinguishable from the real thing and sell for a third to half as much.

● Vinyl. Soffit panels of vinyl can substitute for tongue-and-groove lumber used for exterior overhangs. For arbors, gaze-bos, and trellises there's wood-grained vinyl lattice ($45 for a four-foot-by-eight-foot sheet). Unlike wood, vinyl never needs painting, won't rot, and is unpalatable to wood-chewing insects. Even if you're dedicated to preserving or installing wood clapboard siding, it may be smart to install look-alike vinyl on high-maintenance areas around the house, especially on soffits and on window and door frames.

● Tambour panels. Grooved, four-foot-by-eight-foot sheets of tambour (like rolltop desk covers) are sheathed in plastic laminate, or wood or metal veneer. Because of their built-in flexibility, these sheets ($150 and up)

Weatherproof vinyl lattice never needs painting.

can be applied to flat or curved walls, cabinets, and columns to instantly hide a multitude of surface sins.

● Fiber ceiling panels. Once relegated to basement recreation rooms, the embossed fiberboard panels of suspended ceilings are better-looking than ever. The metal grids that hold them up are now almost invisible. Prices start at about $1 a square foot and even rank amateurs can master the tech-

Wafer-thin marble tile goes on floors and walls.

Laminated tambour panels for curved walls and columns.

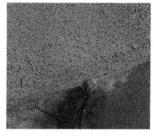

Grainy, brush-on surfacing renews cracked sidewalks.

For a plastered look, use embossed ceiling tiles.

niques for installing them in a couple of hours. Compared to replastering or replacing a defective ceiling with new gypsum board, suspended ceilings can be both cheaper and easier to install.

● Synthetic terra-cotta. Now being used to replace original terra-cotta details on landmark buildings, synthetic terra-cotta will undoubtedly make its way into the home renovation marketplace soon. Lighter, stronger, and far less expensive than the real thing, it's molded at the factory into balusters, cornices, brackets, and even columns.

# PAINT AND WALLPAPER

Decorative treatments—paint, paper, or both—can work for whole or partial walls, ceilings too. A word of caution: If you want the focus on your furnishings, go easy on elaborate backgrounds.

## WALLPAPER

**Reproduction patterns evoke period charm.**

**Paper borders: use with or without wallpaper.**

Except for the heaviest kinds, wallpaper is not a surefire solution for flawed walls. Before papering, patch dents and fill cracks with drywall compound sanded smooth. It's also a good idea to remove old layers before adding new wallpaper. A liquid remover is sponged or

**A Victorian favorite: embossed wallcovering.**

sprayed on and then the paper is scraped and peeled. Next, the wall is prepared with "sizing," a brush-on liquid that roughens the surface so the paper will stick to it. If possible, get prepasted wallpaper (water activates the adhesive). Otherwise, be sure to have the right adhesive—vinyl or wheat paste—for the paper you're using.

## PAINT

**"Combed" paint adds class to a tub enclosure.**

There's a paint for every surface, but no one type of paint can be used in every circumstance. Latex paint comes closest to being the universal coating. It's just as washable and almost as durable as oil-based paints and its dries more quickly. Spatters, spills, and tools can be cleaned up with water. But don't use it on raw wood or it will raise the grain (seal the wood with a priming paint first). And because latex is a water-based coating, it can cause newly painted wallpaper to peel away from the wall. Be certain the paint you're buying is suitable. The same goes for the tools: Cheap brushes or rollers aren't worth the money, and you need different kinds for different jobs (latex requires synthetic bristle brushes; natural bristles absorb water and droop). To make the job easier, paint a room in this order: ceiling, trim, walls.

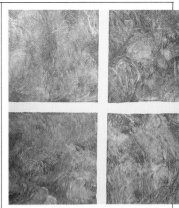

**Sponge-painted hardboard.**

Again, preparation is crucial. Reset popped nails and patch with spackling compound. Patch cracks and holes, and scrape loose paint. Wipe down or wash walls. Degloss shiny surfaces with liquid deglosser or fine steel wool.

With sponges or combs from the paint store you can even master decorative finishes yourself. For glazing or marbelizing, though, call a professional.

**A glazed wall and faux marble baseboard in a bath.**

**Pastel paints yield a subtle rainbow of rafters.**

# ROOFING AND SIDING

Shop around. Roofing can be the most expensive renovation you ever undertake, and the better the materials, the longer it lasts. Choose for the effect you want as well as long wear.

## WOOD AND ASPHALT SHINGLES

Cedar roofing and siding shingles age gracefully.

**Low-cost asphalt offers an enormous range of colors.**

Cedar shingles and shakes ($2 to $3 per square foot) weather naturally, need never be painted, will last up to 75 years, and can change the character of a house. Asphalt shingles are

**Mixed media: fish-scale shingles and clapboard.**

among the least expensive roofing materials (35 cents per square foot), yet will last up to 25 years. For both, installation adds about $1 per square foot.

## SHEET SIDING

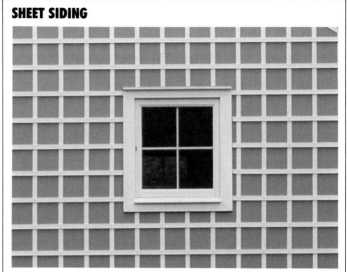

**Painted marine-grade plywood under an applied lath grid.**

Cover big areas fast with weather-resistant marine plywood ($80 per four-foot-by-eight-foot sheet) or ribbed galvanized steel ($14 for a three-foot-by-eight-foot panel).

**Galvanized steel.**

## STUCCO

**The look's adobe . . .**

Earthy colors and gritty textures give stucco a Mediterranean character. Brick, concrete block, or old stucco needs two coats of this plasterlike material. Wood or nonmasonry walls need a metal mesh and three coats. Made of lime, sand, and Portland cement, the real cost is in having it professionally applied. A

**. . . or stonelike.**

typical job: $8,000 for 2,000 square feet. Besides the Spanish mission look, stucco is appealing because it produces an impervious and seamless surface. Have the final coat tinted the color you want and you'll never have to paint.

## SLATE

Genuine slate ($250 per 100 square feet) requires a steep and extra-sturdy roof (get a structural evaluation from an engineer first) and will easily last from 50 to 100 years. An option: Supra-Slate (about $175 per 100 square feet) is a synthetic that looks every bit as good and is lighter and easier to install.

**Castle class: faux slate.**

# SINKS

New colors, shapes, and sizes mean these highly visible fixtures can now fit into the most exacting renovation plans—and look good while working hard.

## KITCHEN SINKS

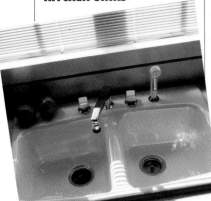

**Cast iron with twin bowls ten inches deep.**

Kitchen sinks come with one, two, or three bowls. Even with a dishwasher, some people prefer to have at least two bowls. Six-, seven-, and eight-inch bowls are most common, but one that's ten inches deep makes washing big pots and pans easier. In descending order of popularity, sinks are made of stainless steel, enameled cast iron, enameled steel, or porcelain on steel. If you want stainless steel (18 gauge is better than 20 gauge), choose one with a high chrome content—it'll age better and show fewer water spots. Cast iron's advantage is that it's more durable than steel, easier to clean, and less likely to chip. Also, choose a self-rimming sink—one that doesn't have a metal ring around it—or one that mounts under the counter.

All faucets will not fit all sinks. Make sure the fixtures will work together before you order.

Prices do vary for double-bowl sinks: less than $100 for enameled steel; $250 to $325 for stainless steel; $200 to $300 for cast iron.

**From a restaurant supplier, custom stainless steel.**

## BATH SINKS

**Vintage pedestal sink.**

If the sink will be set into a vanity, choose a self-rimming type. It's easier to install and keep clean. Prices range from about $100 for a plain white bowl made of enameled steel to $600 for cast iron or vitreous china. And be prepared: A faucet set can often cost as much or more than the sink itself.

Vintage models of pedestal sinks are fairly plentiful at salvage companies. And at $50 to $300, they seem like a bargain. But

**Self-rimming sink with a gooseneck faucet.**

restoring them—new porcelain glazing, new drainpipe, new faucets and handles—can double the price. Plus there may be other problems. Beware of charming old porcelain sinks with old handles they were not born with. Before you shop for a sink, take a look at the water and drainpipes in your bathroom. Most come through the wall. Trouble is, some old pedestals were designed to drain through a pipe in the floor. Naturally, you can rearrange the plumbing, but that will add to the price significantly.

**High-tech enameled steel.**

By comparison, faithful reproductions of the original pedestal designs, in several colors now, cost $400 to $800 (faucets extra).

If economy is a priority and imported tile or structural changes will eat up most of the budget, think about having your existing sink refinished. There are companies that will apply new porcelain to old sinks and tubs right in your home. You can even have a new color applied. Costs run

**Victorian reproduction pedestal sink.**

from $150 to $200 for a pedestal sink and $200 to $300 for a tub. The process takes just a few hours. True, it won't last forever, but most refinishers provide at least a three-year guarantee.

Stock vanities are available through kitchen cabinet or bath dealers. Most are about 34 inches high, which many consider too low for comfort. Ask the installer to add a 1- or 2-inch wood strip onto the bottom of the cabinet. The kickplate can be made to cover the alteration.

# SKYLIGHTS

Say good-bye to gloomy rooms: roof windows deliver up to three times the light of windows in the wall and fresh air to boot.

**Single units, side by side, positioned between roof rafters.**

Most rectangular and square skylights are designed to fit between existing roof rafters, so you can arrange them in rows if you decide on more than one. Round skylights are more dramatic, of course, but require more elaborate—and costly—alterations in the roof. Like regular windows, most skylights come preframed and ready to drop into place. It's a good idea to invest in a "venting" skylight, one that can be opened to provide air flow. Some are domed; others are flat. Either looks good from inside, but domed ones can look obtrusive from the outside. Some models actually rotate so that you can wash both sides from inside the house. Whether you choose glass or plastic,

**Depending on the pitch of the roof, a skylight can bring in a treetop view as well as natural light.**

specify double glazing to reduce heat loss and to help prevent condensation.

Standard small to medium-size skylights cost from $200 to $450. Installation adds from $200 to $500 each.

**Venting skylights let in light and release hot air.**

# STAIRS

It's now possible to build a new stairway—or restore an old one—with standardized, ready-made components that will help lower the carpenter's bill.

**Carpet-wrapped treads soften steel stairs.**

Depending on design, length, and materials, a custom-built stairway can easily cost from $8,000 to $10,000. Chances are you can repair and restore an existing one for from $1,000 to $2,500 or have a

or replace broken treads, risers, and weak spots. Even sagging "carriages" (the sawtooth-shaped side supports the treads rest on) can be jacked up and resecured to fix a sloping stairway. Missing or damaged balusters, rails, and

**Factory fresh: stock balusters, rail, post.**

**Riserless treads lighten the look of steel stairs.**

cheaper because there are no balusters and posts.

● Straight runs are usually less expensive than L- or U-shaped stairways or those that curve.

● Stock stairway components are widely available, although to some degree every stairway is custom built because it must be made to fit between two existing floors.

● If you plan on carpeting the steps, specify a

cheaper grade of lumber for the treads and risers.

Options: An open-riser steel staircase can cost less because it's assembled at the factory and delivered in one piece. Typical cast-aluminum spiral staircases cost from $2,000 to $4,500. Spirals take up relatively little space—often an area measuring only six feet square—but they're really only suitable for use as secondary stairways or mezzanine spaces.

**Custom oak staircase with turquoise grid balusters.**

new one made of stock components for from $3,000 to $6,500.

Groans, squeaks, and wobbly rails are fairly easy to remedy. The tough part is getting access to the bottom side of the stairs, a process that may require some demolition—messy but often necessary to fix

newel posts can be replaced (a millwright can match them to the originals or—less costly—you can buy new or reproduction components).

For new stairways, keep in mind the following:

● The more components, the higher the cost. An enclosed stairway is

**Curved stairway from a prefabricated kit.**

**For tight places: cast-aluminum spiral stairs.**

# STORAGE

Sometimes the need for more storage is reason enough to renovate. With clever planning, you won't need to sacrifice valuable living space to find more room.

**A bedside table disappears into a cabinet.**

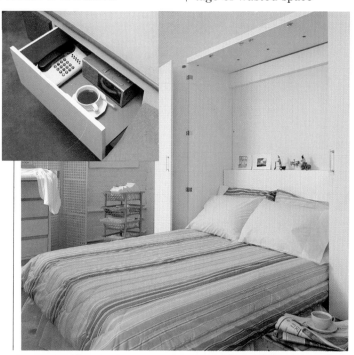

It may not be a glamorous subject, but good storage makes life lots easier. By organizing and holding the things that tend to clutter, well-planned storage can actually yield more livable space, reducing the need for storage furniture—armoires, chests of drawers, dressers, bookshelves, display shelves, and cabinets.

Naturally, a carpenter can build any kind of storage

**In a freestanding cabinet, the traditional Murphy bed can also be built in.**

units you want, and can build them to be taken out and moved as well. You can keep labor costs down by incorporating ready-made pieces into your plan. Frame around freestanding wall units (those sold as furniture) or stock cabinets to make them look built in. The same holds for Murphy beds, which can give you two rooms for the price of one. Take advantage of wasted space—

**Store-bought storage: wire shelves and baskets.**

under the stairs, over the washer and dryer, inside closets—by installing wire shelves, baskets, bins. Prefabricated closet organizers—adjustable shelves, racks, and rods—now come in so many sizes and configurations that you can use them to make almost any closet, pantry, or utility room more efficient.

Kitchen cabinet manufacturers are now making "appliance garages" that turn the space between cupboards and counters into concealed compartments for small appliances.

**Under-the-cupboard "garage" parks appliances.**

**Pop-up stepladder hides behind cabinet kickplate.**

**Mirrored, closed-door storage replaces bulky dressers and chests of drawers.**

# TILE

Long-lived, carefree, and classic, tile is the renovator's choice for almost any surface. Use it wherever color, texture, pattern, and pizzazz are needed.

## FOR WALLS

Out of the locker room and into the living room, glossy finishes and dazzling colors make ceramic tile a high-fashion alternative to paper, paint, and paneling.

**From Italy, high-gloss ceramic wall tiles.**

**A tile tapestry showers a tub enclosure with color.**

## MOSAICS

**Border patrol: outline a room in pattern and color.**

However intricate-looking, mosaics go down fast because most are factory-assembled into 12-inch-by-24-inch paper- or fiber-backed sheets. Specify your own pattern, color, and sizes and some manufacturers will assemble the sheets for you.

Available glazed or unglazed, in solid colors, graduated hues, and an enormous variety of patterns, mosaics are suitable

**Greek key pattern, a classic mosaic motif.**

for floors, walls, and countertops and cost from $5 to $12 per square foot. Professional installation adds another $3.50 to $6 per square foot.

**Different sizes create a customized design.**

## GLAZED VS. UNGLAZED

Impervious to water, grease, and stains, glazed tile is best for countertops (away from the stove though; hot pots can crack the glaze). Glazed tile is widely used on floors, too, but it can be slippery. Unglazed tile is usually less expensive, but it will absorb grease and stains unless periodically treated with a sealant. (It does, however, gain character with age.) Unless you're committed to having the flat-finish surface that only unglazed tiles can produce,

**Earthy and inexpensive Mexican clay pavers.**

**Glazed four-by-fours yield a plaid floor and platform.**

**Matte-finish glazed tiles on countertop.**

stick with glazed types. Matte-finish tile makes a good compromise. Cost: $3 to $8 per square foot, excluding installation.

To keep the grout (the porous cementlike filler between tiles) clean in areas that get lots of abuse seal it with a silicone sealer. Rough-textured and inexpensive clay tiles ($1.45 each for eight-by-eights) can be used indoors or out. A combination of moisture and freezing temperatures can make them crack, however, which makes them impractical outdoors in some climates.

**Curved tiles wrap up a ziggurat divider.**

# TUBS AND TOILETS

Today's baths are turning into home spas that put the emphasis on comfort—physical and emotional—as well as on convenience.

## TUBS

Whirlpool tubs are fast becoming standard equipment. Round, square, oval, octagonal, hexagonal, or rectangular, for the best soaking, get a deep one—24 to 30 inches. Remember: you'll need to reserve space for complex plumbing and a pump, which will need its own electrical circuit. You may also need to shore up the floor. Even

**Oak-trimmed reproduction.**

one-person tubs can top 1,000 pounds when filled. Cost: $2,500 for singles; $4,000 to $8,000 for tubs that will accommodate two or more persons.

If you crave an old-fashioned claw-foot tub, reproductions ($750 to $1,000) can be cheaper than buying and restoring salvaged vintage models.

New standard bathtubs of cast iron, steel, or fiberglass sell for $400 to $1,200. Of the three, cast iron is the best.

**A square fiberglass tub recessed into a platform (below).**

**The live-in tub: speaker phone, stereo, nine jets.**

**Well-preserved claw-foot tub required only new plumbing fixtures.**

## TOILETS

It's more difficult and more costly to rearrange waste lines than water supply lines. So try to retain the toilet's location and just replace the fixture. Otherwise the plumber must reroute the waste drain

**Low-rise Eurostyle toilet has an elongated profile.**

under the floor and tear open a wall to get to the stack pipe (the vertical waste line that leads to the sewer).

Most toilets are 14 inches high, but 16- and 18-inch models are available. Get an elongated version—called an "extended rim"—to better accommodate both sexes.

Among "siphon," "reverse trap," and "washdown" types, the first is the most efficient, effective, and quiet. Prices range from $250 for low-profile models to $700 for top-of-the-line, silent-flush types.

For tight places, toilets with triangular tanks take advantage of corner spaces and leave room for a larger tub or a separate shower.

**A triangular tank toilet makes use of corner space.**

# WINDOWS

Windows are see-through architectural elements that can instantly change the character of a room or even an entire house.

**Postmodern glass block frames steel French doors.**

**On target: a factory-made bull's-eye window.**

**Varied shapes, both indoors and out, delight the eye.**

• Consider the architectural style of your house, but don't be a slave to it. Contrast can be just as important as compatibility. Today, plenty of historically accurate windows are finding their way into ultramodern renovations.

• There is such an enormous range of reproduction styles available as stock windows—those that are factory-made in standard sizes—that only in rare circumstances will you need one custom made. Most quality types are made of wood. On some, the exteriors may be clad in either vinyl or aluminum (no painting). Typical

**Elegant half-round offers privacy and light.**

**Fanlight transom lends stature to an entry.**

double-hung windows cost from $200 to $600, depending on size. Bull's-eye, quarter-round, half-round, and elliptical windows start at about $200 for the smallest and

**Made-to-order Gothic fanlight window.**

**Etched glass pane evokes Victorian style.**

**French doors can turn into big windows.**

There are just too many wonderfully shaped windows on the market today to settle for run-of-the-mill replacements. Never before have renovators had such a vast assortment of architecturally rich shapes and sizes to choose among. Often, just one spectacular window is enough to com-

pletely alter the character of a room for the better, not only by bringing in more light and a worthy view, but also by adding new scale and dimension to the space. The final selection depends mostly on your personal taste and budget, but there are a few pointers worth remembering:

**Reproduction Colonials on bay, bumpouts, dormers.**

Generous Victorian-era double-hung bay windows are well worth restoring.

A two-story bay attached to the outside of the house.

**Factory chic: floor-to-roof steel-frame windows.**

All windows are labeled with U-values (the lower the better) and R-values (the higher the better).

● For doors and windows requiring special treatments, etched, leaded, or stained glass is available from glass suppliers, local artisans, or architectural salvage companies, not window manufacturers.

● Architectural salvage companies often have one-of-a-kind vintage windows that can be recycled.

**Vintage windows were recycled for kitchen cabinets.**

**Transoms set off shuttered French windows.**

go up to several thousand dollars for the large ones.

● For visual impact and variety, think about combining several shapes and sizes in one wall—French doors topped with a half-round fanlight, for example, or an elliptical transom over a single square window.

● Think big. In many cases, one grand and glorious window makes a bigger design statement than two or more small ones.

● And think small, too. In a stairwell, a bathroom, the gable-end of a room with a cathedral ceiling, or an entryway, or a dead-end corridor, a little bull's-eye or diamond-shaped window will sparkle like a lighted gem.

● Don't overlook steel-framed factory windows. Their industrial-strength design is practically timeless and they look good in almost any situation.

● Whenever possible, for energy conservation, invest in windows that are double-glazed. That is, windows that have from a half-inch to one inch of insulating airspace between two panes of glass. They may be more expensive than single-pane windows, but over time they'll pay for themselves in lower heating and cooling bills.

# INSTANT ACCESS
## A PRACTICAL GUIDE TO RENOVATION EXPERTS

The initial decision to renovate—to disrupt your home and life for the improved benefits to come—is tough enough. Even harder are the endless questions and choices that inevitably follow. Do you need an architect, a designer, or a contractor—and how do you go about selecting one? Which mortgage or home improvement loan makes sense? Where do you find that terrific reproduction wall molding you saw a few chapters back? Here are all the answers. This chapter is a complete and trustworthy roundup of the professionals and materials that will help you get the house you want.

# HOW TO HIRE AN ARCHITECT, INTERIOR DESIGNER, OR CONTRACTOR

Home renovation is one of those life dramas where the gods applaud good casting. You want to carefully choose whom you will spotlight for the duration.

It's clear you'll need an expert to help design and execute the changes, but what kind? Are you restoring? Renovating? Or just making a few improvements? Your choices are an architect, an interior designer, a contractor—or all three.

But finding and hiring the right ones can be tricky and intimidating, mostly because you're an amateur hiring professionals. So much depends on you: who you are, who you know, and how much advance planning you do—what all the experts we questioned, from coast to coast, call your "homework."

Before you set up that first interview, decide what you want and *why*. Be clear in your own mind about which problems the renovation should solve. Have a pretty good notion of what style, what look you're after. And (this above all) know how much you're prepared to spend. Your role in this limited partnership is that of producer (your money, your house); you have the power to put it all together. Whoever you hire is the director you'll depend on to guide you though the whole production—on cue, on time, and, one hopes, on budget.

Only you can write the scenario. With an approved, clearcut program—a script—you can understand your role, narrow that experiential gap, and know a great deal about what to expect along the way. You can stay in control of both cost and design, minimize risks and variables. You'll have earned your own applause at the final curtain, when the house is finally done.

## SCENE ONE: WRITE YOUR OWN TICKET

The budget comes first. *Metropolitan Home* design editor Donna Warner, a veteran of several renovations, was quick to respond when asked for her worst horror story: "The final bill," she said.

If you approach an architect or designer without a firm dollar amount in mind, you may get a superb design, but you're likely to find that you also can't afford it all—even when it's *exactly* what you wanted. Well, so's the Taj Mahal. Being unrealistic about money is not fair either to the professionals or to yourself. After deciding on a figure you can afford, make sure your budget includes a contingency or "flow" amount of up to 20 percent. No one will know what's behind that wall until it comes down. In renovating, the only rule is, "Expect the unexpected."

To help determine what amount you should spend, get an appraisal of the house from someone you know and trust in real estate. Will your investment be protected by the ultimate resale value? Will the neighborhood sustain it? No one can give you a guarantee, but this way you'll at least have a ball-park figure. Don't always be afraid to speculate—it depends on what you have.

## SCENE TWO: THE CURTAIN-RAISER

Decide what it is you want and keep your ideas visual. Cut out pictures from magazines, collect book photos. These will give you a mood, a flow, a spirit—many top-dollar ideas without cost. Compare notes. Are you and the design team all talking about the same things? Verbal descriptions and visual actualities can vary a great deal. It's important to express tangible *and* intangible needs, like an unarticulated longing for a space of your own, even a totally new way of life. "We ask clients to make up two lists," says designer John Saladino. "We ask for a must list, and a maybe list. The must list has to do with, 'I must have seating for ten and I am allergic to wool.' Or, 'I hate kelly green and I love white.' The maybe list is, 'I think I want a whirlpool bath, or a disco in the basement, or an exercise room on the third floor.' At any rate, those two lists are very helpful. It's a great start—you really have something to work with."

New York interior designer Kevin Walz reports that many clients come to him when they're going through life-changing phases. They want to start fresh, and their immediate environment is an area they can control. "A house is a kind of form of how people see their destiny," says Marin County, California, architect William Kirsch. "It also may be the most money they'll ever spend, and it can turn into a battle of wills."

One thing we've learned over the years is to hire professionals and then to trust them. Don't try to solve the problems or design the space yourself—that's the reason you're hiring a professional. But do study and analyze your day-to-day routines and needs in a way you can communicate to experts. Without these clues, all agree, they're designing mere space stations.

Look around you. Everything you see—your books, husband, hats, art collection, milkman, Lhasa Apso, wife, old Eames chair, new baby—is a clue. The photos in your scrapbook are clues. Taken together, they are the basis for your program, which is what you want for your house.

Approach the idea of renovation in the spirit of self-discovery, but make this one *tangible*. This isn't Jungian analysis; it's a house. Keep it in focus.

When your kids say they want more personal room, you may see a playroom and they envision what amounts to corporate headquarters. When the lady of the house wants a new entryway, she may really be talking about something else entirely. You may both agree on a "cozy bedroom," but one imagines a cave and the other a treehouse.

If you find you have opposing tastes or goals, don't panic. You're entitled to them. Often they're just the specific data a creative designer needs.

One designer had clients whose tastes really clashed. They had just gotten married and were remodeling a new condominium. But she detested his modern art collection and he hated her Louis

Quinze. "When the job was done," says Sonoma, California, interior designer Nancy Armstrong, "I'd been able to reconcile the tastes *and* the couple. They came to me and said I'd saved their relationship."

So: Work out details visually and do it together. It will save time, money, maybe even your marriage.

## SCENE THREE: AUDITIONS

At some point you just have to dive in, but if you've done that homework, you can try for a double swan instead of a belly flop. Design professionals rarely charge for "get acquainted" interviews. Pick up the phone and get started. Since architects and designers don't advertise (like doctors and most lawyers, they consider it vaguely undignified), begin with a little tribal networking. Ask friends and business associates for suggestions. Look up awards issues of architectural and design magazines. Drive around and look for renovated homes in your area that speak to you. Then ask who worked on them. You have to begin with a little hunch. Throwing darts at the *Yellow Pages* won't work.

You can call local chapters of the AIA (American Institute of Architects) or ASID (American Society of Interior Designers). They're ready with detailed "how to hire" worksheets geared to their respective professions, and the AIA has a list (the "matrix") of their members coded to special interests.

Equip yourself with all the practical and theoretical information you can. You might even go to the extreme of joining a night class like the one restoration/renovation expert Patrick McCrew teaches at the University of California Extension called "Interior Architecture and Design." You'll be exposed to a broader range of design options, make contacts, and acquire expertise all at once.

In Washington, D.C., the Remodelers Council of the National Association of Home Builders can send you brochures about contractors' services, what to look for, and what to ask for when you interview them.

Don't be afraid to request a list of previous clients from any of the professionals. If they're proud of their work, they won't hesitate to give you names and phone numbers of people they've done jobs for, and they might even offer to take you around to meet them. Then, check them out. Ask if the client would hire the same expert again. Check bank references and building materials suppliers to see if the companies are solvent, if they pay their bills.

With contractors, according to Bryan Patchan of the Remodelers Council, make sure they're licensed if your local jurisdiction requires it. Also ask if the contractor carries insurance, workmen's compensation, or property damage liability. If he doesn't, and if somebody falls off a ladder one day, guess who's responsible?

These guidelines apply equally to any structure, whether cottage, loft, town house, or condominium. It's the individual you hire, not the label, that's important. Do you *like* the person? Would you ask her to dinner, take him to a ball game? Whoever you select will become a temporary member of your family— with all the ups and downs that implies. The difference here is that you get

to choose your relatives. "An architect is the owner's alter ego," Kirsch says. "We're in the owner's camp, and that relationship should be strong and bonded. Personality is almost more important than talent."

And San Francisco contractor Jim Gongwer adds: "Remodeling is an act of violence that has to be performed with sensitivity. There's so much fear and anxiety in renovation. We're violating the existence of our clients. It's important for a contractor to have that sensitivity. When it's over, it's the most wonderful thing that could have happened—it's all worth it—but during the process, you're actually going to be living with that contractor. You'd better like him."

Don't forget this process is a two-way street—you're being interviewed as well. Be prepared for a little scrutiny.

"We do our own Rorschach test," one architect said. "We have a slide show that includes every look imaginable—horrible, beautiful, kitschy, minimal, goofy. We test client reactions. Maybe what they really want is a log cabin mood. Well, I can't get my head around that, so they really ought to be with someone else."

Show the designer your scrapbook and describe your needs. He'll show you the company portfolio and outline fee schedules. Ask what you can expect for that fee, the "scope of services," which varies, especially from specialty to specialty. Most architects charge from 15 to 20 percent of the total budget for their fee, but that includes drafting, rendering, blueprints, and other technical time and activity (acquiring permits, interpreting zon-

ing regulations) that are often billed extra by interior designers, who normally charge by the hour at between $40 and $125 per.

During the interview, on another level, be alert for a kind of chemistry that should be starting to percolate. Is there a meeting of the minds, a burgeoning enthusiasm that means creativity? You may be the type who wants someone to take over completely and you might want to collaborate closely through every phase. Are you making that clear?

"Some clients want their lives organized," notes Washington, D.C., architect Patrick Pinnell of Cass & Pinnell. "If you don't figure out who they are early on, or if you confuse them, you're likely to lose the job. I lost one by showing him too many options, the sort most clients find invigorating. I showed him five. This client was very busy, and not visually oriented. He wanted solutions, not options. It threw him into a panic and he went to someone else, a formula person."

Don't be chary of getting involved, though. "The ideal client wants to participate," advises Des Moines architect Cal Lewis of Charles Herbert & Associates. "He wants to be involved and have a reasonable feel for what we're after. He's analyzed his life-style not just for today but for the future, say, after the children have grown and left the house."

But there is still a broad spectrum between the *auteur* tyrant who "refuses to pass the baton" to anyone—including you, the client—and who will insist on perfection, and, at the other end, the *nouveau* organic-view architect who would just as soon see the rules of architecture self-destruct and send everybody out into a meadow to watch the way a tree grows.

Don't get lost in the parameters; you may never find your way out. We're in an "eclectic" period now, a freestyle kaleidoscope of options from a postmodern addition to rugged primitivism. The range isn't from excellent to mediocre, either. It's from what you want to what you don't want. Listen and learn.

## SCENE FOUR: REHEARSALS

By now, you're well on your way. You've studied your needs, decided on your "program" and budget, interviewed a few professionals, and developed a working scrapbook. Don't look now, but you're really enjoying it. This is probably one of the biggest investments you'll ever make, both in cash and quality of life. Now it's time to take that plunge.

Before you do, just step back and—one more time —study the options. It's time for fine tuning. For the same reason you probably won't take the lowest bid from a contractor (in this business you absolutely get what you pay for), you won't necessarily team up with the most aggressive architect or designer.

Test the waters. Say you've met one architect you really like and trust. Without making a major commitment, you can quite legitimately hire him for a preliminary study, for some sketches on which to base a cost estimate. Normally he will charge by the hour, or around 25 percent of the total projected fee, based on the agreed-to budget. (If your budget is $50,000, and his 15 percent fee will be $7,500, he'd charge maybe a quarter of that, or $1,875 for a preliminary study.)

As Santa Rosa, California, architect Jack Jones says, "It's probably the cheapest investment you can make, that beginning paper part. With it, you can ask a contractor for an estimate, not a bid but an estimate. You'll have something real

to measure against and you'll know if you're on track."

Also with the results of the preliminary study, you have something to take to the bank to bolster your loan application. Bankers are not gamblers. They want assurance that the house will be worth the money they're providing. Finally, with a sketch, you'll have an actual design to consider, not just talk.

Take stock of your position. Are you headed in the direction you envisioned? Has the architect or designer interpreted your stated needs and wishes, or has he or she gone into orbit? Now's the time to assess the relationship— before the commitment. Don't get caught up in the details. Back out now if you see warning signs.

## SCENE FIVE: CHARACTER STUDY

Take the time to evaluate the professionals you've met. Which one is right for you? Your project may require all three specialists, working as an all-for-one team, but even so, there will probably be just one your intuition has chosen. And it needn't follow the hierarchy of (1) architect, (2) interior designer, and (3) contractor. Sometimes the interior designer is chosen first, and he then hires the architect. That was a recent case with Ann DuPuy of New Orleans, when an Alabama client hired her by reputation and completely turned over the job to her. DuPuy became responsible for designing the interiors, buying china, linens, silver, and also for hiring the architect to remodel the house.

As for which design professional is the appropriate choice for your project, there are, of course, standard clichés to define the differences among them. These are as roughly accurate as any conventional wisdom. Architects tend to be intellectual, to enjoy theoretical or philosophical challenges. They're the aristocrats of the building trade, articulate and often prima donnas. They've earned it. Their training, experience, and responsibilities are awesome: B.A. and/or graduate degrees in architecture; between three and thirteen years' apprenticeship in the office of a registered architect before being eligible for their own registration exam. Architects must remain up-to-date on zoning restrictions, building codes, costs, contracts. They have expertise in fields as diverse as construction methods, mechanical and electrical engineering, building design, specification writing, drafting, rendering, ethics, and art history. They're likely to be more sophisticated and more innovative in interpreting what you want than interior designers, especially if that means an extensive, expensive project that must look good and work well on the inside *and* the outside. Architects are also likely to be more assertive. Say a client thinks he wants pink walls. In that case, says architect Cal Lewis, who usually undertakes all the interior decoration as well as the architectural design of his residential projects, "I'd better figure out why the client wants pink walls, then give him something that makes him as comfortable as he thinks pink walls would make him." In the end, of course, the client may just have wanted pink walls.

If you're looking for a mood, an image, a flattering color, you may find interior designers more simpatico. Architects are

the *Burke's Peerage* of building to the interior designers' *Vanity Fair*. Their specialty is interior illusion and problem-solving: how to restructure space with light, scale, color, perspective. In recent years, however, designers have been taking on more ambitious structural responsibility than their "decorator" antecedents, who mostly just chose paint color, wallpaper, and furnishings. In most urban areas—Chicago, Boston, Washington, San Francisco, New York, Houston, Los Angeles, Seattle, and so on—where multi-unit buildings vastly outnumber single-family homes, interior designers have come into their own. "In New York," says designer Kevin Walz, who is up to his eyeballs in renovations, "what else is there to do?" Pratt Institute-trained Judith Stockman, a New Yorker also, is a specialist in lofts and apartments. She has learned to deal with the problems that old city buildings turn up. "I did an ambitious project for a client who bought an apartment, then the studio next door to expand into," Stockman says. "After demolition, we saw something we didn't expect. We were turning the next-door studio into a master bath and dressing room and we knew where the pipes were, but they were installed in such a way that we had to raise the floor, and that cost money."

Designer fee procedures have been changing too. In the past, decorators were sometimes called "ten percenters," since their fee, paid by the client, represented the 10 percent discount they usually receive from retail stores and trade showrooms. This is still true in many cases, though designers are also being paid on an hourly basis that can range from $40 to $125 (and up) an hour. It covers the process of working with the contractor, architect, and subcontractors such as lighting designers and interior finishers.

The contractor is usually chosen by the architect or the interior designer, though most will agree to a client-chosen contractor provided they have veto power. "The architect is the agent of the owner," says New York architect Peter Shelton, "and the contractor is seen more as an adversary, someone who must complete the work on time in a quality way." The client wants a sensitive and caring contractor who won't trample gardens or damage furniture. The architect looks for a skilled expert who can fulfill his design dreams—ideally, these talents work for the good of all. If your architect specifies an intricate Japanese joining procedure, you'll need someone with that kind of skill, no matter how high the bid.

Many contractors can successfully complete small renovation projects on their own. "In San Francisco, the majority of remodeling jobs never see an architect," says Bay Area contractor Bruce Helmberger. "At eighty dollars an hour or so, it adds up quickly to a fee most people can't afford. If you have a sixty-year-old house and you want to take out some walls and add some skylights, a contractor will be fine. If you know what you want, chances are you won't need an architect." The key in working with a contractor alone is exactly that—knowing what you want.

Most are highly skilled at the mechanics and can tell you what is or isn't possible, but contractors are not trained to come up with innovative solutions.

Again, it's the individual, not the degree, that's crucial. If you have a one-family house on a valuable lot in a prime area and you want maximum structural change, go for an architect. If you live in a big city, you're probably only restructuring interior space, and if you want to maximize the resale value, then you'd be advised to hire one of the new, sophisticated breed of urban interior designers with contemporary expertise. If you have a comfortable older house or apartment and want to spiff it up, make it work until the kids are grown, or can't afford design fees, hire a creative, empathetic, reliable contractor. But the lines between these professions have gotten blurry here and there in the last few years. And none of these rules work if the design professional is unreliable or untalented. Trust the individual before you trust the rules.

## SCENE SIX: NO TIME FOR COMEDY

You've made your decision and now some money must cross some palms. Expect whoever you've chosen to write down detailed specifications, including every last nail and handle. Carefully monitor this process—you're the one who has to pay for it.

Now you're into working plans and drawings, and you've probably been asked to come up with a deposit that can vary from a few thousand dollars to 25 percent of the budget. The architect, say, will prepare blueprints and specifications; then either you, he, or the pair of you will choose certain contractors to bid on them. Don't automatically go for the lowest bid. The contractor may have "forgotten" thousands of dollars in cabinetry, and have to make up

the difference by cheapening construction or labor time. The attention you pay to costs will really pay off later—just watch the way it adds up. Set up your own financial worksheet and keep it *up to date*. Be wary. The contractor is dying to give you a low bid and you're dying to get one. If the majority of the bids come in far higher than your total figure for the project, be forewarned. You've probably underbudgeted and either need to scale back your plans or seriously reconsider your total cost.

Contract agreements will vary. There are no cut-and-dried rules to follow, because each job will be different. Most architects use standard form contracts suggested by the AIA that they modify for their own use. But whatever legally binding document is best for the circumstances, get a second opinion or consult an attorney or legal service before you sign.

Don't hesitate to go slow in the beginning; if you've got the right architect, designer, or contractor, they'll be as eager as you are to make it right.

You can ask for help and advice at any time. And now is the time, before somebody starts making mistakes, or you start changing your mind halfway through. Change-orders are very expensive, and contractors thrive on them.

"You hire pros because you need their help," Ann DuPuy says. "You're paying them, why not take advantage of it?"

## SCENE SEVEN: STRIKING THE OLD SET

"Home remodeling," one designer says, "is like giving birth, and takes about the same amount of time." One McLean, Virginia, woman described it as a metamorphosis, both painful and disorienting.

If you're like most of us, you'll be living in that house while it's disintegrating around you—only a few fortunates toss their house keys to a contractor and set sail for the Bahamas. If you do that, make sure you have complete confidence in the professional you've installed.

Take your time; listen and learn along the way; keep an open mind. Don't be disappointed if you have to adjust your vision somewhat after the bids are in—the right creative expert can make substitutions and still give you what you want. And don't expect miracles. Remember that this is an emotional experience. Your taste and values are being highlighted. Are you prepared to have your taste monitored or questioned? You want to choose professionals whose standards and tastes dovetail with yours, because you're going to want a lot of the credit. ("How do you like this place?" Woody Allen says in *Casino Royale*. "I hired a decorator, but of course I worked with her.")

If your architect asks for an hourly fee rather than a fixed one, it may mean he's uncertain about you—and that uncertainty communicates. "An hourly fee is often more equitable," suggests architect Ed Farrell. "The client is an amateur trying to act like a professional, but he really knows nothing about architecture. I might end up standing on my head until he decides I've gotten it right."

Negotiate your program with your designer or architect. He will know solutions that might not have occurred to you. Best of all, after hiring the right experts, you get to stop worrying so much. They know what to do *next*.
*by Beth Coffelt*

# HOW TO FINANCE YOUR RENOVATION

**A** decade or so ago, renovation didn't seem worth it. If you outgrew a house, you simply moved on to a new one. Logically, bankers were infinitely suspicious of the investment value of "remodeling" loans, and money was hard to find. Not so anymore. Today costs are so high that the rationale for undertaking a substantial project is persuasive, not only to homeowners, but to bankers as well. Renovation makes great economic sense. As a direct result, the number of financing options is growing, and lenders have become eager for your business.

The first step is to think like a banker or a potential buyer: assess your house's standing in the neighborhood. If it is the most expensive, a major home improvement project may price it out of the market. But if it's one of the least expensive on the block, you can accomplish substantial work and get much of your money back when you eventually sell. Most large projects are financed by a loan that is secured by the equity in the house. Usually a lender will multiply the market value of your home (which you can learn from local real estate agents familiar with the area) by 80 percent, then subtract the outstanding balance on your mortgage. For example, if your house is worth $150,000, and you have a $65,000 mortgage balance, you could borrow up to $55,000. If you're purchasing a house with the idea of renovating right away, the usual route is to take on a first mortgage for the house as well as another loan (second mortgage or whatever you end up choosing) to finance the renovation. That gives you a rough idea of how much of a project you can afford. You can then begin making concrete plans.

Here are some general guidelines of how much common projects are likely to run, and it comes with the predictable caveats. Costs vary. Everywhere. From place to place and from day to day. It's more expensive to buy oak flooring in California, for instance, than it is in New York, because oak is more scarce on the West Coast. It will cost more to get that floor installed in a large city than in a suburb because urban labor runs higher. The bottom line will depend on what kind of flooring exists in your house in the first place—how tough is the job of putting in the new oak floor? You get the idea. Given the flexible parameters, here are the averages:

**KITCHENS:** Using the existing floor space, a revamped kitchen will cost about $10,000—assuming you are just replacing the appliances, cabinetry, counters, and installing a new floor. Once you begin updating electrical and plumbing sources, however, or adding floor space from adjoining areas, a new kitchen can easily cost $20,000 or more. That's great if you're an enthusiastic cook and you really want that kitchen. But it's not necessarily a good investment. As a rule of thumb, figure that if you spend more than 10 percent of the value of the house, you may not get back your money on resale. Balance your current desires with any future selling plans.

**BATHROOMS:** Expect to pay $4,500 for a simple full bathroom with a tub. A more luxurious room, with twin sinks and a sunken soaking tub for two, can cost from $8,000 to $15,000—or more. Again, it depends on your design, the fixtures and materials you choose, and, of course, the cost of labor for installation. But there are lots of possible trade-offs here, as elsewhere too. If you opt for an inexpensive sink, you can afford the hand-tiled floor. If you choose a less expensive vinyl floor, you can add the soaking tub to the budget. There's no need to settle, but there is need of compromise.

**ADDITIONS:** A simple, unadorned 12-foot-by-14-foot addition runs about $15,000. If you include a fireplace, figure another $4,000 to $5,000.

**SWIMMING POOLS:** These vary widely in price. A 24-foot-diameter, above-ground pool might set you back about $2,000, while a 16-foot-by-32-foot in-ground may cost $10,000 to $18,000, depending on the material of the shell. Future buyers might well worry about the cost and effort of maintaining a pool, so make sure you're installing it for your own enjoyment.

Once you have an idea of the scale of your renovation, and perhaps with an architect's preliminary sketch in hand, you can begin shopping the banks, S&Ls, credit unions, and the like for the deal best suited to your circumstances. Here are the choices.

## SECOND MORTGAGES

Traditionally, second mortgages are the bread and butter of the home improvement business, and they're the popular choice for funding a large renovation, whether you've already got equity built up in the house or you're just moving in.

Typically, you can expect to pay 1 percent to 2 percent more than the going rate for first mortgages. In the past year or two, the range for seconds has been around 12 percent to 15 percent. You can reduce that rate if you'll agree to share the interest rate risk with the lender. When interest rates began spiraling in 1979, many banks and savings institutions found themselves in trouble. They were stuck with low-interest-rate loans that had long periods left on them. As an inducement to get borrowers to share the risk of rising rates with them, the banks offer discounts on variable loans.

Flexible seconds have not come into as widespread use as adjustable-rate first mortgages have. Few borrowers want the inherent risk, and a renovation project doesn't usually have the same urgency as buying a home.

Of course, just as with variable-rate first mortgages, variable seconds do not necessarily set up a limitless risk. For one thing, the interest rate is recomputed only occasionally—usually every six months or on every anniversary of your loan. Moreover, there's no prepayment penalty, so if you sense that interest rates are about to take off, you could renegotiate the loan. The drawback is that you'd then have to pay substantial costs.

Variable seconds are best if you intend to pay off your loan in a comparatively short period. For example, if you are borrowing $20,000 to redo the kitchen and you believe you can repay the full amount in three or four years, a variable will probably prove less expensive —even if rates rise during the time of repayment.

If you are willing to gamble on a variable, you can usually drive a good bargain. Rates are as much as two or three percentage points less for variable seconds as for fixed-rate.

Whichever type you choose—fixed or variable —you will encounter the same sort of closing costs that you incur with other loans secured by real estate. Expect to pay one to three "points"—each one being equal to 1 percent of the amount of your loan—plus a discouraging array of other fees and charges. You'll need to get an appraisal of the property, which the lender generally attends to. That can cost $100 or more. A title search can add another $125, and insurance on the loan $25 or so more. An attorney is a necessity to help you close the loan, and typical legal fees range

from $200 to $400. You also face a variety of annoying smaller charges, such as filing fees and the cost of a credit report. Comparison shopping is imperative. Just as interest rates vary dramatically among different institutions within one metropolitan area, so do costs. The points you have to pay for the loan—by far your biggest expense—fluctuate the most, depending on how much money a lender has available at the moment. The looser funds are, the fewer points you'll be required to pay.

Not only do you need significant equity in your house to get a second mortgage, you must also have a good credit rating. There should be no liens, defaults, or judgments, nor should you have neglected many outstanding payments for more than 30 days.

## GOVERNMENT LOANS

Anyone with little equity and a less than sparkling credit record still may be able to get the required money. The Federal Housing Administration's Title I program lets you borrow up to $17,500 for home improvements, and if you are purchasing a place that needs rehabilitation, you can borrow up to $67,000 ($90,000 in some high-cost areas) through the 203(k) program to cover both the first mortgage and the renovation.

Title I and 203(k) loans come from conventional lenders. The government insures them. Since the lending institution has no worry about default, it typically may charge about half a point less interest than would be the case with an uninsured loan. Besides, FHA borrowers don't have to pay appraisal or title fees. As long as you have a steady income and haven't defaulted on any previous government loan, you're likely to get the money for which you apply.

The difficulty lies in finding an institution to lend you the money. Many lenders don't want to bother with

the paper work that FHA loans entail, and thus don't participate in the Title I or 203(k) programs. You'll need to shop around.

## REFINANCING

Paying off your old mortgage and taking out a new, larger one at a lower rate can, under some circumstances, be as effective as taking a second mortgage. Since the rates for first mortgages are lower than for seconds, you might be able to raise money less expensively. However, refinancing is feasible only if you bought your house when interest rates were stratospheric—primarily between 1979 and 1982. That's because when you refinance you must pay points on a larger loan than you would if it were only a second mortgage. Here's a typical example. One couple bought their $90,000 house in 1981. They got a $60,000 mortgage at 14½ percent, with monthly payments for principal and interest of $735 a month. Now they need $30,000 for an addition that would include a second living room, bedroom, and bath. With a second mortgage, they will have to pay $600 for the two points the bank is charging ($30,000 times 2 percent), plus other closing costs. By refinancing, their charges will soar to $1,800 ($90,000 times 2 percent), plus the other costs. However, by refinancing they can get the full $90,000 loan at 11½ percent, so their monthly payments will be only $891. If, instead, they got a $30,000 second mortgage at 12½ percent, and kept their 14½ percent first loan, their payments would go up to $1,105 a month.

As a guideline, figure that refinancing is most economical when it lowers the interest rate on your mortgage by at least two percentage points.

## HOME EQUITY LOANS

This innovation in home improvement financing— it's about seven years old —is a big advance in several important respects. It can be a surprisingly convenient method of paying for a renovation—or just about any other substantial expense you might encounter (except buying stocks or bonds, which is not permitted).

Because you use only the money you need, when you need it, you don't pay ongoing interest on a large, unnecessary sum. For example, say you are planning a $20,000 project that includes building a garage, landscaping, and constructing a patio and gazebo. It might take several months to decide just what you want, find the contractors or architects to draw up plans, and then search out the best financing. If you were finally ready to close on the loan in late February, for example, you could have that $20,000 waiting to be spent for months before the job got started, let alone finished. Work might not begin until the ground thawed in April, and it might be August before it was completed. With a second mortgage, you could have spent over $1,000 in interest during that five- or six-month period. The costs with a home equity loan would have been a fraction of that.

Home equity loans, which are like revolving charge accounts, are especially appropriate for large projects. You can pay for work as it is completed. When the electrical contractor finishes, you write him a check. Same with the carpenter, plumber, and painter. Some may require you to pay a portion of the costs up front. That's also easy.

With a home equity loan, you receive a checkbook. Most lenders insist that your checks be for $500 or more, but, of course, it's simple enough to put multiples of that amount in your bank account and then pay smaller bills from it. The check-writing feature allows you to spend precisely the money you need, and that is all you're charged interest on.

Home equity credit lines are being offered by a growing roster of banks, S&Ls, large brokerage firms, and even some credit unions. As with second mortgages or refinancing, the maximum you can get is based on the worth of your house. However, because repayment is much looser, some institutions let you borrow only up to 70 percent, not the customary 80 percent, of the difference between your home's market value and the amount of your first mortgage.

The interest rate on a home equity loan is adjustable, typically changing each month. The lender pegs the rate to some index. For example, an institution may charge two percentage points more than the current average prime rate.

Because your home is the collateral for an equity loan, you are liable for many of the same costs that you'd pay with a second mortgage. You can expect to be charged for the appraisal and the title search, which together may run $300. You also have to pay points, and they are figured on your entire line, not just the amount you use, so it is unwise to sign up for significantly more than you are likely to need. Unlike other home loans, there's a $35 to $45 annual membership fee with a home equity line, intended to pay administrative costs each year. The one significant saving is in lawyers' fees. There are none.

Be prudent with an equity loan, though. Remember that you are pledging your house as security. If you fall behind in your payments, the lending institution can consider you in default. When that happens, the lender is entitled to accelerate the loan, meaning you must pay the entire principal and interest. If you can't, you risk having the lender foreclose.

Because they are letting you have access to a comparatively large amount of money with a relatively unstructured loan, lenders are cautious about who qualifies for such a credit line. You should have worked at least two years in the same profession and preferably with the same firm, and have a lengthy and flawless credit record. Your debts must be manageable. In most cases, that means total payments —including the credit line —of less than 36 percent of your income.

The danger with most home equity loans is the seductively easy repayment schedule. Many lenders charge interest only. Others include part of the principal as well as interest in the minimum monthly payment that they require. If you are paying only interest, you need to have the self-discipline to regu-larly pay off part of the principal as you go along. Otherwise, when your credit line ends, usually in 10 to 15 years, you'll owe the full amount of the loan. If you can't pay, you could lose the house.

## UNSECURED PERSONAL LOANS

While seconds and equity lines are excellent ways to borrow large sums, you will find them prohibitively expensive for a modest project. Say you are planning to spend $2,500 to upgrade a bath, or $4,000 to have a new roof installed. You would not want the expense of a loan that was secured by your house because you'd have to pay closing costs.

As a rule, if you need $5,000 or less, you are probably a candidate for an unsecured loan. The simplest loan of all, it is guaranteed by only your signature. You can get the money in just a few days, based on the lender's estimate of your ability to repay. Because the institution doesn't have an iron-clad assurance that you will repay—as it does when it can attach your house if you default—you face substantially higher interest rates, typically at least three percentage points more than with seconds or home equity loans. But your savings in fees on a small loan more than outweighs the higher rates.

## OTHER OPTIONS

Although most home improvement loans are either secured by your house or are unsecured personal loans, it pays to consider alternatives that may provide lower rates and more flexibility. For instance:

**YOUR FAMILY:** Approaching your parents or doting Uncle Harold can be the ideal way to get a loan. It's generally inexpensive and need not be secured by collateral. Moreover, on interest-free loans of up to $10,000, the lender is exempt from federal gift taxes on the loan's annual uncollected interest. (One person can also *give* another up to $10,000 a year with no tax consequences. So, your parents could give you up to $40,000 without paying any obeisance to the taxman.)

You might, for instance, borrow $10,000 from your family. An appropriate interest rate might be 10 percent, which you could adjust up or down annually to reflect, say, money market rates. The assumption is that Uncle Harold might have stashed that cash in a money fund if he hadn't lent it to you. You wouldn't necessarily put a term on the loan. But scheduling regular payments is advisable, and at least once a year, either the borrower or the lender should prepare an accounting of the loan's status.

Borrowing from the folks has drawbacks, of course. In exchange for cheap credit, you run the risk of ruining a family relationship. To lessen the strain, you might want to draw up a promissory note, using forms available at many stationery stores.

**WHOLE LIFE INSURANCE:** One of the best ways to raise money at bargain rates is to borrow against your whole life policy's cash value. The amount that's available will depend on the number of years that the policy has been in effect, your age when it was issued, and the size of the policy's death benefit. But you don't have to disclose your reason for the loan, and you can repay at your own pace—or not at all.

In general, you need to have been building your policy's cash value for seven or eight years to borrow at 6 percent. Policies in effect for as few as four years often guarantee rates as low as 8 percent.

Older whole life policies provide access to sizable loans. For instance, a 50-year-old man with a $50,000 policy that he bought in 1969 most likely has built up a cash value of more than $10,000. To borrow that amount, all he has to do is fill out a loan form available from his insurance agent. The rate, typically 6 percent, is stated in the policy. Of course, if you die without retiring the loan, the remaining principal and compounded interest is subtracted from the policy's proceeds.

### CORPORATE SAVINGS PLANS:

Employees at many companies can get below-market loans from their firms. A growing number of company-sponsored savings and profit-sharing funds now let vested employees borrow against their balances in the plans. Most companies base their loan rates on indexes of, say, interest on long-term corporate bonds. Repayments are usually made by payroll deductions.

Federal pension laws place several restrictions on how much you can borrow from your savings plan, though. If you have been thinking of taking such a loan, now is a good time to do so. The proposed tax-law change would restrict your ability to take out money. Right now, you can borrow up to $50,000 against a profit-sharing, savings, or 401(k) salary reduction plan as long as the loan amount doesn't exceed half your benefits. The proposal President Reagan sent to Congress would restrict any new loans you take out to $50,000, minus

the highest amount you owed during the previous 12 months. The idea is to prohibit employees from owing their companies up to $50,000 year after year. If you leave the company, the outstanding balance of your loan is simply subtracted from your nest egg before it is turned over to you.

If you must do so, this is also the time to turn to your individual retirement account for assistance. You cannot borrow against an IRA, but you can withdraw your money early (before you are 59½). Now, there's a 10 percent penalty for early withdrawal, but if the President's tax proposals are enacted, it would increase to 20 percent.

### ASSET AND MARGIN ACCOUNTS:

If you have a sizable portfolio of stocks or bonds, you may be able to use it as collateral for a loan to complete a home improvement project. Borrowing on margin is a service traditionally offered by brokers to clients who pledge a portion of their portfolio as collateral to buy additional stocks and bonds. But you can also get securities-backed loans by opening an asset management account at most brokerage houses and at many large banks.

The amount you can borrow depends to an extent on the type of securities you pledge, and their market value. In general, you can borrow up to half the value of your securities. The interest rate you pay is variable, usually about 1½ percentage points above the so-called broker loan rate that banks charge to brokerage firms. Margin accounts are open-ended, which means that you don't have to repay principal or interest as long as the market value of your stocks is at least 30 percent of the margin loan amount. Interest usually is charged to your brokerage account and compounded once a month. Of course, security

prices usually fall when interest rates rise. Since the margin rate is adjustable, you could take a hammering if rates went up. Not only would you have to pay higher carrying costs, but you might also have to meet your broker's demands for additional collateral.

Asset management accounts, which require initial deposits of from $5,000 to $25,000, let you borrow against your portfolio by cashing checks drawn on the account. They are an excellent way to finance a home improvement, especially a small one, since an asset management account—like a home equity loan, which is meant for much larger projects—lets you pay the bills as they come in. You need not borrow the entire cost of the renovation ahead of time.

This era of high interest rates demands that borrowers be adroit to get the most favorable financing. Explore every possibility, especially if the project you are undertaking is not enormous. Your particular needs will probably eliminate most of the options before you begin. Once you've homed in on the real possibilities, we repeat, it's crucial to shop around. The variation in rates and terms is startling. But you'll be able to enjoy that new kitchen or loft or greenhouse more if you bargain as firmly with the banker as you do with the contractor.

*by Robert Runde*

# DIRECTORY OF ARCHITECTS, INTERIOR DESIGNERS, AND CONTRACTORS

*Page iv*
Designer: Ben Lloyd, *Metropolitan Home* magazine, 750 Third Ave., New York, NY 10017, (212) 551-7008
Architect: Howard Glazbrook III, AIA, Howard Glazbrook III Architects, 2000 N. Lamar St., Suite 206, Dallas, TX 75202, (214) 720-0508
*Page viii*
Design: Philip Sides, Sides/McAlpine, Inc., 407 Cloverdale Rd., Montgomery, AL 36106, (205) 262-8315
*Page xiv*
Architect: Edward Allen, AIA, 129 Eliot St., South Natick, MA 01760, (617) 653-3852

## BIG HOUSE DREAMS
### THE ONCE AND FUTURE HOUSE
*Pages 2–9*
Architect: Robert A.M. Stern., Robert A.M. Stern Architects, 211 W. 61st St., New York, NY 10023 (212) 246-1980
Designer: Ronald Bricke & Assoc., Inc., 333 E. 69th St., New York, NY 10021, (212) 472-9006
### FROM A PORCH TO A POST-MODERN PARLOR
*Pages 10–11*
Architect: Stephen R. Knutson, Knutson Designs, 923 Michigan Ave., Evanston, IL 60202, (312) 869-3850
Designer: Lawrence Boeder, Lawrence Boeder Interior Design, 445 E. Wisconsin Ave., Lake Forest, IL 60045, (312) 295-1393
### PRESERVATION HALL
*Pages 12–17*
Designer: Mary Southworth, Samlesbury Hall, LTD, 730 Forest Ave., Lake Forest, IL 60045, (312) 295-6070
### THE NEW FAMILY HOME
*Pages 18–21*
Architect and designer: Elida Schujman, Architecture Studio, 12 Captain's Landing, Tiburon, CA 94920, (415) 381-3536
### THE NEW GLAMOUR OF COMFORT
*Pages 22–25*
Architect: Michael Carbine, Michael Carbine Designs, 1430 Toledano St., New Orleans, LA 70115, (504) 895-9016
Designers: Ann Holden and Ann Dupuy, Holden & Dupuy Interior Design, 1101 First St., New Orleans, LA 70130, (504) 524-6327

### THE ENLIGHTENED TUDOR
*Pages 26–27*
Owners/designers/photographers: Mary Lou and Gary Whalen, Pittsburgh, PA
### NEW WING FOR AN OLD FARMHOUSE
*Pages 28–31*
Architect: David Jenkins, DIVO Design, 2601 NW Thurman, Portland, OR 97210
Designers: Tiger and Geraldine Warren, Gridlock Construction and Design, 1411 SW Davenport, Portland, OR 97201, (503) 222-7272
Paint decoration specialists: Ron Wagner and Philip Emmerling, 2324 NW Johnson, Portland, OR 97205, (503) 224-7036
### RENOVATING THE RANCH: TRACT HOUSING AND THE SPLIT-LEVEL
### THE SUBURBAN LOFT
*Pages 32–35*
Designers: Daniel Solomon and project associate John Long, Daniel Solomon and Associates, F.A.I.A., 84 Vandewater St., San Francisco, CA 94133, (415) 397-9190
### THE MAGAZINE MAKEOVER
*Pages 36–45*
Architect: Val Glitsch, AIA, P.O. Box 70984, Houston, TX 77008, (713) 864-0984
Designer: Ben Lloyd, *Metropolitan Home* magazine, 750 Third Ave., New York, NY 10017, (212) 551-7008
Contractor: Windham Martin Interests, 5719 Kirby, Suite 27, Houston, TX 77265, (713) 520-1605
### CUSTOMIZING THE COLONIAL
*Pages 46–47*
Architect: Chad Floyd, Centerbrook Architects, P.O. Box 409, Essex, CT 06426, (203) 767-0175
### RE-INVENTING THE SPLIT-LEVEL
*Pages 48–53*
Architect: Calvin Lewis, Charles Herbert and Associates, 202 Fleming Building, Des Moines, IA 50309, (515) 288-9536
Contractor: Rudy Wipperman, The Dallas Home Builders, Dallas Center, IA 50063, (515) 992-3469

### A '60s HOUSE LIGHTENS UP
*Pages 54–55*
Architect: Peter de Bretteville, de Bretteville and Polyzoides, 8067 Willow Glen Rd., Los Angeles, CA 90014, (213) 624-3381
Contractor: John Beug, 7649 Woodrow Wilson, Los Angeles, CA 90046, (213) 876-1944
### RAISING THE ROOF ON A RANCH
*Pages 56–59*
Designers: Barbara Barry and Margy Newman, 621 Tenth St., Santa Monica, CA 90402, (213) 938-7799
### THE SMALL CITY HOUSE
### TRADITION WITH A NEW, FRESH AIR
*Pages 60–65*
Architect: Michael Carbine Designs, 1430 Toledano St., New Orleans, LA 70115, (504) 895-9016
Designers: Ann Holden and Ann Dupuy, Holden & Dupuy Interior Design, 1101 First St., New Orleans, LA 70130, (504) 524-6327
### THE HOUSE THAT ROARED
*Pages 66–67*
Designer: Robert H. Taylor, AIA, Box 2408 Malibu, CA 90265, (213) 395-2456
### THE URBANE RENEWAL
*Pages 68–73*
Architect: Ronald F. Katz, Ronald Katz Design, 795 Burnett Ave., San Francisco, CA 94131, (415) 552-5300, and 1260 Esplanade Ave., New Orleans, LA 70116, (504) 581-9483
### BRAVE NEW BUNGALOW
*Pages 74–77*
Architect and designer: Frederick Fisher, Frederick Fisher Architects, 1422 Second St., Santa Monica, CA 90501, (213) 451-1767
### ADDING ON THE RITZ
*Pages 78–79*
Architects: Robert Lewis and Michael Holt, Lewis & Holt Architects, 1405 12th St., NW, Washington, DC 20005, (202) 234-4972
### THE OUTDOOR ROOM
*Pages 80–83*
Architect: Steven D. Ehrlich, AIA Architects, 76 Market St., Venice, CA 90291, (213) 399-7711
Designer: Wayne Williamson, Insight, Box 8417, Palm Springs, CA 92262

### BUILDING ON THE SKYLINE
*Pages 84–87*
Architects and designers: Jane Siris and Peter Coombs, Siris/Coombs Architects, 2112 Broadway, New York, NY 10023, (212) 580-2220
Contractor: Meader Assoc. Inc., 19 Hubert St., New York, NY 10013
### THE LOFT MOVEMENT
### THE REVISIONIST LOFT
*Pages 88–97*
Designer: Alan Buchsbaum Architect, 12 Greene St., New York, NY 10013, (212) 966-3010
### NEW VIEW ON LOS ANGELES
*Pages 98–99*
Designer: April Sheldon Design, 620 Moulton Ave., Studio 204, Los Angeles, CA 90031, (213) 222-7675
### THE MOVABLE DESIGN
*Pages 100–101*
Designer: Richar, Richar Interiors, Inc., 833 N. Orleans, Chicago, IL 60610, (312) 951-0924
### THE SALON LOFT
*Pages 102–103*
Architects: Joint project of Olson/Walker Architects, 1507 Western, Seattle, WA 98101, (206) 624-5670, and The NBBJ Group, 111 South Jackson, Seattle, WA 98104, (206) 223-5555
Designer: Terry Hunziker, 97 South Jackson, Seattle, WA 98104, (206) 467-1144
### LIVING ON TOP OF THE WORLD
*Pages 104–111*
Architect: Angus John Bruce, Angus John Bruce & Co., LTD, 398 W. Broadway, New York, NY 10012, (212) 226-3658
### THE NEO-CLASSIC LOFT
*Pages 112–113*
Designer: Carol Helms, *Metropolitan Home* magazine, 750 Third Ave., New York, NY 10017, (212) 551-7009
### SALADINO ON LOFTS
*Pages 114–115*
Designer: John Saladino, John Saladino Inc., 305 E. 63rd St., New York, NY 10021, (212) 752-2440
### THE CONVERTIBLE HOME: CHURCHES, CARRIAGE HOUSES, AND ADAPTIVE RE-USE
### HOME IN A VILLAGE CHURCH
*Pages 116–121*
Designer: David Eugene Bell, Design Multiples, Inc., 225 Lafayette Place, New York, NY 10012, (212) 219-8430

### THE DESIGN FACTORY
*Pages 122–125*
Architects and designers: George Pappageorge and David Haymes, Pappageorge Haymes Ltd., 814 N. Franklin St., Chicago, IL 60610, (312) 337-3344
### LIVING IN A LANDMARK
*Pages 126–129*
Designers: Elisabeth Edlefsen (retired), Bend, OR, (503) 389-6135, and Sharon Powell, The Joshua Sears Building, 725 Market St., Kirkland, WA 98033, (206) 828-4444
### THE GAS STATION, REVISITED
*Pages 130–131*
Architect: James F. Gohl Inc., 411 W. 61st St., Kansas City, MO 64113, (816) 361-4828
### CONVERTING A CARRIAGE HOUSE
*Pages 132–135*
Architect: George Suyama Architects, 121 E. Boston St., Seattle, WA 98102, (206) 324-9060
Contractor: Ned Lumpkin, Lumpkin Inc., 1201 Market St., Kirkland, WA 98033, (206) 232-8770
### A BOWLING ALLEY MOVES INTO THE FAST LANE
*Pages 136–137*
Architect: Martin Sexton, 858 N. Orleans, Chicago, IL 60610, (312) 642-5456
### THE URBAN PLANNER: LIVING IN A HIGH-RISE
### THE STREAMLINED CONDO
*Pages 138–143*
Architect: David Estreich and Associates, Architects, 100 Fifth Ave., New York, NY 10011, (212) 242-1060
### THE ENGINEERED APARTMENT
*Pages 144–145*
Designer: Joseph Paul D'Urso Design, 80 W. 40th St., New York, NY 10018, (212) 905-7250
### THE NEWS IN DETAIL
*Pages 146–151*
Architect: Peter M. Wheelwright Associates, 125 Cedar St., New York, NY 10006, (212) 619-2010
### PRIVATE PENTHOUSE
*Pages 152–155*
Architect: Douglas Peix, Peix & Crawford Architecture, 208 Fifth Ave., New York, NY 10010, (212) 683-9888
### THE NEW CLASSICS
*Pages 156–159*
Architects and designers: Lee Mindel and Peter Shelton, Shelton-Mindel Assoc., 216 W. 18th St., New York, NY 10011, (212) 243-3939

# THE GREAT VICTORIANS: TOWN HOUSES, BROWNSTONES, AND PAINTED LADIES

## THE LIGHT-FILLED GINGERBREAD
*Pages 160–163*
Designers: Paula and Gary Fracchia, San Francisco, CA
Design advisors: Robert H. Hersey Architects, 1 Lombard St., Suite 306, San Francisco, CA 94111, (415) 989-9250, and Phyllis Podesto, Box 334, Modesto CA 95353

## STATE-OF-THE-ART TOWN HOUSE
*Pages 164–167*
Architect: Henry Smith-Miller Architects, 305 Canal St., New York, NY 10013, (212) 334-9100

## PERFECT RETROFIT
*Pages 168–173*
Architect: Sidney Weinberg, 820 Ridge Road, Highland Park, IL 60035, (312) 831-4684

## THE VICTORIAN IMPULSE
*Pages 174–179*
Designer: Clem Labine, *The Old-House Journal*, 69A Seventh Ave., Brooklyn, NY 11217, (718) 636-4514

## TOWN HOUSE WITH A SECRET
*Pages 180–183*
Architects: George Pappageorge and David Haymes, Pappageorge Haymes Ltd., 814 N. Franklin St., Chicago, IL 60610, (312) 337-3344

## THE POSSIBLE DREAM HOUSE
*Pages 184–187*
Architects: Lubotsky, Metter, Worthington & Law Architects, 200 E. Ontario St., Chicago, IL 60611, (312) 642-3878

## THE GREENHOUSE EFFECT
*Pages 188–189*
Architect: Kenneth A. Schroeder & Associates, 714 S. Dearborn St., Chicago, IL 60605, (312) 786-9030

## THE URBAN VILLA
*Pages 190–197*
Designer: Ben Lloyd, *Metropolitan Home* magazine, 750 Third Ave., New York, NY 10017, (212) 551-7008

## A LABOR OF LOVE
*Pages 198–201*
Architect: Ralph Gillis, AIA, Gillis Associates, 156 Fifth Ave., New York, NY 10010, (212) 243-5330

# CHARM AND HOW TO GET IT: COTTAGES AND BUNGALOWS

## THE ROMANTIC COTTAGE
*Pages 202–211*
Designer: Theadora Van Runkle, 6363 Wilshire Blvd., Suite 520, Los Angeles, CA 90048, (213) 655-7147

## INSTANT HERITAGE FOR A NEW HOUSE
*Pages 212–213*
Designers: Gary Holt and William Summers, 1697 Missoula Ave., Missoula, MT 59802, (406) 721-4169

## THE CITY-SLICK BARN
*Pages 214–219*
Architect: Edwin Cady, (203) 355-2217
Designers: John and Janet Jay, 1000 Third Ave., New York, NY 10021, (212) 705-2427

## SHAKER CHIC
*Pages 220–223*
Designers: Tait and Philip Weigel, 615 S. Locust St., Freeport, IL 61032, (815) 232-2763

## THE APPEAL OF HAND-CRAFTING
*Pages 224–229*
Architect: Val Glitsch, AIA, P.O. Box 70984, Houston, TX 77008, (713) 864-0984

## THE SUNSHINE STATE
*Pages 230–233*
Designers: Michael Tedrick and Tom Bennett, Michael Tedrick & Partners, 761 Bay St., San Francisco, CA 94109

# THE THINKING COOK'S KITCHEN

## INSTALLING THE KITCHEN SYNC
*Pages 234–239*
Architect: Dan Phipps, Dan Phipps & Assoc., 1652 Stockton St., San Francisco, CA 94133, (415) 986-0414

## AN OLD-TIME KITCHEN THAT COOKS
*Pages 240–241*
Architect: Michael Carbine, 1430 Toledano St., New Orleans, LA 70115 (504) 895-9016
Designer: Clancy Dupépé, % Provincial Hotel, 1024 Charter Street, New Orleans, LA 70116, (504) 581-4995

## A CONTEMPORARY WAY WITH WOOD
*Pages 242–243*
Architect: David Jenkins, DIVO Design, 2601 NW Thurman, Portland, OR 97210
Designers: Tiger and Geraldine Warren, Gridlock Construction and Design, 1411 SW Davenport, Portland, OR 97201, (503) 222-7272

## THE CHEF'S SPECIAL
*Pages 244–245*
Architect: Martin E. Rich, Architect, 2112 Broadway, New York, NY 10023, (212) 580-1746

## BUILDING ON YOUR DREAM
*Pages 246–251*
Architects: Jefferson B. Riley, AIA, and James A. Coan, AIA, Centerbrook Architects, P.O. Box 409, Essex, CT 06426, (203) 767-0175
Designer: Donna Warner, *Metropolitan Home* magazine, 750 Third Ave., New York, NY 10017, (212) 551-7006

## A KITCHEN TO LIVE IN
*Pages 254–257*
Designer: Keren Williams, St. Charles Kitchens of New York City Inc., 150 E. 58th St., New York, NY 10155, (212) 838-2812, and Donna Warner, *Metropolitan Home* magazine, 750 Third Ave., New York, NY 10017, (212) 551-7006

## LIMITED ADDITION
*Pages 258–259*
Architect: Stephen Banigan, Harpole-Banigan Architects, 2104 18th St., NW, Washington, DC 20009, (202) 745-7456

## THE MODULE PLAN
*Pages 260–263*
Architect and Designer: Hobbs Fukwi Davison, 300 E. Pike, Seattle, WA 98122, (206) 625-0270

## THE EUROSTYLE KITCHEN
*Pages 264–265*
Architect: Barry Berkus, Berkus Group, 223 E. Be La Guerra, Santa Barbara, CA 93101, (805) 963-8901

## BUILDING INTO THE BACKYARD
*Pages 266–267*
Designers: Stuart Cohen and Anders Nereim, in association with Lubotsky, Metter, Worthington & Law, Architects, 200 E. Ontario, Suite 700, Chicago, IL 60611, (312) 642-3878

## OPENING UP THE GALLEY
*Pages 268–269*
Designer: Donna Warner, *Metropolitan Home* magazine, 750 Third Ave., New York, NY 10017, (212) 551-7006
Contractors: Ed Costello, John McGuire, Douglas R. Berry, ECCM Corporation, 300 E. 59th St., New York, NY 10022, (212) 688-4329

## PINK AND BLACK IS COMING BACK
*Pages 270–271*
Designers: Deborah and William McDowell, Cagney and McDowell, 711 S. Dearborn, Chicago, IL 60605

## THE WARMTH OF WOOD
*Page 272*
Architect: George Suyama Architects, 121 E. Boston St., Seattle, WA 98102, (206) 324-9060
Contractor: Ned Lumpkin, Lumpkin Inc., 1201 Market St., Kirkland, WA 98033, (206) 232-8770

## THE SURPRISE OF CONCRETE
*Page 273*
Designers: James Olson and Gordon Walker, Olson/Walker Architects, 1507 Western Ave., Seattle, WA 98101, (206) 624-5670

## THE NEO-FIFTIES KITCHEN
*Pages 274–275*
Designer: Eric Owen Moss Architect, 3964 Ince Blvd., Culver City, CA 90230, (213) 839-1199

## THE SEMI-PROFESSIONAL KITCHEN
*Pages 276–277*
(*left*) Designers: Stephen Lloyd and William Grover, Centerbrook Architects, P.O. Box 409, Essex, CT 06426, (203) 767-0175
(*right*) Designer: Dorothy Slover, Isabel O'Neil Studio Workshop, 177 E. 87th St., New York, NY 10128, (212) 348-4464

# THE PERSONAL SPA: BATHS AND DRESSING ROOMS

*Page 278*
Designer: Dorothy Slover, Isabel O'Neil Studio Workshop, 177 E. 87th St., New York, NY 10128, (212) 348-4464
*Page 279*
Designer: Ralph Gillis, AIA, Gillis Associates, 156 Fifth Ave., New York, NY 10010, (212) 243-5330

## THE MASTERFUL BATH
*Page 281*
Designer: Randy Engel, R.L. Engel and Company, Architects, 2905 Dean Parkway, Minneapolis, MN 55416

## THE WET ROOM
*Pages 282–283*
Designer: Kevin Walz, Walz Designs, 141 Fifth Ave., New York, NY 10011, (212) 477-2211
*Pages 284–285*

## THE NEW RETREAT
*Pages 284–285*
Designer: Val Glitsch, AIA, P.O. Box 70984, Houston, TX 77008, (713) 864-0984

## A JAPANESE BATHHOUSE
*Pages 286–287*
Architect: Tom Hoffman
Designer: Susan K. Okamoto, Inc., ASID, 317 E. Pine, Seattle, WA 98122, (206) 623-4888

## BATH, WITH A CITY VIEW
*Page 288*
Designer: Ugo Sap, 301 Upper Terrace, San Francisco, CA 94117, (415) 863-0103

## BATH, WITH A CANYON VIEW
*Page 289*
Designer: Peter de Bretteville, de Bretteville and Polyzoides, 8067 Willow Glen Rd., Los Angeles, CA 90014, (213) 624-3381

## THE GLAMOUR BATH
*Pages 290–291*
Designers: Ben Lloyd, *Metropolitan Home* magazine, 750 Third Ave., New York, NY 10017, (212) 551-7008, with Kohler Company, Kohler, WI 53044, (414) 457-4441

## THE FRENCH LINE
*Pages 292–293*
Designer: Howard Kaplan, Howard Kaplan's French Country Store, 827 Broadway, New York, NY 10003

## THE BEDSIDE SPA
*Pages 294–295*
Designer: Victor Belcic

## A SOLUTION IN BOLD STROKES
*Page 296*
Designer: David James Design, 8262 Fountain, Los Angeles, CA 90046, (213) 656-9440

## A SOLUTION IN OLD-FASHIONED FANTASY
*Page 297*
Designer: Ben Lloyd, *Metropolitan Home* magazine, 750 Third Ave., New York, NY 10017, (212) 551-7008

## ROSES AND THE RETRO LOOK
*Pages 298–299*
Designer: Betsey Johnson, 248 Columbus Ave., New York, NY 10023 (plus other store locations), (212) 226-0251

## CALIFORNIA, COUNTRY STYLE
*Page 300*
Designers: Andrew and Hope Batey, 1540 Yount Mill Rd., Yountville, CA 94599, (707) 944-8664

## JAPAN, CONTEMPORARY STYLE
*Page 301*
Designers: Bromley/Jacobsen Architecture & Design, 242 W. 27th St., New York, NY 10001, (212) 620-4250
*Page 302*
Architect: Steven David Ehrlich, AIA, 76 Market St., Venice, CA 90068, (213) 399-7711
*Page 334*
Architect: Stuart Silk, 1932 First Ave., Seattle, WA 98101, (206) 624-5275
Designer: Steven Wagner, *Metropolitan Home* magazine, 750 Third Ave., New York, NY 10017, (212) 551-7007
*Page 335*
Carol Helms, *Metropolitan Home* magazine, 750 Third Ave., New York, NY 10017, (212) 551-7009

# DIRECTORY OF WHOLESALERS, MANUFACTURERS, AND RETAILERS

## APPLIANCES
(see page 304)

**Refrigerators, ranges, cooktops, ovens, dishwashers, trash compactors, garbage disposals, clothes washers and dryers**

**Admiral**
1701 E. Woodfield Road
Schaumburg, IL 60196
(312) 884-2600

**Amana Refrigeration Co.**
Amana, IA 52203
(319) 622-5511

**Broan Mfg. Co., Inc.**
P.O. Box 140
Hartford, WI 53027
(414) 673-4340

**Caloric Corp.**
403 N. Main Street
Topton, PA 19562-1499
(215) 682-4211

**Frigidaire Co.**
P.O. Box WC 4900
3555 S. Kettering
Boulevard
Dayton, OH 45449
(513) 297-3629

**Gaggenau USA Corp.**
5 Commonwealth Avenue
Woburn, MA 01801
(617) 938-1655

**General Electric**
Major Appliance Division
Appliance Park
Building 6, Room 143
Louisville, KY 40225
800-626-2000

**Gibson Appliance Co.**
Gibson Appliance Center
Greenville, MI 48838
(616) 754-5621

**Hot Point**
2100 Gardiner Lane
Suite 301
Louisville, KY 40205
(502) 452-5364

**Jenn-Air Co.**
Consumer Services Dept.
3035 Shadeland
Indianapolis, IN 46226-0901
(317) 545-2271

**Kenmore**
Sears, Roebuck and Co.
Sears Tower
Dept. 703 BSC 40-15
Chicago, IL 60684
(312) 875-2500

**KitchenAid**
Division Hobart Corp.
Troy, OH 45374
(513) 332-3000

**Litton Microwave**
Cooking Products
1405 Xenium Lane North
Minneapolis, MN 55440
(612) 553-2000

**Magic Chef**
740 King Edward Avenue
Cleveland, TN 37311
(615) 472-3371

**The Maytag Company**
Newton, IA 50208
(515) 792-7000

**Modern Maid Co.**
403 N. Main Street
Topton, PA 19562-1499
(215) 682-4211

**Monarch Range Co.**
Beaver Dam, WI 53916
(414) 887-8131

**Panasonic Major Appliance Dept.**
One Panasonic Way
Secaucus, NJ 07094
(201) 348-7000

**Sub-Zero Freezer Co.**
P.O. Box 4130
Madison, WI 53711
(608) 271-2233

**Tappan Appliances**
Tappan Park
Mansfield, OH 44901
(419) 755-2011

**Thermador/Waste King**
5119 District Boulevard
Los Angeles, CA 90040
(213) 562-1133

**Toshiba America, Inc.**
Microwave Divison
82 Totowa Road
Wayne, NJ 07470
(201) 628-8000

**WCI Appliance Group**
300 Phillipi Road
Columbus, OH 43228
(614) 761-7020

**Whirlpool Corp.**
2000 U.S. 3 North
Benton Harbor, MI 49022
800-253-1301
800-632-2243 (in MI)

### COMMERCIAL REFRIGERATORS

**Traulsen and Co., Inc.**
114-02 15th Avenue
College Point, NY 11356
(212) 463-9000

### GARBAGE DISPOSALS

**In-Sink-Erator**
Emerson Electric Co.
4700 21st Street
Racine, WI 53406
800-558-5712
(414) 552-7303 (in WI)

**Sinkmaster**
Anaheim Mfg.
4240 E. La Palma Avenue
Anaheim, CA 92803
(714) 524-7770

### RESTAURANT STOVES

**Blue Flame Corp.**
523 W. 125th Street
New York, NY 10027
(212) 662-6990

**Chambers Corp.**
P.O. Box 927
Oxford, MS 38655
(601) 234-3131

**Garland Commercial Ind.**
185 E. South Street
Freeland, PA 18224
(717) 636-1000

**Majestic Range Works**
P.O. Box 139
Mascoutah, IL 62258
(618) 566-2371

**Roper Sales Corp.**
P.O. Box 867
Kankakee, IL 60901
(814) 937-6000

**Southbend Escan Corp.**
201 S. Cherry Street
South Bend, IN 46627
(219) 287-6585

**U.S. Range**
14501 S. Broadway
Gardena, CA 91105
(213) 770-8800

**Vulcan-Hart**
3600 N. Point Boulevard
Baltimore, MD 21222
(301) 284-0660

**Wolf Range Co.**
19600 S. Alameda Street
Compton, CA 90224
(213) 637-3737

### WASHERS/DRYERS

**Admiral**
1701 E. Woodfield Road
Schaumburg, IL 60196
(312) 884-2600

**Amana Refrigeration Co.**
Amana, IA 52203
(319) 622-5511

**Frigidaire Co.**
P.O. Box WC 4900
3555 S. Kettering
Boulevard
Dayton, OH 45449
(513) 297-3629

**General Electric**
Major Appliance Division
Appliance Park
Building 6, Room 143
Louisville, KY 40225
800-626-2000

**Gibson Appliance Co.**
Gibson Appliance Center
Greenville, MI 48838
(616) 754-5621

**Hot Point**
2100 Gardiner Lane
Suite 301
Louisville, KY 40205
(502) 452-5364

**Kenmore**
Sears, Roebuck and Co.
Sears Tower
Dept. 703 BSC 40-15
Chicago, IL 60684
(312) 875-2500

**Magic Chef**
740 King Edward Avenue
Cleveland, TN 37311
(615) 472-3371

**The Maytag Company**
Newton, IA 50208
(515) 792-7000

**Panasonic Major Appliance Dept.**
One Panasonic Way
Secaucus, NJ 07094
(201) 348-7000

**Speed Queen Co.**
Ripon, WI 54971
(414) 748-3121

**Toshiba America, Inc.**
Microwave Division
82 Totowa Road
Wayne, NJ 07470
(201) 628-8000

**WCI Appliance Group**
300 Phillipi Road
Columbus, OH 43228
(614) 761-7020

**Whirlpool Corp.**
2000 U.S. 3 North
Benton Harbor, MI 49022
800-253-1301
800-632-2243 (in MI)

## ARCHITECTURAL ARTIFACTS
(see pages 308, 310, 313, 323, 328, 331)

**Doors, mantels, newel posts, columns, corbels, wainscoting, cornices, stair rails, bath fixtures, etc.**

See also MOLDING for sources of antique and reproduction building materials, and COLUMNS.

**Architectural Antiques**
1321 E. Second
Little Rock, AR 72202
(501) 372-1744

**Architectural Antiques Exchange**
709-15 N. Second Street
Philadelphia, PA 19123
(215) 922-3669

**Architectural Emporium**
1011 S. 9th Street
Lafayette, IN 47905
(317) 423-1500

**Art Directions**
6120 Delmar Boulevard
St. Louis, MO 63112
(314) 863-1895

**The Bank**
1824 Felicity Street
New Orleans, LA 70113
(504) 523-2702

**Barewood Inc.**
141 Atlantic Avenue
Brooklyn, NY 11201
(718) 875-9037

**1874 House**
8070 SE 13th
Portland, OR 97202
(503) 233-1874

**Great American Salvage**
34 Cooper Square
New York, NY 10003
(212) 505-0070

**Irreplaceable Artifacts**
1046 Third Avenue
New York, NY 10021
(212) 223-4411

**Florida Victoriana Architectural Antiques**
901 W. First Street
Sanford, FL 32771
(305) 321-5767

**Lost City Arts**
257 W. 10th Street
New York, NY 10014
(212) 807-6979

**Nostalgia, Inc.**
307 Stiles Avenue
Savannah, GA 31401
(912) 232-2324

**Old Mansions Co.**
1305 Blue Hill Avenue
Mattapan, MA 02126
(617) 296-0445

**Old Theatre Architectural Salvage Co.**
1309 Westport Road
Kansas City, MO 64111
(816) 931-0987

**Pelnik Wrecking Co., Inc.**
1749 Erie Boulevard, East
Syracuse, NY 13210
(315) 472-1031

**Renovation Source**
3512-14 N. Southport
Chicago, IL 60657
(312) 327-1250

**Salvage One**
1524 S. Peoria Street
Chicago, IL 60608
(312) 733-0098

**SAVE**
339 Berry Street
Brooklyn, NY 11211
(718) 388-4527

**Stamford Wrecking Co.**
1 Barry Place
Stamford, CT 06904
(203) 324-9537

**Structural Antiques, Inc.**
3005 Classen Boulevard
Oklahoma City, OK 73106
(405) 528-7734

**United House Wrecking**
328 Selleck Street
Stamford, CT 06902
(203) 348-5371

**Urban Archaeology**
137 Spring Street
New York, NY 10012
(212) 431-6969

**The Wrecking Bar**
292 Moreland Avenue, NE
Atlanta, GA 30307
(404) 525-0468

## BATHROOM FIXTURES
(see pages 312, 317, 326, 331)
Grab bars, tissue dispensers, towel racks, soap dishes, etc.

See also TUBS AND TOILETS, SINKS, and FAUCETS.

**Auburn Brass**
2501 W. 5th Street
Santa Ana, CA 92703
(714) 547-0333

**Baldwin Hardware Corp.**
P.O. Box 82
841 Wyomissing Boulevard
Reading, PA 19603
(215) 277-7811

**The Charles Parker Co.**
290 Pratt Street
Meriden, CT 06450
(203) 235-6365

**Conran's**
160 East 54th Street
New York, NY 10022
(212) 371-2225

**IKEA**
Plymouth Meeting Hall
Plymouth Meeting, PA 19462
(215) 834-0150

**Union Hardware and Decorator Center**
7810 Wisconsin Avenue
Bethesda, MD 20814
(301) 654-7810

## CABINETS
(see page 306)
Kitchen and bath

**Allmilmo Corp.**
P.O. Box 629
Fairfield, NJ 07006
(201) 227-2502

**Alno . . . The World of Kitchens**
109 Wappoo Creek Drive
Suite 4B
Charleston, SC 29412
(803) 795-8683

**Aristokraft**
P.O. Box 420
14th and Aristokraft Square
Jasper, IN 47546
(812) 482-2527

**Coppes**
401 East Market Street
Nappanee, IN 46550
(219) 773-4141

**Crystal Cabinet Works, Inc.**
1100 Crystal Drive
Box 158
Princeton, MN 55371
(612) 389-4187

**Downsview Kitchens**
2635 Rena Road
Mississauga, Ontario
CANADA L4T 1G6
(416) 677-9354

**Dura Supreme**
10750 County Road 15
Minneapolis, MN 55441
(612) 544-9316

**Dwyer Compact Kitchens**
Calumet Avenue
Michigan City, IN 46360
(219) 874-5236

**Euroform**
6501 NW 37th Avenue
Miami, FL 33147
800-327-0014
(305) 836-8810 (in FL)

**EXCEL**
One Excel Plaza
Lakewood, NJ 08701
(201) 364-2000
800-526-2365

**Formica Corp.**
Information Center
Dept. 09
1 Stanford Road
Piscataway, NJ 08854
(201) 469-1555

**Haas Cabinet Co, Inc.**
625 W. Utica Street
Sellersberg, IN 47172
(812) 246-4431

**Heinrich Lager USA, Inc.**
35 Agnes Street
East Providence, RI 02914
(401) 438-8320

**Kitchen Kompact, Inc.**
KK Plaza
P.O. Box 868
Jeffersonville, IN 47130
(812) 282-6681

**Merillat Industries, Inc.**
P.O. Box 1946
Adrian, MI 49221
(517) 263-0771

**Milbrook Custom Kitchens**
Nassau, NY 12123
(518) 766-3033

**Poggenpohl USA Corp.**
222 Cedar Lane
Teaneck, NJ 07666
(201) 836-1550

**Quaker Maid**
Route 61
Leesport, PA 19533
(215) 926-3011

**Riviera Cabinets, Inc.**
825 Greenbrier Circle
Suite 200
Chesapeake, VA 23320
(804) 424-7400

**Roseline Products, Inc.**
120 Schmitt Boulevard
Farmingdale, NY 11735
(516) 293-8234

**Rutt Custom Kitchens**
Route 23
Goodville, PA 17528
(215) 445-6751

**St. Charles Mfg. Co.**
St. Charles, IL 60174
(312) 584-3800

**Scheirich Cabinetry**
P.O. Box 37120
250 Ottawa Avenue
Louisville, KY 40233-7120
(502) 363-3583

**Sears, Roebuck and Co.**
Sears Tower
Chicago, IL 60684
(312) 875-2500

**SieMatic Corp.**
919 Santa Monica Boulevard
Santa Monica, CA 90401
(213) 395-8394

**Snaidero Canada, Ltd.**
481 Hanlan Road
Woodbridge, Ontario
CANADA L4L 3T1
(416) 851-7777

**Wood-Mode Cabinetry**
Kreamer, Snyder County, PA 17833
(717) 374-2711

## CEILING FANS
(see page 318)

**Beverly Hills Fan Co.**
12612 Raymer Street
North Hollywood, CA 91605
(818) 982-1002

**Casablanca Fan Co.**
P.O. Box 37
182 S. Raymond Avenue
Pasadena, CA 91109
(213) 960-6441

**The Ceiling Fan Co.**
4212 SW 75th Avenue
Miami, FL 33155
(305) 261-3356

**The Ceiling Fan Place**
20 Round Swamp Road
Huntington, NY 11743
(516) 367-3835

**Homestead Ceiling Fans**
114 Fourteenth Street
Ramona, CA 92065-2192
800-833-8833
(619) 789-2314 (in CA)

**Hunter Fans**
Robbins and Myers, Inc.
2500 Frisco Avenue
Memphis, TN 38114
(901) 743-1360

**Panasonic**
One Panasonic Way
Secaucus, NJ 07094
(201) 348-7000

## CEILINGS
(see page 323)

### DROP-IN PANELS

**Armstrong World Industries**
P.O. Box 3001
Lancaster, PA 17604
800-233-3823
(717) 397-0611 (in PA)

### POLYURETHANE/GYPSUM PANELS THAT LOOK LIKE TIN

**Entol Industries, Inc.**
8180 NW 36th Avenue
Miami, FL 33147
(305) 696-0900

### TIN

**AA-Abbingdon Ceiling Co.**
2149 Utica Avenue
Brooklyn, NY 11234
(718) 236-3251

**Chelsea Decorative Metal Co.**
6115 Cheena
Houston, TX 77096
(713) 721-9200

**Hi-Art East**
6 N. Rhodes Center, NW
Atlanta, GA 30309
(404) 876-4740

**Shanker Steel Corp.**
70-32 83rd Street
Glendale, NY 11385
(718) 326-1100

**W.F. Norman Corp.**
Box 323
214-32 N. Cedar Street
Nevada, MO 64772
800-641-4038
(417) 667-5552 (in MO)

## COLUMNS
(see page 308)

**A. F. Schwerd**
3215 McClure Avenue
Pittsburgh, PA 15212
(412) 766-6322

**American Wood Column Corp.**
913 Grand Street
Brooklyn, NY 11211
(718) 782-3163

**Hartmann-Sanders Co.**
4340 Bankers Circle
Atlanta, GA 30360
(404) 449-1561

**Moultrie Manufacturing Co.**
P.O. Box 1179
Moultrie, GA 31768
800-841-8674
(912) 985-1312 (in GA)

**Somerset Door and Column Co.**
P.O. Box 328
Somerset, PA 15501
(814) 445-9608

**Turncraft**
P.O. Box 2429
White City, OR 97503
(503) 826-2911

**Worthington Group**
P.O. Box 53101
Atlanta, Georgia 30355
(404) 872-1608

## COOKTOPS
(see page 304)

See also APPLIANCES

**Admiral**
1701 E. Woodfield Road
Schaumburg, IL 60196
(312) 884-2600

**Blanco**
P.O. Box 24190
Tampa, FL 33623
(813) 855-1488

**Chambers Corp.**
P.O. Box 927
Oxford, MS 38655
(601) 234-3131

**Dacor**
950 S. Raymond Avenue
Pasadena, CA 91105
(213) 682-2803

**Gaggenau USA Corp.**
5 Commonwealth Avenue
Woburn, MA 01801
(617) 938-1655

**General Electric**
Major Appliance Division
Appliance Park
Building 6, Room 143
Louisville, KY 40225
800-626-2000

**Jenn-Air Co.**
Consumer Services Dept.
3035 Shadeland
Indianapolis, IN 46226-0901
(317) 545-2271

**Kenmore**
Sears, Roebuck and Co.
Sears Tower
Dept. 703 BSC 40-15
Chicago, IL 60684
(312) 875-2500

**KitchenAid**
Division Hobart Corp.
Troy, OH 45374
(513) 332-3000

**Magic Chef**
740 King Edward Avenue
Cleveland, TN 37311
(615) 472-3371

**Modern Maid Co.**
403 N. Main Street
Topton, PA 19562-1499
(215) 682-4211

**Roper Sales Corp.**
P.O. Box 867
Kankakee, IL 60901
(815) 937-6000

**Thermador/Waste King**
5119 District Boulevard
Los Angeles, CA 90040
(213) 562-1133

**U.S. Range**
14501 S. Broadway
Gardena, CA 91105
(213) 770-8800

**Whirlpool Corp.**
2000 U.S. 3 North
Benton Harbor, MI 49022
800-253-1301
800-632-2243 (in MI)

**Wolf Range Co.**
19600 S. Alameda
Compton, CA 90224
(213) 637-3737

## COUNTERTOPS
(see page 309)
See also MARBLE

### LAMINATES

**Formica Corp.**
Information Center
Dept. 09
1 Stanford Road
Piscataway, NJ 08854
(201) 469-1555

**Indesco**
330 Nassau Avenue
Brooklyn, NY 11222
(718) 387-8001

**Lamin-Art, Inc.**
1330 Mark Street
Elk Grove Village, IL 60007
(312) 860-4300

**Nevamar Corp.**
Odenton, MD 21113
(301) 569-5000

**COUNTERTOPS (cont.)**

**Wilsonart**
600 General Bruce Drive
Temple, TX 76501
(817) 778-2711

**SYNTHETIC MARBLE**

**Corian**
E.I. Du Pont de Nemours
& Co.
1007 Market Street
Wilmington, DE 19898
(302) 774-1000

# DOORS
(see page 310)

**See also**
ARCHITECTURAL ARTIFACTS

**Andersen Corp.**
Bayport, MN 55003
(612) 439-5150

**Atrium**
Moulding Products, Inc.
P.O. Box 226957
Dallas, TX 75222-6957
(214) 438-2441

**Caradco Corp.**
P.O. Box 920
Rantoul, IL 61866
(217) 893-4444

**Castlegate Doors**
Division U.S. Gypsum
101 S. Wacker Drive
Chicago, IL 60606
800-323-2274
(312) 321-4000 (in IL)

**Creative Openings**
1013 W. Holly Street
Bellingham, WA 98225
(206) 671-7435

**Door Facing Products**
P.O. Box 158
Maumee, OH 43537
(419) 893-8787

**E.A. Nord Co.**
P.O. Box 1187
Everett, WA 98206
(206) 259-9292

**Elegant Entries**
65 Water Street
Worcester, MA 01604
(617) 755-5237

**Gibbons Sash and Door**
Route 1
P.O. Box 76
Hurley, WI 54534
(715) 561-3904

**Ideal Company, Inc.**
P.O. Box 2540
Waco, TX 76702-2540
(817) 752-2494

**Jack Wallis Doors**
Route 1
P.O. Box 22a
Murray, KY 42071
(502) 485-2613

**Kenmore Industries**
44 Kilby Street
Boston, MA 02109
(617) 523-4008

**Marvin Doors**
Warroad, MN 56763
800-346-5128
800-552-1167 (in MN)

**Maurer and Shepherd Joyners, Inc.**
122 Naubuc Avenue
Glastonbury, CT 06033
(203) 633-2383

**Morgan Products Ltd.**
Oshkosh, WI 54903
800-435-7464

**Moulding Products, Inc.**
P.O. Box 157158
Irving, TX 75015
800-527-5249
(214) 438-2441 (in TX)

**Peachtree Windows and Doors, Inc.**
P.O. Box 5700
Norcross, GA 30091
(404) 449-0880

**Pella Rollscreen Co.**
102 Main Street
Pella, IA 50219
(515) 628-1000

**Pine Crest**
2118 Blaisdell Avenue
Minneapolis, MN 55404
(612) 871-7071

**Renovation Concepts**
213 Washington Avenue, N.
Minneapolis, MN 55401
(612) 333-5766

**Semco**
Semling-Menke Co., Inc.
P.O. Box 378
Merrill, WI 54452
(715) 536-9411

**Therma-Tru Corp.**
P.O. Box 7404
Toledo, OH 43615
(419) 537-1931

**Weather Shield Mfg., Inc.**
P.O. Box 309
Medford, WI 54451
(715) 748-2100

**Zeluck, Inc.**
5300 Kings Highway
Brooklyn, NY 11234
(718) 251-8060

# FAUCETS
(see page 312)

**Abbaka**
435 23rd Street
San Francisco, CA 94107
(415) 648-7210

**American Standard**
P.O. Box 2003
New Brunswick, NJ 08903
(201) 980-3000

**Artistic Brass**
4100 Ardmore Avenue
South Gate, CA 90280
(213) 564-1100

**Auburn Brass**
2501 W. 5th Street
Santa Ana, CA 92703
(714) 547-0333

**Blanco**
P.O. Box 24190
Tampa, FL 33623
(813) 855-1488

**Brass Menagerie**
524 St. Louis Street
New Orleans, LA 70130
(504) 524-0921

**Chicago Faucet Co.**
2100 S. Nuclear Drive
Des Plaines, IL 60018
(312) 694-4400

**Delta Faucet Co.**
P.O. Box 40980
55 E. 111th Street
Indianapolis, IN 46280
(317) 848-1812

**Epic Faucets**
8630 E. 33rd Street
Indianapolis, IN 46226
(317) 897-1142

**Euro Building Supply, Inc.**
7170 NW 50th Street
Miami, FL 33166
(305) 592-7739

**Gamma Distributors**
2508 Arapahoe Street
Denver, CO 80205
800-426-6232
(303) 292-0422 (in CO)

**Grohe America**
900 Lively Boulevard
Wood Dale, IL 60101
(312) 350-2600

**Kohler Co.**
44 Highland Drive
Kohler, WI 53044
(414) 457-4441

**Kolson**
Dept. T35
653 Middle Neck Road
Great Neck, NY 11023
(516) 829-4150

**KWC**
Western States Mfg.
Corp.
42 Woodgrove
Irvine, CA 92714
(714) 557-1933

**Luwa Corp.**
Builder Products Division
P.O. Box 16348
Charlotte, NC 28297-6348
(704) 394-8341

**Moen**
377 Woodland Avenue
Elyria, OH 44036
(216) 323-3341

**Peerless Faucet Co.**
P.O. Box 40980
Indianapolis, IN 46280
(317) 848-7933

**Sherle Wagner, Inc.**
60 E. 57th Street
New York, NY 10022
(212) 758-3300

**U.S. Plumbing Products**
P.O. Box 2003
New Brunswick, NJ 08903
(201) 885-1900

**U.S. Tap**
P.O. Box 369
800 W. Clinton
Frankfort, IN 46041
(317) 659-5415

**Watercolors**
Garrison, NY 10524
(914) 424-3327

**REPRODUCTION**

**A-Ball Plumbing Supply**
1703 W. Burnside Street
Portland, OR 97209
(503) 228-0026

**Nostalgia Inc.**
307 Stiles Avenue
Savannah, GA 31401
(912) 232-2324

**Steptoe & Wife Antiques Ltd.**
322 Geary Avenue
Toronto, Ontario
CANADA M6H 2C7
(416) 530-4200

**Sunrise Specialty**
2210 San Pablo Avenue
Berkeley, CA 94702
(415) 845-4751

# FIREPLACES
(see page 313)

**Flue Works, Inc.**
86 Warren Street
Columbus, OH 43215
(614) 291-6918

**Heatilator**
1915 W. Saunders
Mt. Pleasant, IA 52641
(319) 385-9211

**Heat-N-Glo Fireplaces**
3850 W. Hwy. 13
Burnsville, MN 55337
(612) 890-8367

**Majestic**
P.O. Box 800
Huntington, IN 46750
(219) 356-8000

**Martin Industries**
P.O. Box 128
Florence, AL 35631
(205) 767-0330

**Preway, Inc.**
1430 Second Street, N.
Wisconsin Rapids, WI
(715) 423-1100

**Superior Fireplace**
4325 Artesia Avenue
Fullerton, CA 92633
(714) 521-7302

**Wilshire Colonial Fireplace Shop**
8636 Wilshire Boulevard
Beverly Hills, CA 90211
(213) 657-8183

# FLOORING
(see page 314)

**RESILIENT**

**Armstrong World Industries**
P.O. Box 3001
Lancaster, PA 17604
800-233-3823
(717) 397-0611 (in PA)

**Congoleum Corp.**
195 Belgrove Drive
Kearny, NJ 07032
800-447-2882
(201) 991-1000 (in NJ)

**GAF Corp.**
140 W. 51st Street
New York, NY 10020
(212) 628-3000

**Mannington Mills**
P.O. Box 30
Salem, NJ 08079
800-447-4700
(609) 935-3000 (in NJ)

**Tarkett, Inc.**
P.O. Box 264
Parsippany, NJ 07054
800-225-6500
(201) 428-9000 (in NJ)

**RUBBER**

**Allstate Rubber Corp.**
105-12 101st Avenue
Ozone Park, NY 11416
(212) 526-7890

**American Floor Products**
5010 Boiling Brook Pkwy.
Rockville, MD 20852
(301) 770-6500

**Jason Industrial**
Rubber Flooring Division
340 Kaplan Drive
P.O. Box 365
Fairfield, NJ 07006
(201) 227-4904

**Mondo Rubber Canada Ltd.**
2655 Francis Hughes
Parc Industriel
Chomedey Laval
Quebec
CANADA H7L 358

**U.S. Mat and Rubber Co.**
P.O. Box 152
Brockton, MA 02403
(617) 587-2252

**VINYL TILE**

**Kentile Floors, Inc.**
58 Second Avenue
Brooklyn, NY 11215
(718) 768-9500

**National Floor Products Co., Inc.**
P.O. Box 354
Florence, AL 35631
(205) 766-0234

**Terralast**
Vinyl Plastics, Inc.
3123 S. 9th Street
Sheboygan, WI 53081
(414) 458-4664

**WOOD**

**Anderson Hardwood Floors**
P.O. Box 1155
Clinton, SC 29325
(803) 833-6250

**Bangkok Industries, Inc.**
Gillingham and Worth
Streets
Philadelphia, PA 19124
(215) 537-5800

**Bruce Hardwood Floors**
16803 Dallas Pkwy.
Dallas, TX 75248
(214) 931-3000

**Caribbean Lumber Co.**
P.O. Box 2687
Savannah, GA 31498-2687
(912) 234-3485

**Carlisle Restoration Lumber**
Route 123
Stoddard, NH 03464
(603) 446-3937

**E. T. Moore Jr., Co.**
119 E. Second Street
Richmond, VA 23224
(804) 231-1823

**Harris-Tarkett, Inc.**
383 Maple Street
Johnson City, TN 37601
(615) 928-3122

**Hartco, Inc.**
Oneida, TN 37841
(615) 569-8526

**Kentucky Wood Floors, Inc.**
4200 Reservoir Avenue
Louisville, KY 40213
(502) 451-6024

**Lebanon Oak Flooring Co.**
P.O. Box 669
Lebanon, KY 40033
(502) 692-2128

**Memphis Hardwood Flooring**
P.O. Box 7253
Memphis, TN 38107
(901) 526-7306

**Tiresias, Inc.**
P.O. Box 1846
Orangeburg, SC 29116
(803) 534-8478

## GLASS BLOCK
(see page 315)

**American Glass Block**
485 Victoria Terrace
Ridgefield, NJ 07657
(201) 945-4303

**Beinenfeld Industries**
1539 Covert Street
Palisades, NY 10964
(914) 359-0061

**Pittsburgh-Corning Corp.**
800 Presque Isle Drive
Pittsburgh, PA 15239
(412) 327-6100

**Supro Building Products Corp.**
48-16 70th Street
Woodside, NY 11377
(718) 429-5110

## GREENHOUSES AND ATRIUMS
(see page 316)

**Brady and Sun**
97 Webster Street
Worcester, MA 01603
(617) 755-9580

**English Greenhouses**
11th and Linden
Camden, NJ 08102
(609) 966-6161

**Evergreen Distributors**
P.O. Box 128
Burnett, WI 53922
(414) 689-2471

**Florian Greenhouses**
P.O. Box 763
Union City, NJ 07087
800-624-0026
(201) 863-4770 (in NJ)

**Four Seasons Solar Products Corp.**
425 Smith Street
Farmingdale, NY 11735
800-645-9527
(516) 694-4400 (in NY)

**Gammans Industries**
P.O. Box 1181
Newnan, GA 30264
(404) 253-8692

**Garden Way Sun Rooms**
430 Hudson River Road
Waterford, NY 12188
800-343-1908

**Green Mountain Homes**
Royalton, VT 05068
(802) 763-8384

**Habitat**
123 Elm Street
South Deerfield, MA 01373
(413) 665-4006

**Janco Greenhouses**
J.A. Nearing Co., Inc.
9390 Davis Avenue
Laurel, MD 20707
(301) 498-5700

**Lord and Burnham**
CSB-3181
Melville, NY 11747
(914) 591-8800

**Pella Rollscreen Co.**
102 Main Street
Pella, IA 50219
(515) 628-1000

**Solar Additions**
15 W. Main Street
Cambridge, NY 12816
800-833-2300
(518) 677-8511 (in NY)

**The Sun Company**
3241 Eastlake Avenue, E.
Seattle, WA 98102
(206) 323-2377

**Sun System Solar Greenhouses**
60 Vanderbilt Motor Parkway
Commack, NY 11725
(516) 543-7600

**Sunwrights, Inc.**
334 Washington Street
Somerville, MA 02143
(617) 547-0352

**Vegetable Factory**
Solar Structures Division
100 Court Street
Copiague, NY 11726
(516) 842-9300

## HARDWARE
(see page 317)
Door knobs, drawer pulls, hinges, handles, etc.

**Baldwin Hardware Corp.**
P.O. Box 82
841 Wyomissing Boulevard
Reading, PA 19603
(215) 777-7811

**Ball and Ball**
463 W. Lincoln Hwy.
Exton, PA 19341
(215) 363-7330

**Blaine Window Hardware**
1919 Blaine Drive
RD4
Hagerstown, MD 21740
(301) 797-6500

**Bradley Corp.**
P.O. Box 309
Menomonee Falls, WI 53051
(414) 251-6000

**Broadway Collection**
250 Troost
Olathe, KN 66061
(913) 782-6244

**Chown Hardware**
333 NW 16th
Portland, OR 97209-2688
(503) 243-6500

**Crawford's Old House Store**
301 McCall Street
Waukesha, WI 53186
(414) 542-0685

**Forms and Surfaces**
P.O. Box 5215
Santa Barbara, CA 93108
(805) 969-4767

**Gainsborough Hardware Industries**
P.O. Box 569
Chesterfield, MO 63017
(314) 532-8466

**The Ironmonger**
1822 N. Sheffield
Chicago, IL 60614
(312) 935-2784

**Kwikset**
516 Santa Ana Street
Anaheim, CA 92803
(714) 535-8111

**Normbau Design Systems**
1040 Westgate Drive
Addison, IL 60101
(312) 628-8373

**Omnia, Inc.**
P.O. Box 263
Montclair, NJ 07042
(201) 746-4300

**Plastiglide Ltd.**
80 Sante Drive
Concord, Ontario
CANADA L4K2W5
(416) 663-7720

**Schlage Lock Co.**
P.O. Box 3324
San Francisco, CA 94119
(415) 467-1100

**Valli and Colombo**
1540 Highland Avenue
Duarte, CA 92010
(818) 359-2569

**VSI Hardware**
Donner Mfg. Co.
P.O. Box 4445
12930 Bradley Avenue
Sylmar, CA 91342
(818) 367-2131

**W. J. Weaver & Sons, Inc.**
1208 Wisconsin Avenue, NW
Washington, D.C. 20007
(202) 333-4200

### REPRODUCTION

**Antique Hardware Co.**
P.O. Box 1592
Torrance, CA 90505
(213) 378-5590

**Cirecast, Inc.**
380 7th Street
San Francisco, CA 94103
(415) 863-8319

**P.E. Guerin**
23 Jane Street
New York, NY 10014
(212) 243-5270

**Renovator's Supply**
182 Northfield Road
Millers Falls, MA 01349
(413) 659-2211

**Restoration Hardware**
438 Second Street
Eureka, CA 95501
(707) 443-3152

**Restoration Works**
4122½ Virginia Street
Buffalo, NY 13201
(716) 856-8000

**Roy Electric**
1054 Coney Island Avenue
Brooklyn, NY 11230
(718) 339-6311

**Sunrise Specialty**
2210 San Pablo Avenue
Berkeley, CA 94702
(415) 845-4751

## HEATING AND COOLING
(see page 318)
Furnaces, air conditioners, boilers, heat pumps, exhaust fans, etc.

See also CEILING FANS.

**Borg-Warner Corp.**
York Division
P.O. Box 1592
York, PA 17405
(717) 771-7890

**Bryant Heating and Air Conditioning**
7310 W. Morris Street
Indianapolis, IN 46231
(317) 243-0851

**Burnham Boiler Co.**
Lancaster PA 17604
(717) 397-4701

**Carrier Corp.**
Carrier Parkway
P.O. Box 4808
Syracuse, NY 13221
(315) 432-6000

**Fedders Corp.**
Edison, NJ 48817
(201) 549-7200

**General Electric**
Appliance Park, Bldg. 6
Louisville, KY 40225
(502) 452-4971

**Grumman Energy Systems, Inc.**
445 Broadhollow Road
Melville, NY 17747
(516) 454-8600

**Honeywell, Inc.**
10400 Yellow Circle Drive
Minnetonka, MN 55343
(616) 931-4142

**Intertherm, Inc.**
10820 Sunset Office Drive
St. Louis, MO 63127
(314) 822-9600

**Lennox Industries, Inc.**
7920 Beltline Road
Dallas, TX 75240-8145
(214) 980-6000

**Preway Industries, Inc.**
P.O. Box 534
Evansville, IN 47704
(812) 424-3331

**Trane Co.**
Tyler, TX 75711
(214) 581-3200

**Weil-McLain**
Blaine Street
Michigan City, IN 46360
(219) 879-6561

**Whirlpool Heating & Cooling Products**
Heil-Quaker Corp.
635 Thompson Lane
P.O. Box 40566
Nashville, TN 37204-0566
(615) 244-0450

### EXHAUST FANS

**Allmilmo Corp.**
P.O. Box 629
70 Clinton Road
Fairfield, NJ 07006
(201) 227-2502

**Broan Mfg. Co., Inc.**
P.O. Box 140
Hartford, WI 53027
(414) 673-4340

**Dacor**
950 S. Raymond Avenue
Pasadena, CA 91105
(213) 682-2803

**Gaggenau USA Corp.**
5 Commonwealth Avenue
Woburn, MA 01801
(617) 938-1655

**Kool Matic Corp.**
1831 Terminal Road
P.O. Box 684
Niles, MI 49120
(616) 683-2600

**Lomanco, Inc.**
2102 W. Main Street
P.O. Box 519
Jacksonville AR 72076
(501) 982-6511

**NuTone**
Madison and Red Bank Roads
Cincinnati, OH 45227
800-543-8687
(513) 527-5100 (in OH)

**Thermador/Waste King**
5119 District Boulevard
Los Angeles, CA 90040
(213) 562-1133

**Vent-A-Hood**
1000 N. Greenville
Richardson, TX 65080
(214) 235-5201

### RADIATORS

**Burnham Corp.**
P.O. Box 255
Irvington, NY 10533
(914) 591-8800

**N.A.E.S., Inc.**
Hampton, NH 03842
(603) 926-1771

### THERMOSTATS

**Honeywell**
Inquiries Supervisor
Honeywell Plaza
Minneapolis, MN 55408
(612) 931-4186

**Jade Controls**
P.O. Box 271
Montclair, CA 91763
800-854-7933
(714) 985-7273 (in CA)

**Robert Shaw Controls Co.**
Consumer Products Marketing Group
100 W. Victoria Street
Long Beach, CA 90805
800-421-1130
800-262-1173 (in CA)

## INSULATION
(see page 318)

**Accurate Metal Weatherstrip Co., Inc.**
725 S. Fulton Avenue
Mount Vernon, NY 10550
(914) 668-6042

## INSULATION (cont.)

**CertainTeed Corp.**
P.O. Box 860
Valley Forge, PA 19482
(215) 568-3771

**Dow Chemical Co.**
Fabricated Products Div.
2020 Willard H. Dow
Center
Midland, MI 48674
(517) 636-1000

**Monsanto Co.**
800 N. Lindbergh Blvd.
Dept. 198
St. Louis, MO 63167
(314) 694-1000

**Mortell Co.**
Kankakee, IL 60901
(815) 933-5514

**Owens-Corning Fiberglas Corp.**
Fiberglas Tower
Toledo, OH 43659
(419) 248-8000

**Thermwell Products Co., Inc.**
150 E. 7th Street
Patterson, NJ 07524
(201) 684-5000

**U.S. Gypsum Co.**
101 S. Wacker Drive
Chicago, IL 60606
(312) 321-3852

## LIGHTING
(see page 319)

**Ceiling and wall fixtures, track lighting, recessed lighting, outlets, and wall switches**

**Artemide Inc.**
150 E. 58th Street
New York, NY 10155
(212) 980-0710

**Atelier International Lighting**
595 Madison Avenue
New York, NY 10022
(212) 644-0400

**Basic Concept**
141 Lanza Avenue
Garfield, NJ 07026
(201) 742-5600

**Boyd Lighting Co.**
56 12th Street
San Francisco, CA 94103
(415) 431-4300

**George Kovacs Lighting, Inc.**
24 W. 40th Street
New York, NY 10018
(212) 944-9606

**Harry Gitlin Lighting Co.**
305 E. 60th Street
New York, NY 10022
(212) 243-1080

**Halo Lighting**
Division McGraw Edison
Co.
333 W. River
Elgin, IL 60120
(312) 956-8404

**Juno Lighting, Inc.**
2001 S. Mt. Prospect
Road
Des Plaines, IL 60017-
50605
(312) 827-9880

**Koch and Lowy, Inc.**
21-24 39th Avenue
Long Island City, NY
11101
(718) 786-3520

**Light, Inc.**
1162 Second Avenue
New York, NY 10021
(212) 838-1130

**The Lighting Center**
1097 Second Avenue
New York, NY 10017
(212) 758-1562

**Lightolier, Inc.**
346 Claremont Avenue
Jersey City, NJ 07035
(201) 333-5120

**Progress Lighting**
Erie Avenue and G
Streets
Philadelphia, PA 19134
(215) 289-1200

**Ron Rezek**
5522 Venice Boulevard
Los Angeles, CA 90019
(213) 931-2488

**Tech Lighting, Inc.**
300 W. Superior
Chicago, IL 60611
(312) 642-1586

**Thunder and Light**
147 41st Street
Brooklyn, NY 11232
(718) 499-3777

**Trak Lighting, Inc.**
14625 E. Clark
City of Industry, CA
91746
(818) 330-3106

## REPRODUCTION/ANTIQUE

**Brass Light of Historic Walker's Point**
719 S. 5th Street
Milwaukee, WI 53204
(414) 383-0675

**City Lights**
2226 Massachusetts
Avenue
Cambridge, MA 02140
(617) 547-1490

**Roy Electric Co.**
1054 Coney Island
Avenue
Brooklyn, NY 11230
(718) 339-6311

**St. Louis Antique Lighting Co.**
25 N. Sarah
St. Louis, MO 63108
(314) 863-1414

## MANTELS
(see page 313)

**See also**
**ARCHITECTURAL ARTIFACTS, FIREPLACES**

**Decorators Supply Corp.**
3610-12 S. Morgan Street
Chicago, IL 60609
(312) 847-6300

**Designer Resource**
5160 Melrose Avenue
Los Angeles, CA 90038
(213) 465-9235

**Jerard Paul Jordan Gallery**
Box 71, Slade Road
Ashford, CT 06278
(203) 429-7954

**La Cheminee**
Dalton-Gorman
1508 Sherman Avenue
Evanston, IL 60201
(312) 527-5555

**Log Power Distributors**
R.D. 1
P.O. Box 2224
Allentown, NJ 08501
(609) 259-9709

**Morgan Products Ltd.**
Oshkosh, WI 54903
800-435-7464
(414) 235-7170 (in WI)

**Mountain Lumber**
1327 Carlton Avenue
Charlottesville, VA 22901
(804) 295-1922

**William H. Jackson Co.**
3 E. 47th Street
New York, NY 10017
(212) 953-9400

**New York Marble Works**
1399 Park Avenue
New York, NY 10029
(212) 534-2242

**Readybuilt Products Co.**
P.O. Box 4425
Baltimore, MD 21223
(301) 233-5833

**Sunshine Architectural Woodworks**
Rte. 2, P.O. Box 434
Fayetteville, AR 72701
(501) 521-4329

**Western Art Stone Co., Inc.**
541 Tunnel Avenue
P.O. Box 315
Brisbane, CA 94005
(415) 467-2175

**Ye Olde Mantel Shoppe**
3800 NE Second Avenue
Miami, FL 33137
(305) 576-0225

## MOLDINGS
(see page 322)

**Balmer Architectural Art, Inc.**
69 Pape Avenue
Toronto, Ontario
CANADA M4M 2V5
(416) 466-6306

**Bendix Mouldings, Inc.**
235 Pegasus Avenue
Northvale, NJ 07647
(201) 767-8888

**Classic Architectural Specialties**
5302 Junius
Dallas TX 75214
(214) 827-5111

**Classic Moulders**
P.O. Box 466
Palm Beach. FL 33480
(305) 659-4200

**Cumberland Woodcraft Co., Inc.**
2500 Walnut Bottom Road
Carlisle, PA 17013
(717) 243-0063

**Decorators Supply**
3610-12 S. Morgan Street
Chicago, IL 60609
(312) 847-6300

**Dovetail, Inc.**
P.O. Box 1569
750 Suffolk Street
Lowell, MA 01853-2769
800-344-5570
(617) 454-2944 (in MA)

**Driwood Moulding Co.**
P.O. Box 1729
Florence, SC 29503
(803) 662-0541

**The Emporium**
2515 Morse Street
Houston, TX 77019
(713) 528-3808

**Felber Studios**
110 Ardmore Avenue
P.O. Box 551
Ardmore, PA 19003
(215) 642-4710

**Focal Point, Inc.**
2005 Marietta Road, NW
Atlanta, GA 30318
(404) 351-0820

**Fypon, Inc.**
22 W. Pennsylvania
Avenue
Stewartstown, PA 17363
(717) 993-2593

**Mad River Woodworks**
P.O. Box 163
4935 Boyd Road
Arcata, CA 95521
(707) 826-0629

**San Francisco Victoriana**
2245 Palou Avenue
San Francisco, CA 94124
(415) 648-0313

**Silverton Victorian Mill Works**
P.O. Box 877
Silverton, CO 81433
(303) 387-5716

**Victorian Collectibles Ltd.**
845 E. Glenbrook Road
Milwaukee, WI 53217
(414) 352-6910

**Vintage Wood Works**
Dept. 382
513 S. Adams Street
Fredricksburg, TX 78624
(512) 997-9513

## NEW MATERIALS
(see page 323)

### MARBLE

**Colonna and Co., Inc.**
3446 Vernon Blvd.
Long Island City, NY
11106
(212) 274-1111

**General Marble Corp.**
9407 Arrow
Rancho Cucamonga, CA
91730
800-845-7957
(714) 987-4636 (in CA)

**Georgia Marble Co.**
2575 Cumberland
Parkway, NW
Atlanta, GA 30339
(404) 432-0131

**Granite and Marble World Trade**
2434 W. Fulton
Chicago, IL 60612
(312) 243-9007

**Marble Modes**
15-25 130th Street
College Point, NY 11356
(718) 539-1334

**New York Marble Works**
1399 Park Avenue
New York, NY 10029
(212) 534-2242

**Ventura Marble**
12595 Foothill Boulevard
Sylmar, CA 91342
(818) 890-1886

**Vermont Marble Co.**
61 Main Street
Proctor, VT 05765
(802) 459-3311

**Westchester Marble and Granite, Inc.**
179 Summerfield Street
Scarsdale, NY 10583
(914) 472-5666

### SLATE

**Evergreen Slate Co.**
P.O. Box 248
Granville, NY 12832
(518) 642-2530

**Hilltop Slate Co.**
Middle Granville, NY
12849
(518) 642-2270

**Peacock Valley Stone and Slate Co.**
400 Demarest Avenue
Closter, NJ 07624
(201) 768-2133

**Rising and Nelson Slate Co.**
West Pawlet, VT 05775
(802) 645-0150

**The Structural Slate Co.**
P.O. Box 187
222 E. Main Street
Pen Argyl, PA 18072
(215) 863-4141

**Vermont Structural Slate Co.**
P.O. Box 98
Fair Haven, VT 05743
(802) 265-4933

### SYNTHETIC MARBLE

**Corian**
E.I. Du Pont de Nemours
& Co.
1007 Market Street
Wilmington, DE 19898
(302) 774-1000

## PAINT
(see page 324)

**Benjamin Moore**
51 Chestnut Ridge Road
Montvale, NJ 07645
(201) 573-9600

**DeSoto, Inc.**
1700 S. Mount Prospect
Road
Des Plaines, IL 60017
(312) 391-9000

**Devoe and Reynolds**
4000 Dupont Circle
Louisville, KY 40207
(502) 897-9861

**Duron**
10406 Tucker Street
Beltsville, MD 20705
(301) 792-2616

**Fuller-O'Brien**
450 E. Grand Avenue
San Francisco, CA 94080
800-227-6159
(415) 761-2300 (in CA)

**Glidden Coatings
and Resins**
900 Union Commerce
Bldg.
Cleveland, OH 44115
(216) 344-8140

**Illinois Bronze
Paint Co.**
Lake Zurich, IL 60047
(312) 438-8201

**Janovic Plaza**
1150 Third Avenue
New York, NY 10021
(212) 772-1400

**Martin-Senour Co.**
1370 Ontario Avenue, NW
Cleveland, OH 44113
(216) 566-3178

**The Muralo
Company, Inc.**
148 E. 5th Street
Bayonne, NJ 07002
(201) 437-0770

**Olympic Stain**
2233 112th Avenue, NE
Bellevue, WA 98004
800-426-6306

**Pittsburgh Paints**
1 Gateway Center
Pittsburgh, PA 15227
(412) 434-3131

**Pratt and Lambert**
2145 Schultz Street
St. Louis, MO 63122
(314) 993-6116

**Sherwin-Williams**
P.O. Box 6939
Cleveland, OH 44101
(216) 566-2332

**Wolf Paints and
Wallcoverings**
771 Ninth Avenue
New York, NY 10019
(212) 245-7777

**Zolatone**
Division of Surface
Protection Industries
3411 E. 15th Street
Los Angeles, CA 90023
(617) 281-4742

## ROOFING
(see page 325)

### ASPHALT SHINGLES
**CertainTeed Corp.**
P.O. Box 860
Valley Forge, PA 19482
(215) 568-3771

**Elk Roofing Products**
P.O. Box 37
Stepens, AR 71764
800-643-1304
(501) 836-5836 (in AR)

**Georgia Pacific**
133 Peachtree Street, NE
Atlanta, GA 30303
(404) 521-4000

**Masonite Corp.**
29 S. Wacker Drive
Chicago, IL 60606
(312) 372-5642

**Timberline Shingles**
GAF Corp.
1361 Alps Road
Wayne, NJ 07470
(201) 628-3000

**Weyerhaeuser Co.**
Tacoma, WA 98477
(206) 924-2345

### CLAY
**Gladding, McBean
and Co.**
P.O. Box 97
Lincoln, CA 95648
(916) 645-3341

**Lifetile Corp.**
P.O. Box 21516
San Antonio, TX 78221
(512) 626-2771

**Monier Roof Tile Co.**
P.O. Box 5567
Orange, CA 92666
(714) 538-8822

**Terra Cotta
Productions, Inc.**
P.O. Box 99781
Pittsburgh, PA 15233
(412) 321-2109

### METAL
**W. F. Norman Corp.**
P.O. Box 323
Nevada, MO 64772-0323
(417) 667-5552

### SLATE
**Evergreen Slate Co.**
P.O. Box 248
Granville, NY 12832
(518) 642-2530

**The Structural Slate
Co.**
P.O. Box 187
222 E. Main Street
Pen Argyl, PA 18072
(215) 863-4141

### SYNTHETIC SLATE
**Supradur Mfg. Co.**
P.O. Box 908
Rye, NY 10580
(914) 967-8230

### WOOD, TILE, SLATE
**Celestial Roofing Co.**
1710 Thousand Oaks
Boulevard
Berkeley, CA 94707
(415) 549-3421

## SHUTTERS
See also
ARCHITECTURAL ARTIFACTS
and MOLDING

**Beech River Mill Co.**
Old Route 16
Center Ossipee, NH
03814
(603) 539-2636

**Cell-Wood**
Bisbee Brothers
East Street
Chesterfield, MA 01012
(413) 296-4755

**Carado Corp.**
201 Evans Drive
Rantoul, IL 61866
(217) 893-4444

**Island City Wood
Working Co.**
1801 Mechanic Street
Galveston TX 77550
(409) 765-5727

**Mid-American Bldg.
Products**
9146 Hubbell Street
Detroit, MI 48228
(313) 838-4520

## SIDING
(see pages 323, 325)

### BRICK
**Acme Brick Co.**
P.O. Box 425
2821 W. 7th Street
Ft. Worth, TX 76101
(817) 332- 4101

**Architectural Brick
Co.**
425 Washington Avenue
North Haven, CT 06473
(203) 239-2504

**Belden Brick Co.**
P.O. Box 910
700 Tuscarawas Street,
W.
Canton, OH 44701
(216) 456-0031

**Binghamton Brick
Co., Inc.**
P.O. Box 1256
Binghamton, NY 13902
(607) 722-0420

**General Shale
Products Co.**
P.O. Box 3547 CRS
Johnson City, TN 37602
(615) 282- 4661

**Glen-Gery Corp.**
P.O. Box 5
Rte. 61
Shoemakersville, PA
19555
(215) 562-3076

**Hoiss-Kuhn-Chuman
Co.**
2723 W. 47th Street
Chicago, IL 60632
(312) 927-6414

**Mutual Materials Co.**
P.O. Box 2009
605 119th NE
Bellevue, WA 98009
(206) 455-2869

**Ochs Brick and Tile
Co.**
15300 State Highway 5
Eden Prairie, NM 55344
(612) 937-9430

**Robinson Brick Co.**
P.O. Box 5243
500 S. Santa Fe Drive
Denver, CO 80217
(303) 744-3371

**Summit Pressed
Brick and Tile Co.**
P.O. Box 533
Pueblo, CO 81002
(303) 542-8278

**Victor Cushwa and
Sons, Inc.**
P.O. Box 228
Williamsport, MD 21795
(301) 223-7700

### WOOD
**American Plywood
Association**
P.O. Box 11700
Tacoma, WA 98411
(206) 565-6600

**CertainTeed Corp.**
P.O. Box 860
Valley Forge, PA 19482
(215) 568-3771

**Champion
International Corp**
1 Champion Plaza
Stamford, CT 06921
(203) 358-7000

**Forest Fiber Products
Co.**
P.O. Box 68
Forest Grove, OR 97116
(503) 648-4194

**Georgia-Pacific**
133 Peachtree Street, NE
Atlanta, GA 30303
(404) 521-4000

**ITT Rayonier, Inc.**
Peninsula Plywood
Division
439 Marine Drive
Port Angeles, WA 98362
(206) 457-4421

**Masonite Corp.**
29 S. Wacker Drive
Chicago, IL 60606
(312) 372-5642

**Specialty
Woodworking Co,
Inc.**
1434 NW 22nd
Portland, OR 97210-2688
(503) 224-5465

### WOOD SHINGLES
**Shakertown Corp.**
P.O. Box 400
Winlock, WA 98596
800-426-8970
(206) 785-3501 (in WA)

## VINYL
**Mastic Corp.**
P.O. Box 65
131 S. Taylor Street
South Bend, IN 46624-
0065
(219)288-4621

**VIPCO**
P.O. Box 498
Columbus, OH 43216
800-848-3490
(614) 443-4841 (in OH)

### VINYL, ALUMINUM
**Alcan Aluminum
Products**
280 N. Park Avenue
Warren, OH 44481
(216) 841-3331

**Alcoa Building
Products**
P.O. Box 716
2615 Campbell Road
Sidney, OH 45365
(513) 492-1111

**Wolverine
Technologies**
Building Products Division
1650 Howard Street
Lincoln Park, MI 48146
(313) 386-0800

## SINKS
(see page 326)
Kitchen and bath
sinks

See also
ARCHITECTURAL ARTIFACTS
and TUBS AND TOILETS

**Abbaka**
435 23rd Street
San Francisco, CA 94107
(415) 648-7210

**American Standard**
P.O. Box 2003
New Brunswick, NJ 08903
(201) 980-3000

**Blanco**
P.O. Box 24190
Tampa, FL 33623
(813) 855-1488

**Delta Faucet Co.**
P.O. Box 40980
55 E. 111th Street
Indianapolis, IN 46280
(317) 848-1812

**Eljer Plumbingware**
Three Gateway Center
Pittsburgh, PA 15222
800-441-9422
(412) 553-7200 (in PA)

**Elkay Mfg. Co.**
2222 Camden Court
Oak Brook, IL 60512
(312) 986-8484

**Franke, Inc.**
Kitchen Systems Division
212 Church Road
North Wales, PA 19454
(215) 699-8761

**Kallista, Inc.**
200 Kansas Street
San Francisco, CA 94103
(415) 552-2500

**Kohler Co.**
44 Highland Drive
Kohler, WI 53044
(415) 457-4441

**La France Imports**
2008 Sepulveda Boulevard
Los Angeles, CA 90025
(213) 478-6009

**Luwa Corp.**
Builder Products Division
P.O. Box 16348
Charlotte, NC 28297-6348
(704) 394-8341

**Sherle Wagner, Inc.**
60 E. 57th Street
New York, NY 10022
(212) 758-3300

**Villeroy and Boch, Inc.**
I-80 at New Maple Avenue
Pine Brook, NJ 07058
(201) 575-0550

### PEDESTAL REPRODUCTION

**A. Ball Plumbing**
1703 Burnside
Portland, OR 97209
(503) 228-0026

**Barclay Products Co.**
424 N. Oakley Boulevard
Chicago, IL 60612
(312) 243-1444

**The Sink Factory**
2140 San Pablo Avenue
Berkeley, CA 94702
(415) 540-8193

**Stringer's Environmental Restoration and Design**
2140 San Pablo Avenue
Berkeley, CA 94702
(415) 548-3967

### SKYLIGHTS AND ROOF WINDOWS
(see page 327)

**Andersen Corp.**
P.O. Box 12
Bayport, MN 55003
(612) 439-5150

**APC Corporation**
50 Utter Avenue
P.O. Box 515
Hawthorne, NJ 07507
(201) 423-2900

**Caradco, Corp.**
P.O. Box 920
Rantoul, IL 61866
(217) 893-4444

**Pella Rollscreen Co.**
102 Main Street
Pella, IA 50219
(515) 628-1000

**Plasteco, Inc.**
P.O. Box 24158
Houston, TX 77229-4158
(713) 453-8696

**Velux-America, Inc.**
6180-A Atlantic Boulevard
Norcross, GA 30071
800-241-5611
800-282-3342 (in GA)

**Ventarama Skylight Corp.**
140 Cantiague Rock Road
Hicksville, NY 11801
(516) 931-0202

**Wasco Products**
P.O. Box 351
Sanford, ME 04073
(207) 324-8060

### STAIRS
(see page 328)

**American General Products**
1735 Holmes Road
Ypsilanti, MI 48197
800-732-0609
(313) 483-1833 (in MI)

**Cooper Stair Co.**
1331 Leithton Road
Mundelein, IL 60060
(312) 362-8900

**Curvoflite**
205 Spencer Avenue
Chelsea, MA 02150
(617) 889-0007

**Duvinage Corp.**
P.O. Box 828
Hagerstown, MD 21741
(301) 733-8255

**The Iron Shop**
P.O. Box 128
400 Reed Road
Broomall, PA 19008
(215) 544-7100

**James R. Dean**
62 Pioneer Street
Cooperstown, NY 13326
(607) 547-2625

**Mansion Industries, Inc.**
P.O. Box 2220
14711 E. Clark Ave.
City of Industry, CA 91746
800-423-6589
(213) 968-9501 (in CA)

**Mestel Stair Building Corp.**
3480 Fulton Street
Brooklyn, NY 11208
(718) 647-4022

**Midwest Spiral Stair Co.**
2153 W. Division Street
Chicago, IL 60622
800-621-3887
(312) 227-8461 (in IL)

**Morgan Products Ltd.**
Oshkosh, WI 54903
800-435-7464
(414) 235-7170 (in WI)

**Mylen Industries, Inc.**
P.O. Box 350
650 Washington Street
Peekskill, NY 10566
800-431-2155
(914) 739-8486 (in NY)

**Piedmont Home Products, Inc.**
111 E. Church Street
Orange, VA 22960
800-622-3399
(703) 672-3888 (in VA)

**St. Louis Ornamental Iron Works**
5269 Northrup
St. Louis, MO 63110
(314) 664-8811

**Stairways, Inc.**
4323-A Pinemont
Houston, TX 77018
(713) 680-3110

**Steptoe & Wife Antiques Ltd.**
322 Geary Avenue
Toronto, Ontario
CANADA M6H 2C7
(416) 530-4200

**Woodbridge Ornamental Iron Co.**
2715 N. Clybourn Avenue
Chicago, IL 60614
(312) 935-1500

**York Spiral Stair**
N. Vassalboro, ME 04962
(207) 872-5558

### STORAGE
(see page 329)

**Amerock Corp**
4000 Auburn Street
Rockford, IL 61101
(815) 963-9631

**Closet Maid Corp**
720 SW 17th Street
Ocala, FL 32670
(904) 732-8734

**Closet Systems Corp**
1175 Broadway
Hewlett, NY 11557
(516) 569-1400

**Dorz Manufacturing Co.**
P.O. Box 456
Bellevue, WA 98009
(206) 454-5472

**Elfa**
Scan-Plast Industries, Inc.
One Industrial Park
Rutherford, NJ 07070
(201) 933-7330

**Ello Furniture Mfg. Co.**
1034 Elm Street
Rockford, IL 61101
(815) 964-8601

**George C. Brown and Co.**
Super Cedar Closet Lining
P.O. Drawer B
Greensboro, NC 27402
(919) 292-2961

**Hafele America Co.**
P.O. Box 1590
High Point, NC 27261
(919) 889-2322

**Iron-A-Way, Inc.**
220 W. Jackson
Morton, IL 61550
(309) 266-7232

**Murphy Door/Bed Co., Inc.**
Lew Raynes, Inc.
40 E. 34th Street
New York, NY 10016
(212) 682-8936

**Rubbermaid**
Home Products Division
1147 Akron Road
Wooster, OH 44691
(216) 264-6464

**SICO Incorporated**
P.O. Box 1169
7525 Cahill Road
Minneapolis, MN 55440
(612) 941-1700

**Schulte Corp.**
11450 Grooms Road
Cincinnati, OH 45242
(513) 489-9300

**Storage Systems**
Division Lee/Rowan
6333 Etzel Avenue
St. Louis, MO 63133
800-325-6150
(314) 721-3363 (in MO)

**Store 'N Save**
The Innovators
57 Hamilton Avenue
Waterbury, CT 06702
800-431-1904
(203) 575-9992 (in CT)

### STUCCO
(see page 325)

**Simplex Products Division**
P.O. Box 10
Adrian, MI 49221
(517) 263-0169

**U.S. Gypsum**
101 S. Wacker Drive
Chicago, IL 60606
(312) 321-4101

### TILE
(see page 330)

**American Olean Tile Co.**
P.O. Box 271
1000 Cannon Avenue
Lansdale, PA 19446
(215) 855-1111

**Architectural Terra Cotta & Tile Ltd.**
932 W. Washington Boulevard
Chicago, IL 60607
(312) 666-1181

**Country Floors**
300 E. 61st Street
New York, NY 10021
(212) 758-7414

**Dal-Tile Corp**
7834 Hawn Freeway
Dallas, TX 75217
(214) 389-1411

**Florida Tile**
Lakeland, FL 33802
(813) 665-4646

**Franciscan Ceramic Tile**
2901 Los Feliz Boulevard
Los Angeles, CA 90039
(213) 663-3361

**Hastings Tile**
201 E. 57th Street
New York, NY 10022
(212) 755-2710

**Laura Ashley**
P.O. Box 5308
Melville, NY 17114
800-367-2000

**Mid State Tile**
P.O. Box 1777
Lexington, NC 27292
(704) 249-3931

**Summitville Tiles, Inc.**
P.O. Box 73
Summitville, OH 43962
(216) 223-1511

**Taos Clay Products**
P.O. Box 15
Taos, NM 87571
(505) 758-9513

**Tile Distributors, Inc.**
7 Kings Highway
New Rochelle, NY 10801
(914) 633-7200

**Tilecraft**
101 Henry Adams
San Francisco, CA 94103
(415) 552-1913

**Villeroy and Boch, Inc.**
I-80 at New Maple Avenue
Pine Brook, NJ 07058
(201) 575-0550

### TUBS AND TOILETS
(see page 331)

**American Standard**
P.O. Box 2003
New Brunswick, NJ 08903
(201) 980-3000

**Colton-Wartsila, Inc.**
P.O. 887
330 W. Citrus Street
Colton, CA 92324
(714) 825-3032

**Eljer Plumbingware**
Three Gateway Center
Pittsburgh, PA 15222
(800) 441-9422
(412) 553-7300 (in PA)

**Hastings Tile**
201 E. 57th Street
New York, NY 10022
(212) 755-2710

**Jacuzzi Whirlpool Bath**
P.O. Drawer J
298 N. Wiget Lane
Walnut Creek, CA 94596
(415) 938-7070

**Kallista, Inc.**
200 Kansas Street
San Francisco, CA 94103
(415) 552-2500

**Kohler Co.**
44 Highland Drive
Kohler, WI 53044
(415) 457-4441

**WaterJet Corp.**
8431 Canoga Avenue
Canoga Park, CA 91304
800-423-3542
(818) 998-3884 (in CA)

**FIBERGLASS BATHTUBS**

**Delta Faucet Corp.**
P.O. Box 40980
55 E. 111th Street
Indianapolis, IN 46280
(317) 848-1812

**Owens-Corning Fiberglas Corp.**
Fiberglas Tower
Toledo, OH 43659
(419) 248-8000

**REPRODUCTION**

**Barclay Products Limited**
424 North Oakley Boulevard
Chicago, IL 60612
(312) 243-1444

**Nostalgia, Inc.**
307 Stiles Avenue
Savannah, GA 31401
(912) 232-2324

**Steptoe & Wife Antiques Ltd.**
322 Geary Avenue
Toronto, Ontario
CANADA M6H 2C7
(416) 530-4200

**Sunrise Specialty and Salvage Co.**
2210 San Pablo Avenue
Berkeley, CA 94702
(415) 845-4751

**WALLPAPER**
(see page 324)

**Bentley Brothers**
918 Baxter Avenue
Louisville, KY 40204
(502) 589-2939

**Bradbury and Bradbury Wallpapers**
P.O. Box 155
Benicia, CA 94510
(707) 746-1900

**Brunschwig and Fils**
979 Third Avenue
New York, NY 10022
(212) 838-7878

**F. Schumacher and Co.**
939 Third Avenue
New York, NY 10022
(212) 644-5900

**Greeff Fabrics, Inc.**
155 E. 56th Street
New York, NY 10022
(212) 888-5060

**Katzenbach and Warren, Inc.**
979 Third Avenue
New York, NY 10022
(212) 751-4470

**Laura Ashley**
P.O. Box 5308
Melville, NY 17114
800-367-2000

**Louis W. Bowen, Inc.**
979 Third Avenue
New York, NY 10022
(212) 392-5810

**Mile Hi Crown**
1230 S. Inca Street
Denver, CO 80223
(303) 777-2099

**San Francisco Victoriana**
2245 Palou Avenue
San Francisco, CA 94124
(415) 648-0313

**Scalamandre, Inc.**
950 Third Avenue
New York, NY 10022
(212) 361-8500

**Thomas Strahan**
National Gibson
Corporate Place 128
Building 3
Wakefield, MA 01880
(617) 246-5130

**Victorian Collectibles Ltd.**
845 E. Glenbrook Road
Milwaukee, WI 53217
(414) 352-6910

**WINDOWS**
(see page 332)

**Andersen Corp.**
P.O. Box 12
Bayport, MN 55003
(612) 439-5150

**Biltbest**
175 10th Street
Ste. Genevieve, MO 63670
(314) 883-3575

**Capitol Products Corp.**
P.O. Box 3070
Harrisburg, PA 17105
(717) 766-7661

**Caradco, Corp.**
P.O. Box 920
Rantoul, IL 61866
(217) 893-4444

**Crestline**
P.O. Box 1007
910 Cleveland Avenue
Wausau, WI 54401
(715) 845-1161

**John F. LaVoie**
P.O. Box 15
Springfield, VT 05156
(802) 886-8253

**Louisiana-Pacific**
Weather Seal Division
Building Products
324 Wooster Road, N.
Barberton, OH 44203
(216) 745-1661

**Marvin Windows**
P.O. Box 100
Warroad, MN 56763
800-346-5128
(218) 386-1430 (in MN)

**Moulding Products, Inc.**
P.O. Box 157158
Irving, TX 75051
(214) 438-2441

**Pella Rollscreen Co.**
102 Main Street
Pella, IA 50219
(515) 628-1000

**Roblin Architectural Products**
Battle Creek, MI 49106
(616) 962-5571

**Sealrite Windows, Inc.**
P.O. Box 4468
Uni Place Station
3500 North 44th Street
Lincoln, NE 68504
(402) 464-0202

**Semco**
Semling-Menke Co., Inc.
P.O. Box 378
Merrill, WI 54452
(715) 536-9411

**Weather Shield Mfg., Inc.**
P.O. Box 309
Medford, WI 54451
(715) 748-2100

**Webb Mfg., Inc.**
P.O. Box 707
Conneaut, OH 44030-0707
(216) 593-1151

**The Woodstone Co.**
P.O. Box 223
Patch Road
Westminster, VT 05158
(802) 722-4784

**WOOD STOVES**
(see page 318)

**Ashley Heater Co.**
P.O. Box 128
Florence, AL 35631
(205) 767-0330

**Ceramic Radiant Heat**
3849 Pleasant Drive
Lochmere, NH 03252
(603) 524-9663

**The Coalbrookdale Co.**
P.O. Box 477
Stowe, VT 05672
800-633-9200
802-253-9727 (in VT)

**Consolidated Dutchwest**
P.O. Box 1019
Plymouth, MA 02360
800-225-8277
(617) 747-1963 (in MA)

**Greenbriar Products, Inc.**
P.O. Box 473
Spring Green, WI 53588
(608) 588-2923

**Jotul USA, Inc.**
P.O. Box 1157
343 Forest Avenue
Portland, ME 04104
(207) 775-0757

**Kent Heating Ltd.**
P.O. Box 40507
Portland, OR 97240
800-547-4577

**Lopi International Ltd.**
10850 117th Place, NE
Kirkland, WA 98033
(206) 827-9505

**New Buck Corp.**
P.O. Box 69
Spruce Pine, NC 28777
(704) 765-6144

**Quaker Stove Co., Inc.**
P.O. Box E
Kumry Road
Trumbauersville, PA 18970
(215) 538-2610

**Svendborg Co.**
85 Mechanic Street
Lebanon, NH 03766
(603) 448-5065

**Thelin-Thompson**
P.O. Box 459
Kings Beach, CA 95719
(916) 265-2121

**Turning Point**
South Strafford, VT 05070
(802) 765-4066

**Vermont Castings, Inc.**
9338 Prince Street
Randolph, VT 05060
(802) 728-3111

**Vermont Iron Stove Works**
299 Prince Street
Waterbury, VT 05676
(802) 244-5254

**Webster Stove Foundry**
3112 LaSalle
St. Louis, MO 63104
(314) 772-0454

**Wesland Stoves**
P.O. Box 4003
Gastonia, NC 28053
(704) 864-0540

# INDEX

Aalto, Alvar, 43, 165
Adri, 282
air-conditioners, 318
Aldoco, Marco, 22
American Federalist architecture, 148
American Olean, 72
Andrews, Colman, 62
antiques, 102, 206, 208
apartments, 138–59
*Apocalypse Now,* 62
appliances, kitchen, 257
    cooktops, 72, 238, 240, 257, 304
    dishwashers, 305
    exhaust fans, 305
    ranges, 276, 304
    refrigerators, 305
    stoves, 20, 200, 252, 263, 268, 276
    wall ovens, 45, 305
    washers/dryers, 304
architects, 8
architectural artifacts, 213
architectural salvage companies, 179, 213, 307, 333
architecture:
    American Federalist, 148
    controlled demolition and, 136
    Greek Revival, 178
    International Style, 54
    Italianate, 17, 162
armoires, 292, 329
atriums, *see* greenhouses; solariums; sun rooms
Augusto, Charles, 276

balconies, 50
balloon shades, 17, 31
balusters, 17
balustrades, 12
    carved, 188
    refinishing of, 17
Banigan, Stephen, 259
Barry, Barbara, 57–59
baseboards, 70
Batey, Andrew, 300
Batey, Hope, 300
bathhouses, Japanese, 286–87
bathrooms, 151
    accessories, 317
    antique fixtures in, 298–99
    circuit breakers in, 289
    skylights in, 182, 208, 209, 284, 287, 288, 301
    stock vanities in, 290, 326

    tiles in, 282, 285, 286, 289
    towel racks, 290, 292
    vent fans in, 294
    whirlpool, 97, 158, 280, 282–283, 286, 292
    *see also* shower enclosures; toilets; tubs; whirlpool baths
Bauhaus, 218
bay windows, 4, 17, 53, 258–59, 332, 333
beams, 82
    I-, 187
    roof, 207
    sandblasting, 100, 102
    Tinkertoy I-, 84
    wooden, 102
bedrooms, 150, 173, 218
beds:
    cannonball, 223
    Gustavian, 218
    Murphy, 329
Belcic, Victor, 295
Bell, David Eugene, 120
Benite oil, 286
Bernard, Eric, 280
Beug, John, 54–55
bins, slide out, 269, 306, 307
blinds, 151
    built-in adjustable, 86
    thin-slat, 171
    vertical, 180
Boeder, Larry, 10
bookshelves, 329
brackets, 17
Bretteville, Peter de, 54
Breuer, Marcel, 204
brick row houses, 162
bricks, acid washes for, 168
broilers, salamander, 236
Bromley/Jacobsen, 301
brownstones, 160
Bruce, Angus, 106–9
Buatta, Mario, 4
Buchsbaum, Alan, 90, 93–94
Buckley, Michael, 118
bulbs, halogen, 320
bull's-eye windows, 332
bungalows, 62

cabinet pulls, porcelain, 59
cabinets, 20, 25, 59, 244, 259, 263, 306–7, 329
    birch, 272
    buffets, 307
    floor-to-ceiling, 251
    glass-door, 195, 238, 242
    hutches, 307
    laminated, 171, 257
    metal, 269
    oak, 252
    pine, 44
    plywood, 45, 226
    self-closing doors on, 307

*Cabins du Bain in Brittany,* 171
Cape Code houses, 34
Cappeto, Rocco, 98
Carbine, Michael, 22, 64
Carlock, Jim, 130–31
Carpenter Gothic cottages, 10, 162
carpets:
    dhurries, 254
    flat-weave rugs, 6
    Oriental, 292
    stair, 328
    wall-to-wall, 12, 90
casement windows, 233
caulk, types of, 286
ceiling fans, 9, 72, 154, 318
ceiling medallions, 92, 140, 179, 188, 323
ceilings:
    barrel-vault, 35
    Bermuda tray, 64
    cathedral, 333
    dropped, 106
    fiber panels for, 322
    insulation, 217, 218
    joists, 214
    lattice-board, 143, 266
    raising, 57, 64, 132, 238
    Robert Adam, 114
    timbered, 27
    tongue-in-groove slat, 8
ceilings, tin, 200
    cleaning, 92, 322
    repainting, 92, 93
    repairing, 92, 93
chairs:
    Adirondack, 107, 218
    Alvar Aalto, 43, 165
    Angelo Donghia, 157
    arm, 31
    bentwood, 252
    Biedermeier, 102
    bistro, 252
    Bugatti, 100
    "Chippendale," 14
    Duncan Phyfe, 193
    Eliel Saarinen, 150
    Empire, 102
    English wicker, 94
    Josef Hoffman, 138–39, 163
    Le Corbusier, 180, 214–15
    Louis XV, 101
    Louis XVI, 64
    Mackintosh, 145
    Mallet-Stevens, 237
    mismatched, 153
    Queen Anne, 166
    Regency, 14
    Richard Meier, 45
    wingback, 14, 165
chaises, 40, 68, 286
chandeliers, 193, 204, 240
Chesterfield sofas, 31
chest of drawers, 329
chimneys, 251
    flues, 251, 318
    hearths, 318
Claiborne, Craig, 276

cleaning fluids, 262
closet organizers, 329
closets, 142, 173, 284
Cohen, Stuart, 266
collar ties, 29
Colonial houses, 4
Colorcore, 309
columns:
    aluminum, 308
    cast plaster capitals on, 308
    Corinthian, 179
    decorative, 25, 308
    Doric, 78
    fiberglass, 308
    freestanding, 308
    load-bearing, 132
    marble, 308
    Palladian, 78, 90
    steel, 10, 134, 308
    wooden, 308
condominiums, 140, 142–43
    platforms in, 165
    restrictions for renovation of, 140
conversions:
    bank, 127–29
    barn, 118, 214–19
    bowling alley, 136–37
    carriage house, 118, 132–35
    church, 119–21
    gas station, 130–31
    grain elevator, 118
    guidelines for, 118
    restructured plumbing and, 120
    rewiring and, 120
    schoolhouse, 118
convertible houses, 116–37
cooktops, 238
    exhaust systems of, 72, 304
    induction, 257
    restaurant, 240, 304
cooling systems, 318
Coombs, Peter, 84
co-ops, *see* apartments; condominiums
Corian, 309
cottages, Carpenter Gothic, 10, 162
countertops:
    butcher-block, 108, 237, 238, 263, 309
    ceramic tile, 309
    concrete, 273
    granite, 309
    laminated, 309
    marble, 237, 238, 242, 251, 252, 254, 268, 309
    slate, 309
Crawford, William, 153
Cusack, Yvette, 188

dadoes, 176
decks, 82, 130
    joists, 55

decks (*cont.*)
  lattice work on, 67
  ranch house, 57, 59
  wraparound, 288
dentils, 168, 213
dishwashers, 305
dividers, 102
  column-and-truss, 35
  glass block 143
  shoji-style, 291
  windowed partitions, 148
  ziggurat, 315, 330
door hinges, 317
doorknobs, 17, 317
door pulls, 317
doors:
  custom-made entryways for, 310
  French, 6, 8, 25, 42, 78, 300, 311
  Louis XV-style, 240
  louver, 193–94
  pine panel, 310
  pocket, 147
  sliding glass, 130, 136, 137, 267, 310
  tambour, 242
  wraparound, 286
doorways, enlarging, 68
dormers, 185, 332
double glazing, 137, 294, 316, 327
drains, 293
draperies, 14, 17
drawer pulls, 317
drawers:
  dovetail joints for, 306
  metal vs. plastic glides for, 307
  mortise-and-tenon corners for, 306
  reinforced bottoms of, 306
Dresser, Christopher, 176
dressers, 329
dryers, 304
drywall compound, 322, 324
dumpsters, roll-off, 164
Dupépé, Clancy, 240
duplexes, 22, 66
Du Pont, 309
Dupuy, Ann, 22–26, 64
D'Urso, Joe, 45, 140, 145
Dutch colonial houses, 34, 220–23

Ehrlich, Steven David, 81–83
electrical systems:
  in kitchens, 253
  perimeter wiring, 181
Emmerling, Philip, 28
  escutcheons, 17
  Estreich, David, 142–43

factory windows, 333
family rooms, 43

fans:
  ceiling, 9, 72, 154, 318
  exhaust, 305
  kitchen, 200
  paddle, 125
  single-lever, 312
  swivel-spout sink, 312
  vent, 294
farmhouses, 28–31, 204
faucets, 312
  gooseneck, 262, 297, 312
faux granite, 77
faux marble, 30–31, 324
Fellini, Federico, 296
fireplaces, 8, 173, 313
  in kitchens, 251
  prefab, 182, 313
  stone, 27, 214
Fisher, Frederick, 74–77
flatroofs, *see* ranch houses
floors:
  bleaching, 57
  concrete, 246, 284, 297, 314
  faux marble, 30–31
  flagstone, 23, 25
  marble, 148
  marbelizing techniques for, 30
  Mexican tile, 82, 244, 300
  no-wax, 314
  parquet, 4, 14, 314
  raising, 78
  refinishing, 170, 192
  sanding, 12, 79, 93, 187, 199
  tiled, 72, 112, 180, 242, 314
  vinyl, 77, 314
  wooden, 314
  wooden, painted, 65
Floyd, Chad, 46
Formica, 309
Fracchia, Paula, 163
French Country Store, 292
French doors, 6, 8, 25, 42, 78, 300, 311
French windows, 64, 252, 254
friezes, 176, 178
furniture:
  Duncan Phyfe, 113
  Hepplewhite, 113, 223
  neo-classic, 31, 102, 112
  Shaker antique, 222, 223
  Shaker style, 20
  Sheraton, 113

gables, 10, 266
gallerias, 50–51
Gillis, Ralph, 198, 200
glass blocks, 50, 143, 298, 315
Glitsch, Val, 36, 37, 38, 224–29
granite tiles, 323
Graves, Michael, 28
Graziano, Bob, 130

Greek Revival architecture, 178
greenhouses, 188, 316
grills, woodburning, 252
Ground Fault Circuit Interrupters (GFCIs), 289
grouting, 289
gypsum wallboards, 290, 323

Halcyon Ltd., 118
halogen bulbs, 320
halogen ceiling fixtures, 321
hand-held showers, 280, 288
Harpole, Jerry, 259
Haymes, David, 122, 180, 182
heat conservation:
  by caulking, 318
  by damper adjustment, 318
  by thermostat, 318
  by weatherstripping, 318
  *see also* insulation
heat guns, 15, 233
heating ducts, concealing, 229
Hester, Paul, 224–29
hinges, concealed, 307, 317
historical restoration, 178
Hoffman, Tom, 286
Holden, Ann, 22, 64
Holt, Gary, 212–13
Holt, Michael, 78–79, 236
home improvement loans, 36
houses:
  brick row, 162
  brownstones, 160
  Cape Cod, 34
  Colonial, 4
  convertible, 116–37
  Dutch Colonial, 34, 220–23
  extensions of, 50, 226
  farm, 28–31, 204
  Italianate villas, 162
  Mansard town, 162
  New Traditional, 4
  painted ladies, 160, 163
  Queen Anne, 162
  ranch, 32–34, 36–45, 57–59
  Shingle Style, 2, 6–9
  shotgun, 60, 62, 63–65
  split-level, 34
  stucco, 82
  town, 160
  Tudor, 4, 27
  Victorian, 162
Huffman, Brenda, 47
Hunziker, Terry, 102

I-beams, 187
insulation, 318

aluminum-foil-faced urethane sheathing, 246
ceiling, 217, 218
of concrete slab houses, 42, 246
fiberglass batting, 246
kiln-dried hardwood, 310
interest rates, 36
International Style, 54
Italianate architecture, 17, 162

jabots, 17
Jacobsen, Arne, 45
James, David, 296
Japanese bathhouses, 286–87
Jay, Janet, 214, 216, 218, 219
Jay, John, 214, 216, 219
Jenkins, David, 28, 242
Johnson, Betsey, 298
joists:
  ceiling, 214
  deck, 55
  pine, 114
Jordano, Jeanette, 180
Josef Hoffman sofas, 138–39

Kaplan, Howard, 292
Kaplan Brothers, 276
Katz, Ronald, 68, 72
Kita, Toshiyuki, 153
kitchens, 20–21, 25
  "appliance garages" in, 329
  butcher-block countertops in, 108, 237, 238, 263
  ceramic tile in, 195, 274
  circuit breakers in, 289
  electrical systems in, 253
  fans, 200
  fireplaces in, 251
  galley, 136, 194–95, 270
  heating units in, 239
  high-intensity storage in, 257
  in lofts, 94–95
  marble countertops in, 237, 238, 242, 251, 252, 254, 268
  modules, 262
  open shelving in, 59, 171, 240
  planning, 236
  semi-professional, 276–77
  skylights in, 72
  wall ovens in, 45
  work islands in, 25, 72, 108–9, 232, 236, 246, 251, 252, 254
  work triangles in, 236
  *see also* appliances, kitchen
Knutson, Stephen, 10

Labine, Claire, 174
Labine, Clem, 162, 174, 176–78
latches, touch, 317
lattices, vinyl, 323
laundries, 8, 226
lazy susans, 306
Le Corbusier:
    love seats, 214–15
    tables, 180
Lewis, Cal, 49–53
Lewis, Robert, 78
lighting, 115
    chandeliers, 193, 204, 240
    exposed, 232
    factory, 321
    halogen bulbs, 320
    halogen ceiling fixtures, 321
    industrial, 95, 232, 263
    recessed, 28, 171, 232, 286
    rheostats for, 320
    swivel-base spotlights, 249
    Tiffany-style, 292
    track, 141, 154, 194, 218, 321
    see also sconces
little bricks, 62
Lloyd, Ben, 190, 192, 193, 196
loans, home improvement, 36
lofts, 35, 90–115
    inspections by strutural engineers, 90
    kitchens in, 94–95
    mezzanines in, 93
    neo-classic, 112–13
    raised floor levels in, 104–6
    rewiring, 106
love seats, Le Corbusier, 214–15
Lubotsky, Bob, 185, 187

McDuff, Frederick, 171
McGraw-Hill, 174
mantels, 313
    marble, 17, 190, 313
    neo-classic, 254
marble:
    Cararra, 17
    columns, 308
    countertops, 237, 238, 242, 251, 252, 254, 268, 309
    faux, 30–31, 324
    mantels, 17, 190, 313
    rojo alicante, 269
    staircases, 158
    -topped table, 45
    tubs, 288
marbleizing, 30, 324
Martin, Bill, 36, 45
masonite, 298
mats, tatami, 286
Meier, Richard, 45, 204

Metropolitan Home, 36, 114, 178, 190, 236, 246
mezzanines, 66
Mies van der Rohe, Ludwig, 17
milk cans, decoupaged, 204
Mindel, Lee, 157–58
moldings, 140
    capitals, 322
    ceiling medallions, 92, 140, 179, 188, 322
    corbels, 322
    cornices, 92, 168, 188, 322
    decorative, 17, 25
    faux plaster, 323
    garlands, 323
    quarter-round, 70
    stock, 120, 158, 322
    see also ceilings
mortgages, 36
Moss, Eric, 274
Mount, Charles Morris, 236

National Register of Historic Plalces, 126
neo-classic:
    lofts, 112–13
    mantels, 254
Nereim, Anders, 266
Neutra, Richard, 54
newel posts, 213, 328
    refinishing, 17
Newman, Margy, 57, 59
New Traditional houses, 4
"nonwall walls," 148
Nouvelle Maison, 57

Okamoto, Susan, 286
Old-House Journal, The, 162, 174, 178
Olson, James, 273
ovens:
    convection, 263
    conventional, 238, 257, 263
    microwave, 238, 257, 263
    wall, 45, 305

paddle fans, 125
paint:
    glaze coats, 28
    latex, 324
    plextone, 76
    selection of, 13, 47
    zolatone, 76–77
painted ladies, 160, 163
Palladian windows, 10, 120
panels:
    fiber ceiling, 323
    soffit vinyl, 322
    styrene, 207
    tambour, 323
    tongue-in-groove, 8, 207
pantries, 8, 271

Pappageorge, George, 122, 125, 180, 182
parquet floors, 4, 14, 314
particleboard, 306–7
partitions, windowed, 148
Peix, Douglas, 153, 154
penthouses, 152–55
    studio, 84–87
    period furnishings, 17
Phipps, Dan, 238
platforms, "floating," 189
plextone, 76
plumbing, restructured, 286, 293, 326
pools, 82
porches, 12
    indoor, 10–11
    see also decks; sun porches
Portlandia building, 28

Queen Anne houses, 162

raceways, 106
railings, 165, 166
    steel, 132, 135
    wooden, 229
ranch houses:
    decks, 57, 59
    raised roofs in, 57
    renovation of, 32, 34, 36–45, 57–59
    skylights in, 38–39, 42
ranges, see cooktops; ovens, stoves
refrigerators, professional, 252–253
renovations:
    apartment, 138–59
    bathroom, 280–301
    brownstone, 174–79, 198–200
    factory, 98–99
    kitchen, 236–77
    loft, 91–97
    ranch house, 34, 36–45, 57–59
    split-level house, 48–53
    Tudor house, 27
restaurant stoves, 20, 200, 252, 263, 268, 276
    commercial stoves vs., 276
restorations:
    historical, 178
    rules for, 178
    of Victorian houses, 174–79
rheostats, 320
Rich, Martin E., 244
Richar, 100
rojo alicante marble, 269
rolled-arm sofas, 68
roof beams, 207
roofs:
    asphalt shingled, 325
    cedar shingled, 325
    insulating, 57, 207, 217
    mansard, 12, 162
    peaked, 29, 53, 57, 208

roof windows, see skylights
rugs, flat-weave, 6

Saladino, John, 114–15
salamander broilers, 276
sandblasting, 100, 168, 226
Schroeder, Kenneth, 188
Schujman, Elida, 18, 21
sconces, 254, 280, 320
    halogen bulbs for, 320
screens:
    art-furniture, 112
    Japanese shoji, 106, 107
servants' quarters, 8, 162
Sexton, Martin, 136
shades, balloon, 17, 31
Shaker antique furniture, 222, 223
Sheldon, April, 98
Shelton, Peter, 157–58, 159
shelves:
    adjustable, 306, 329
    display, 329
    glass, 269
    laminated, 173
    open, 59, 171, 240
    pine, 238
    pivoting corner, 307
    rolling wire, 43, 200, 329
Shingle Style houses, 2, 6–9
shotgun houses, 60, 62, 63–65
shower curtains, 298
shower enclosures, 66, 284, 292, 296, 301
    caulking, 286
    tiled, 286
shower rings, 298
showers, hand-held, 280, 288
siding:
    aluminum, 184
    sheet, 325
    slate, 325
    stucco, 325
sinks, 326
    cast-iron, 326
    pedestal, 326
    porcelain, 240, 274, 292, 326
    self-rimming, 326
    stainless steel, 25, 108, 240, 252, 262, 326
    zinc, 297
    see also faucets
Siris, Jane, 84
skylights, 18, 46, 74, 124–25, 134
    in bathrooms, 182, 208, 209, 284, 287, 288, 301
    in bedrooms, 208–9
    blinds for, 86
    copper flashing in, 287
    double bubbles in, 287
    frosted, 154
    in kitchens, 72

skylights (*cont.*)
    movable, 229
    in ranch houses, 38–39, 42
    types of, 327
slate tiles, 322
Slover, Dorothy, 278
Smith-Miller, Henry, 165–66
sofas:
    Chesterfield, 31
    Josef Hoffman, 138–39
    rolled-arm, 68
solariums, 196–97
Solomon, Daniel, 32, 35
spackling compound, 324
spiral staircases, 241, 328
split-level houses, 34
spotlights, swivel-base, 249
staircases:
    carpeting, 328
    marble, 158
    problems, 198, 328
    spiral, 241, 328
    straight vs. curved, 328
    wooden, 229
stair rails:
    staining, 224
    wobbly, 328
stairwells, 66, 125, 333
stencil designs, 176, 178
Stern, Robert A. M., 2, 4, 6–8
stools, Alvar Aalto, 165
storage space, 329 *see also* cabinets
storm windows, 152
stoves:
    commercial, 95
    restaurant, 20, 200, 252, 263, 268, 276
    *see also* cooktops
stucco houses, 82
sun porches, 210–11
    wraparound, 184
    *see also* decks
sunrooms, 8, 18, 182
Suyama, George, 132, 134
synthetic terra cotta, 323

tables:
    gateleg, 193
    Le Corbusier, 180
    marble-topped, 45
tambour doors, 242
tambour panels, 323
tatami mats, 286
Taylor, Robert H., 66
terra-cotta, synthetic, 323
Tiffany-style light, 292
tiles, 20, 72
    in bathrooms, 282, 285, 286, 289
    ceramic, 39, 40, 96, 309, 330
    glazed vs. unglazed, 330
    granite, 323
    mosaic, 259, 298, 330
    quarry, 27, 40–41, 180
    Saltillo, 300
    slate, 323
    terra-cotta, 31, 53, 242
tin ceilings, 200
cleaning, 92, 322
    repainting, 92, 93
    repairing, 92, 93
Tinkertoy I-beams, 84
toilets:
    "extended rim," 331
    "reverse trap," 331
    "siphon," 331
    triangular tanks for, 331
    "washdown," 331
towel racks, 290, 292
townhouses, 160, 162
track lighting, 141, 154, 194, 218, 321
transoms, 310, 333
trim work:
    on ceilings, 224
    on moldings, 224, 226
    staining, 224
    on windows, 224, 226
True, Clarence, 198
tubs:
    cast iron, 288, 331
    caulking, 300
    fiberglass, 288, 331
    marble, 288
    porcelain, 16–17, 288
    steel, 331
    Victorian, 213, 331
Tudor houses, 4, 27

Valerio, Joseph, 204
Van Runkle, Theadora, 203, 206, 208–11
venting hoods, 21, 129, 242, 257, 263, 265
    down-draft, 72, 304
    self-contained filters for, 257
Victorian houses, 162
Victorian tubs, 213, 331
vinyl:
    floors, 77, 314
    lattices, 323

Wagner, Ron, 28
wainscoting, 120, 140, 176, 190, 232
    highlighting, 120
    refinishing, 121
wallpaper, 12, 324
    stock solutions to dissolve, 70, 324
walls:
    fabric-covered, 14, 208
    load-bearing, 134, 171, 188
    "nonwall," 148
    room-divider, 93
    stucco, 82
    treatment, textured, 140
Walz, Kevin, 282–83
Warner, Donna, 246, 251
Warner Brothers, 296
Warren, Geraldine, 28, 31
Warren, Tiger, 28
washers/dryers, 304
weatherstripping, 318
Weigel, Phil, 220–21
Weigel, Tait, 220–22
Weinberg, Sydney, 168, 171–73
Wells Fargo, 300
W. F. Norman Corporation, 92
Wheelwright, Peter, 146–50
whirlpool baths, 97, 158, 280, 282–83, 284, 286, 292
White, Stanford, 210

Windham, Burke, 36, 280
windowed partitions, 148
window frames, Egyptian Revival, 190
windows:
    bay, 4, 17, 53, 258–59, 332, 333
    bull's-eye, 332
    bumpout, 332
    casement, 233
    dormer, 185, 332
    double-glazed, 137, 184, 186, 200, 333
    double height, 96
    elliptical, 332
    factory, 333
    floor-to-roof, 66, 288, 289
    French, 64, 252, 254
    guidelines for installing, 332–33
    half-moon, 10, 254, 332
    lunette, 133
    Palladian, 10, 120
    peaked, 246
    problems with casement, 233
    quarter-round, 332
    R-values of, 207, 333
    special treatments for, 332–33
    storm, 152
    transoms over, 333
    trim work on, 224, 26
    U-values of, 333
    wall-to-wall, 28
    wraparound, 286
wiring, perimeter, 181
woodburning grills, 252
wood flourishes, 168
wood sheathing, 207
wood stoves, 173, 318
    building codes for, 318
work islands, 25, 72, 108–9, 232, 236, 246, 251, 252, 254, 266

*Yucca rostrata,* 70

zolatone, 76–77

# PHOTOGRAPHY CREDITS

Peter Aaron/ESTO, 222 Valley Pl., Mamaroneck, NY 10543, (914) 698-4060. *Pages 152–155; 275*

Jim Ball, Seattle, WA, (206)630-2486. *Pages 126–129*

Peter Bosch, 477 Broome St., New York, NY 10013, (212) 925-0707. *Pages 282–283*

Langdon Clay, 42 West 28th St., New York, NY 10001, (212) 689-2613. *Pages xiv; 22–25; 60–65; 104–111; 138–143; 240–241*

Jacques Dirand, 10 Passage Doisy, Paris, France 75017. *Pages 276–277*

Oberto Gili and Jeff McNamara, % Rattazzi, 20 E. 17th St., New York, NY 10009, (212) 243-5454. *Pages 156–159*

Joshua Greene, 448 West 37th St., 8d, New York, NY 10018, (212) 239-1394. *Pages 244–245*

Jim Hedrich/Hedrich-Blessing, 11 West Illinois St., Chicago IL 60610, (312) 321-1151. *Pages iv; 10–17; 48–53; 68–73; 100–101; 122–125; 130–131; 136–137; 168–173; 180–189; 264–267; 270–271; 281*

Paul Hester, P.O. Box 70984, Houston, TX 77270, (713) 864-0984. *Pages 224–229*

Lizzie Himmel, 117 E. 83rd St., New York, NY 10028, (212) 737-4737. *Pages 146–151; 252–253*

Thomas Hooper, 126 Fifth Ave., New York, NY 10011, (212) 691-0122. *Pages 2–9; 88–97; 114–121; 174–179; 292–295; 298–299*

Norman McGrath, 164 W. 79th St., New York, NY 10024, (212) 799-6422. *Pages 164–167*

Nick Merrick, Hedrich-Blessing, 11 West Illinois St., Chicago, IL 60610, (312)321-1151. *Pages 290–291*

John Parsekian, 56 East Craig Rd., Basking Ridge, NJ 07920, (201) 766-6103. *Pages 87–88*

Laura Rosen, 1380 Riverside Dr., New York, NY 10033, (212) 923-0705. *Page 198*

April Sheldon, April Sheldon Design, 620 Moulton Ave., Studio 204, Los Angeles, CA 90031, (213) 222-7675. *Pages 98–99*

Joseph Standart, 5 West 28th St., New York, NY 10011, (212) 924-4545. *Pages 36–47; 78–79; 84–87; 112–113; 190–197; 214–219; 254–259; 284–285; 297*

Bill Stites, 1600 Park, Houston, TX 77019, (713) 523-6439. *Page viii*

Tim Street-Porter, 6938 Camrose Dr., Hollywood, CA 90068, (213) 874-4278. *Pages 54–59; 66–67; 74–77; 80–83; 202–211; 274–275; 289; 296; 300; 302*

John Vaughan, Russell MacMasters & Assoc., Inc., 128 Texas St., San Francisco, CA 94107, (415) 431-1318. *Pages 18–21; 28–35; 102–103; 132–135; 230–239; 242–243; 260–263; 272–273; 286–288; 334*

Peter Vitale, 157 E. 71st St., New York, NY 10022, (212) 249-8412. *Pages 144–145*

John Waggaman, 2746 N. 46th St., Philadelphia, PA 19131, (215) 473-2827. *Page 301*

Bruce Wolf, 123 W. 28th St., New York, NY 10001, (212) 695-8042. *Pages 198–201; 246–251; 268–269; 276–279*